Key Concepts for Understanding Curriculum

The Teachers' Library

The prime intention of *The Teachers' Library* is to provide impetus and support to analytical and research-oriented teaching practice. Each book in the series has been written to satisfy the needs of teachers wishing to study education and reflect upon their own practice.

Series Editor: Professor Ivor F. Goodson, Warner Graduate School, University of Rochester, USA and Applied Research in Education, University of East Anglia, Norwich, UK

Search and Re-search: What the Inquiring Teacher Needs to Know
Rita S. Brause and John S. Mayher

Doing Qualitative Research: Circles Within Circles
Margot Ely, Margaret Anzul, Teri Freidman, Diane Garner and Ann McCormack

Beginning Qualitative Research
P. Maykut and R. Morehouse

Becoming a Teacher
Gary Borich

Participatory Evaluation in Education
J. Bradley Cousins and Lorna M. Earl

Schooling for Change
Andy Hargreaves and Lorna M. Earl and J. Ryan

Studying School Subjects
Ivor F. Goodson and Colin J. Marsh

On Writing Qualitative Research: Living by Words
Margot Ely, Ruth Vinz, Maryann Downing and Margaret Anzul

Subject Knowledge: Readings for the Study of School Subjects
Ivor F. Goodson with Christopher J. Anstead and J. Marshall Mangan

Fundamentals of Education Research (New Edition)
Gary Anderson

Students as Researchers: Creating Classrooms that Matter
Shirley R. Steinberg and Joe L. Kinchloe

Teachers as Researchers: Qualitative Inquiry as a Path to Empowerment, 2nd edition
Joe L. Kincheloe

Key Concepts for Understanding Curriculum

Third Edition

Colin J. Marsh

RoutledgeFalmer
Taylor & Francis Group

LONDON AND NEW YORK

This edition published 2004 by RoutledgeFalmer
2 Park Square, Milton Park, Abingdon, Oxon OX14 4RN.

Simultaneously published in the USA and Canada
by RoutledgeFalmer
20 Madison Ave, New York, NY 10006

RoutledgeFalmer is an imprint of the Taylor & Francis Group

© 1997, 2003, 2004 Colin J. Marsh

Typeset in 10/12 Times by Keyword Typesetting Services Ltd
Printed and bound in Great Britain by TJ International Ltd, Padstow, Cornwall

British Library Cataloging in Publication Data
A catalogue record for this book is available from the British Library

Library of Congress Cataloging in Pubication Data
Marsh, Colin J.
    Key concepts for understanding curriculum / Colin J. Marsh. – 3rd ed.
      p. cm.
    Includes bibliographical references.
    ISBN 0-415-31917-X (hardback : alk. paper) – ISBN 0-415-31918-8 (pbk. : alk.
paper) 1. Education–Curricula. 2. Curriculum planning. 3. Education–Curricula–
Philosophy. 4. Educational tests and measurements. I. Title.
    LB1570.M3668 2004
    317′.001–dc22   2004002221

ISBN 0-415-31918-8

To Glen; my soulmate, and the support given
by Ross, Jenny and Alison

Contents

Contents

Contents

List of Tables

List of Figures

Preface

As we move almost half-way into the first decade of the twenty-first century it could be useful to pause and consider some important curriculum questions, such as:

- Are we developing a more relevant curriculum for students – a curriculum that has the power to make a difference?
- Are we really addressing complex curriculum dilemmas in a clear and unambiguous fashion?
- Are we becoming more successful at integrating theoretical issues and practical positionings?

An honest and candid response to these questions might well be: very little, or not at all.

The diversity and pace of change in curriculum policy and implementation continues unabated in many countries. In addition, the players who are taking leading roles in policy formulation are changing, with increasing pressures coming from politicians and employer groups, as well as from community interest groups, parents, teachers and students.

A number of these individuals and groups have very limited understanding of curriculum theories, principles and processes, even though they are prepared to commit enormous amounts of energy to advance their preferred solutions to specific curriculum problems.

Key Concepts for Understanding the Curriculum is aimed at assisting various personnel concerned about and involved in curriculum decision-making. Of course, a major clientele are those pre-service teachers who will be commencing full-time careers in schools, namely students who are taking teacher education degrees (BA (Education), Bachelor of Education, Diploma of Education, Diploma of Teaching and PGCEs). Another major group who are likely to be very interested in the book include those practising teachers who are embarking upon professional development programmes. Parents and community members involved as school governors and members of school councils, boards and districts, will obtain considerable assistance from the succinctly stated commentaries about major curriculum concepts.

The book provides details about twenty-one major concepts in curriculum. In such a small space each chapter cannot provide an exhaustive treatment of each concept, but every attempt has been made to highlight major features, controversies, strengths and weaknesses. In particular, the follow-up questions challenge the reader to reflect further upon specific issues relating to each concept and the listing of recent references at the end of the book.

I acknowledge various colleagues in curriculum, both within Australia, and in the United Kingdom, the United States of America and Canada, who have helped me hone my ideas over the decades about curriculum. They include Michael Fullan, Gene Hall, Paul Klohr, Michael Huberman, Elliot Eisner, Bill Reid, Helen Simmons, Kerry Kennedy, Eric Hoyle, Ray Bolam, Michal Connelly, Christine Deer, David Smith, Noel Gough, Chris Day, Ivor Goodson, Brian Caldwell, Paul Morris, David Tripp and John Elliott.

The third edition includes a number of new concepts which are having considerable impact during the beginning of the twenty-first century.

For permission to reproduce figures and tables I am most grateful to Patricia Broadfoot, Brian Caldwell, Chris Day, Stephen Kemmis and Barry Fraser. A special word of thanks is due to Peta Edwards for her expert secretarial assistance in the preparation of the manuscript.

Colin Marsh

Part I

Introduction

1   What Is Curriculum?

Introduction

Defining the word *curriculum* is no easy matter. Perhaps the most common definition derives from the word's Latin root, which means 'racecourse'. Indeed, for many students, the school curriculum is a race to be run, a series of obstacles or hurdles (subjects) to be passed. It is important to keep in mind that schools in Western civilization have been heavily influenced since the fourth century B.C. by the philosophies of Plato and Aristotle and that the word *curriculum* has been used historically to describe the subjects taught during the classical period of Greek civilization. The interpretation of the word *curriculum* broadened in the twentieth century to include subjects other than the classics. Today, school documents, newspaper articles, committee reports, and many academic textbooks refer to any and all subjects offered or prescribed as 'the curriculum of the school'.

Consequently, it is not surprising that writers such as Longstreet and Shane (1993) consider that 'curriculum is an historical accident – it has not been developed to accomplish a clear set of purposes. Rather, it has evolved as a response to the increasing complexity of educational decision making' (p. 7).

Some Definitions of Curriculum

Many writers advocate their own preferred definition of *curriculum*, which emphasizes other meanings or connotations, particularly those the term has taken on recently. According to Portelli (1987), more than 120 definitions of the term appear in the professional literature devoted to curriculum, presumably because authors are concerned about either delimiting what the term means or establishing new meanings that have become associated with it.

Hlebowitsh (1993) criticizes commentators in the curriculum field who focus 'only on certain facets of early curriculum thought while ignoring others' (p. 2).

We need to be watchful, therefore, about definitions that capture only a few of the various characteristics of curriculum (Toombs and Tierney, 1993), especially those that are partisan or biased. Portelli (1987), drawing on a metaphor developed by Soltis (1978), notes, 'Those who look for the definition of curriculum are like a sincere but misguided centaur hunter, who even with a fully provisioned safari and a gun kept always at the ready, nonetheless will never require the services of a taxidermist' (p. 364).

The incompleteness of any definition notwithstanding, certain definitions of the term can provide insights about common emphases and characteristics within the general idea of curriculum. Consider, for example, the following definitions of curriculum.

- Curriculum is the 'permanent' subjects that embody essential knowledge.
- Curriculum is those subjects that are most useful for contemporary living.
- Curriculum is all planned learnings for which the school is responsible.
- Curriculum is the totality of learning experiences so that students can attain general skills and knowledge at a variety of learning sites.
- Curriculum is what the students construct from working with the computer and its various networks, such as the Internet.
- Curriculum is the questioning of authority and the searching for complex views of human situations.

Definition 1

Curriculum is such 'permanent' subjects as grammar, reading, logic, rhetoric, mathematics, and the greatest books of the Western world that best embody essential knowledge.
An example is the National Curriculum enacted in the United Kingdom in 1988, which prescribed the curriculum in terms of three core and seven foundational subjects, including specific content and specific goals for student achievement in each subject.

Problems Posed by the Definition

This definition suggests that the curriculum is limited to only a few academic subjects. It assumes that what is studied is what is learned. It does not address questions such as: Does the state of knowledge change? If so, shouldn't the subjects making up the curriculum also change? What makes learning such subjects essential? Goodson and Marsh (1996) point out that the National Curriculum in the United Kingdom is simply a reconstitution of the subjects included in the Secondary Regulations of 1904, suggesting that 'historical amnesia allows curriculum reconstruction to be presented as curriculum revolution' (p. 157). Griffith (2000) contends that a knowledge-based curriculum such as the National Curriculum does not exist independently of space and time. It should not be considered ahistorically, for it is neither neutral, factual, nor value free.

Definition 2

Curriculum is those subjects that are most useful for living in contemporary society.
The subjects that make up this curriculum are usually chosen in terms of major present-day issues and problems within society, but the definition itself does not preclude individual students from making their own choices about which subjects are most useful.

Problems posed by the Definition

This definition seems to imply that what is contemporary has more value than what is long-lasting. It encourages schools and students to accommodate themselves to society as it exists instead of attempting to improve it. It leaves open questions such as: What accounts for stability in the curriculum? What is useful knowledge? If useful practical skills are increasingly emphasized, what becomes of intellectual development?

Definition 3

Curriculum is all planned learnings for which the school is responsible.
'Planned learnings' can be long written documents specifying content, shorter lists of intended learning outcomes, or simply the general ideas of teachers about what students should know. Exponents of curriculum as a plan include Saylor, Alexander, and Lewis (1981), Beauchamp (1981), and Posner (1998).

Problems Posed by the Definition

This definition seems to assume that what is studied is learned. It may limit 'planned learnings' to those that are easiest to achieve, not those that are most desirable. It does not address questions such as: On what basis does the school select and take responsibility for certain learnings while excluding others? Is it possible for teachers to separate the ends of instruction from the means? Are unplanned, but actual, learnings excluded from the curriculum?

Definition 4

Curriculum is the totality of learning experiences provided to students so that they can attain general skills and knowledge at a variety of learning sites.
Emphasis is on learning rather than teaching, especially learning skills and knowledge at sites other than schools. The assumption is that all sites – including workplace sites – can be conducive to learning general knowledge. This approach to curriculum has been heavily publicized in a number of countries recently and is usually supported for economic reasons by business organiza-

tions, other vocationally oriented groups, and advocates of explicit competency standards.

Problems Posed by the Definition

This definition usually leads to a narrow technical-functionalist approach to curriculum, requiring that unduly large numbers of outcomes and high levels of specificity be identified. Walker (1994) and Cairns (1992) are critical of the uniformity and the focus on minimum standards the definition encourages. Moore (2000) points out that the economic well-being of a nation depends on much besides vocational training.

Definition 5

Curriculum is what the student constructs from working with the computer and its various networks, such as the Internet.
Obviously, this is a modern definition. It assumes that computers are everywhere – in the home, school, and office – and students, perceiving them as part of the natural landscape, are thriving. Although teachers have been slow in developing computer skills, many are now becoming involved. Advocates argue that the new computing technologies have created a culture for increasingly active learning; students can construct their own meanings as they locate sources on the Internet, explore issues and communicate with others. Social skills are also developed through chat groups, conferences, and e-mail communications.

Problems Posed by the Definition

Although some writers such as Vine *et al.* (2000) contend that schools in the near future will change drastically as students access more electronic resources from the home, others such as Reid (2000) and Westbury (2000) believe that schools will remain long-enduring institutions. Budin (1999) reminds us that technology is not a neutral tool. What is now available on the Internet, for example, is not necessarily what should be on it or what will be on it tomorrow. Furthermore, not all students have the same level of access to the Internet, and the learning it promotes may prove to be far more passive than now commonly believed. We should, therefore, be wary of excessive claims about active or constructivist learning made possible by computers.

Definition 6

Curriculum is the questioning of authority and the searching for complex views of human situations.
This definition is consistent with the ancient Socratic maxim 'The unexamined life is not worth living'. However, it may also overly encourage rejection of

what is, making it a postmodernist definition. The term *postmodernist* implies opposition to widely used ('modern') values and practices. Hence, postmodernists are disparate in their own views, usually sharing only a desire to challenge what is modern, a readiness to accept the unaccepted, and a willingness to conceptualize new ways of thinking.

Problems Posed by the Definition

Postmodernism reduced simply to the process of questioning may not be helpful in identifying in practice how students should spend their time and energy. Although many authors are enthusiastic about the general potential of postmodernist thinking (Slattery, 1995; Atkinson, 2000; Parker, 1997), others (Barrow, 1999) contend that it is overly general, vague, and confused. It is subject to the charge of relativism. Moore (2000) contends there is a fatal, internal contradiction among those postmodernists who state that all truth is relative, when this statement itself would have to be nonrelative in order to be true.

Characteristics of Curriculum

Some curriculum experts, such as Goodlad (1979), contend that an analysis of definitions is a useful starting point for examining the field of curriculum. Other writers argue that there are important concepts or characteristics that need to be considered and which give some insights into how particular value orientations have evolved and why.

Walker (1990) argues that the fundamental concepts of curriculum include:

- content: which may be depicted in terms of concept maps, topics, and themes, all of which are abstractions which people have invested and named;
- purpose: usually categorized as intellectual, social and personal; often divided into superordinate purposes; stated purposes are not always reliable indicators of actions;
- organization: planning is based upon scope and sequence (order of presence over time); can be tightly organized or relatively open-ended.

Other writers such as Beane *et al.* (1986) produce principles of curriculum but they are more value-oriented and less generic. For example, they list five major principles about curriculum:

- concern with the experiences of learners;
- making decisions about both content and process;
- making decisions about a variety of issues and topics;
- involving many groups;
- decision-making at many levels.

It is evident that these authors have a particular conception of curriculum; perhaps a combination of student- and society-centred. Inevitably, if specific principles are given a high priority, then a particular conception of curriculum emerges. Longstreet and Shane (1993) refer to four major conceptions of curriculum:

- society-oriented curriculum: the purpose of schooling is to serve society;
- student-centred curriculum: the student is the crucial source of all curriculum;
- knowledge-centred curriculum: knowledge is the heart of curriculum;
- eclectic curriculum: various compromises are possible including mindless eclecticism!

The conceptions or orientations of curriculum produced by Eisner and Vallance (1974) are often cited in literature, namely:

- a cognitive process orientation: cognitive skills applicable to a wide range of intellectual problems;
- technological orientation: to develop means to achieve prespecified ends;
- self-actualization orientation: individual students discover and develop their unique identities;
- social reconstructionist orientation: schools must be an agency of social change;
- academic rationalist orientation: to use and appreciate the ideas and works of the various disciplines.

It is interesting to note that Vallance (1986) modified these orientations 12 years later by deleting 'self-actualization' and adding 'personal success' (pursuing a specific, practical end) and a 'curriculum for personal commitment' (pursuing learning for its inherent rewards).

These conceptions of curriculum are useful to the extent that they remind educators of some value orientations that they may be following, whether directly or indirectly. Yet others, such as Pinar *et al.* (1995), argue that these conceptions are stereotypes and are of little value.

Who Is Involved in Curriculum?

Curriculum workers are many and include school-based personnel such as teachers, principals, and parents and university-based specialists, industry and community groups, and government agencies and politicians.

Jackson (1992) suggests that a large number of those working in the curriculum field are involved in serving the daily and technical needs of those who work in schools. This has been the traditional role over the decades where the focus has been upon curriculum development for school contexts.

Pinar *et al.* (1995) refer to the 'shifting domain of curriculum development as politicians, textbook companies, and subject-matter specialists in the university, rather than school practitioners and university professors of curriculum, exercise leadership and control over curriculum development' (p. 41). It is certainly the case in most OECD (developed) countries that a wider range of interest groups are now involved in curriculum development (Ross, 2000).

Curriculum in the twenty-first century is indeed moving in many directions and some would assert that this reflects a conceptual advance (Jackson, 1992) and a more sophisticated view of the curriculum. Others would argue that curriculum as a field of study is still conceptually underdeveloped (Goodlad and Su, 1992) and rather like trying to nail Jell-O to the wall!! (Wright, 2000).

Reflections and Issues

1. There are very divergent views about the nature of curriculum. What definition of curriculum do you support? Justify your choice.
2. Trying to clarify central concepts by proposing definitions for them has been popular in many fields (Portelli, 1987). Have these concepts and definitions proven useful in the field of curriculum?
3. 'The struggle over the definition of curriculum is a matter of social and political priorities as well as intellectual discourse' (Goodson 1988, p. 23). Reflect upon a particular period of time and analyse the initiatives, successes and failures which occurred in terms of curriculum development or policy development.
4. 'If the curriculum is to be the instrument of change in education, its meanings and operational terms must be clearer than they are currently' (Toombs and Tierney, 1993, p. 175). Discuss.
5. 'The term "social subjects" rarely occurs in the current formulations of the National Curriculum or the whole curriculum in the United Kingdom; indeed the very work "society" is notable by its infrequency.' (Campbell, 1993, p. 137) Does this indicate deficiencies in the conceptions of curriculum incorporated into the National Curriculum? Discuss.

---

2   Introducing Key Concepts

Introduction

We make sense of our world and go about our daily lives by engaging in *concept building*. We acquire and develop concepts so that we can gain meaning about persons and events and in turn communicate these meaning to others.

Some concepts are clearly of more importance than others. The *key concepts* provide us with the power to explore a variety of situations and events and to make significant connections. Other concepts may be meaningful in more limited situations but play a part in connecting unrelated facts.

Every field of study contains a number of key concepts and lesser concepts which relate to substantive and methodological issues unique to that discipline/field of study. Not unexpectedly, scholars differ over their respective lists of key concepts, but there is, nevertheless, considerable agreement. With regard to the curriculum field there is a moderate degree of agreement over key concepts.

Searching for Key Concepts

To be able to provide any commentary on key concepts in curriculum assumes of course that we have access to sources of information that enable us to make definitive statements.

A wide range of *personnel* are involved in making curriculum including school personnel, researchers, academics, administrators, politicians, and various interest groups. They go about their tasks in various ways such as via planning meetings, informal discussions, writing reports, papers, handbooks, textbooks, giving talks, lectures, workshops, etc.

To ensure that a list of key concepts is comprehensive and representative of all these sources would be an extremely daunting task. A proxy often used by researchers is to examine textbooks, especially *synoptic textbooks* (those books which provide comprehensive accounts and summaries of a wide range of concepts, topics and issues in curriculum).

Schubert (1980) and Schubert *et al.* (2002) undertook a detailed analysis of textbooks over the period 1861–2000 and this volume provides a valuable overview of curriculum thought over major historical periods. Marsh and Stafford (1988) provided a similar historical analysis of major curriculum books written by Australian authors over the period 1910–88.

Rogan and Luckowski (1990) undertook an analysis of nine major synoptic curriculum texts produced by American authors.

Major synoptic texts published in the USA include Doll (1996), Oliva (1997) and Marsh and Willis (2003). All of these are long-standing texts in the USA and have undergone subsequent editions.

Pinar *et al.*'s (1995) *Understanding Curriculum: An Introduction to the Study of Historical and Contemporary Curriculum Discourses*, an encyclopaedic volume of diverse discourses, represents a very important but different form of synoptic text.

These texts tend to be very comprehensive and cover a number of key concepts within the broad categories of:

- conceptions of curriculum/models/approaches;
- curriculum history;
- curriculum policy and policy makers, politics of curriculum;
- curriculum development procedures/change/improvement/planning steps;
- issues and trends/problems/future directions;
- discourses of gender, race, postmodern, political, historical, phenomenological (especially Pinar *et al.*, 1995).

A recent text published in the United Kingdom, Ross (2000), has a major focus upon historical developments in curriculum in that country, but also includes sections on curriculum and reproduction, hidden curriculum, content-driven, objectives-driven and process-driven curricula.

In Australia, three major texts focus directly upon curriculum concepts. Brady and Kennedy (2003) examine social contexts, curriculum planning models, assessment and evaluation, and curriculum change. Marsh (2000) examines student learning, curriculum planning models, providing for individual differences, assessment and reporting, school culture, standards, innovation, and change. Smith and Lovat (2003) examine the origins and nature of curriculum, curriculum and ideology, curriculum and the foundational disciplines, critical theory, assessment and evaluation, curriculum change, and curriculum futures.

Taken overall, it is very evident that there are a number of common key concepts that are included in these synoptic texts.

Categories of Concepts Included in this Volume

After examining a wide range of synoptic curriculum texts, including those described above, a decision was made to include material relating to two sets of categories:

- generic issues in curriculum; and
- alternative perspectives.

By concentrating upon a single concept in each chapter, it is possible, of course, to have many different groupings, and readers are encouraged to explore their own interests and swap around their order of reading chapters. Each chapter focuses upon a *key concept* in terms of its major characteristics, strengths, and weaknesses. Follow-up questions and references are also included in each chapter.

Generic Categories

The generic categories include the following.

- Curriculum planning and development.
- Curriculum management.
- Teaching perspectives.
- Collaborative involvement in curriculum.
- Curriculum ideology.

Curriculum Planning and Development

This is the second section in the book (after the introductory section) and, together with the opening chapter, includes six chapters dealing with the following topics.

- What is curriculum? (Chapter 1).
- Curriculum frameworks (Chapter 3).
- Objectives, learning outcomes and standards (Chapter 4).
- Selecting and organizing teaching and learning modes (Chapter 5).
- Assessment, grading and reporting (Chapter 6).
- Curriculum implementation (Chapter 7).

These chapters represent the standard planning processes in developing curriculum.

Curriculum orientations have moved over the decades and previous inviolable principles have been overtaken by postmodern uncertainties (Chapter 1).

In many countries curriculum frameworks have been established to guide (some would argue, enforce) curriculum planning and development (Chapter 3).

'Objectives', 'Outcomes' and 'Standards' continue to stir educationalists. Arguments for outcomes approaches were very dominant in the 1990s but subsequently standards, especially subject standards, are being given a higher priority (Chapter 4).

Teaching and learning modes are widening as teachers attempt to match teacher and student priorities. There is considerable research support for specific learning modes, such as cooperative learning (Chapter 5).

Assessment and grading methods are also diversifying due to pressures from educators proposing 'authentic' and 'performance-based' assessment (Chapter 6).

Curriculum implementation is a critical phase in curriculum development because this is where a plan becomes a reality with real students in a real classroom (Chapter 7).

Curriculum Management

This is the third section in the book and includes five chapters dealing with the following topics.

- Innovation and planned change (Chapter 8).
- Leadership and the school principal (Chapter 9).
- School-based management (Chapter 10).
- School evaluations/reviews (Chapter 11).
- Curriculum reform (Chapter 12).

These span recurring and ongoing issues in curriculum, largely viewed from a management perspective. Curriculum reform (Chapter 12) can also, of course, be a grass-roots/teacher-driven initiative, but over recent times curriculum reform has been decidedly top-down by political/executive directives.

Teaching Perspectives

This is the fourth section in the book and includes two chapters dealing with the following topics.

- Learning environments (Chapter 13).
- Teacher appraisal (Chapter 14).

Learning environments both within and outside the school are an integral part of the learning process and are of major concern to teachers and students (Chapter 13). Teacher appraisals have loomed large in recent years as account-ability pressures continue to increase. However, there are some positive elements which can lead to improved teacher performances and skills (Chapter 14).

Collaborative Involvement in Curriculum

This is the fifth section in the book and includes four chapters dealing with the following topics.

- Collaborative teacher planning and empowerment (Chapter 15).
- Decision-makers, stakeholders and influences (Chapter 16).
- Action research/teachers as researchers (Chapter 17).
- Parent–teacher participation (Chapter 18).

Collaboration in curriculum-making can involve many players including teachers, students, principal and parents (Chapter 16). There are a myriad of stakeholders in curriculum and the list continues to grow (see Chapter 16)!

Action research is a powerful tool for individual teachers and groups of teachers to enquire about and improve their practices (Chapter 17).

Parents' work with schools can vary enormously but there is a powerful pedagogical reason for their close involvement (Chapter 18).

Curriculum Ideology

This is the sixth section in the book and includes three chapters dealing with the following topics.

- Curriculum theorizing (Chapter 19).
- Gender inequalities and the curriculum (Chapter 20).
- Postmodernism and the curriculum (Chapter 21).

Curriculum theorizing is a general process whereby individuals discern emerging patterns in curriculum, identify common patterns and issues and relate these patterns to their own teaching context. There are many diverse approaches to curriculum theorizing ranging from prescriptive to critical-exploratory theorizers (Chapter 19).

Theorizing about the unequal ways in which people are treated because of their gender and sexuality is the focus of gender studies. This includes an analysis of feminist pedagogy and theorizing about male identity, especially challenges to heteronormativity (Chapter 20).

Postmodernism refers to both social conditions and practices. Postmodernists challenge the standardized and traditional, positivist approaches to curriculum development.

Alternative Perspectives

As indicated above, every reader of curriculum will have his or her unique experiences and priorities and may want to read the book in different ways. A small number of possible alternative perspectives are listed below.

Student-centred Perspective

The concepts included in the following chapters emphasize student interests and problems of unequal power relationships between students and teachers. Questions are raised about functions of schools, about schools as a source of conflict for students and about the legal and moral rights of students as clients and consumers.

The following chapters have relevant sections.

- student outcomes (Chapter 4).
- student-oriented modes of learning (Chapter 5).

- authentic assessment (Chapter 6).
- classroom and out-of-school learning environments (Chapter 13).
- collaborative planning (Chapter 15).
- students as stakeholders (Chapter 16).
- gender inequalities (Chapter 20).

Politics of Curriculum Perspective

A perspective which is very evident in the curriculum literature relates to 'politics of curriculum'. According to Longstreet and Shane (1993, p. 93), 'Politics of every sort and at every level of society affect the processes of curriculum, complicating many times over what appear at first glance to be no more than a simple process of translating the overall curriculum design in to a practical plan for students learning'.

The following chapters have relevant sections.

- restriction of curriculum frameworks (Chapter 3).
- standards and political mandates (Chapter 4).
- assessment uses and accountability (Chapter 6).
- measuring curriculum implementation (Chapter 7).
- change leaders (Chapter 8).
- school-based management (Chapter 10).
- reform reports (Chapter 12).
- why do teacher appraisals? (Chapter 14).
- decision-makers and influences (Chapter 16).
- critical exploratory theorizers (Chapter 19).
- poststructuralism and postcolonialism (Chapter 21).

Future Studies and the Curriculum Perspective

Another theme which is also frequently cited in the literature is 'future studies and the curriculum'. As we reach half-way in the first decade of a new millennium there are new emerging pressures and priorities. Various predictions have been made about likely issues for teachers and students in the twenty-first century. Yet the most daunting aspect of all is the profound uncertainty of the future and the need to make decisions despite the uncertainty.

Chapters which allude to future orientations include the following.

- making use of technology (Chapter 5).
- change strategies and tactics (Chapter 8).
- categories of reform (Chapter 12).
- learning settings outside school (Chapter 13).
- decision-makers (Chapter 16).
- critical exploratory theorizers (Chapter 19).
- gender analysis and feminist pedagogy (Chapter 20).
- gender analysis and male identity (Chapter 20).
- postmodernism and schooling (Chapter 21).

Many other themes might be also described but these examples are sufficient to illustrate the combination that can be formed. There are benefits for the reader in reflecting upon each concept and considering examples from their teaching experiences which tend either to support or not to support the statements included in a chapter. The questions at the end of each chapter should also stimulate the reader to ask probing questions and to explore matters further, perhaps by making use of the references at the end of the book.

There are no simple answers or recipes for major issues in curriculum. However, the time spent in reflecting extensively over curriculum matters can be most rewarding. It is to be hoped that the key concepts presented in this volume provide as accessible entry-point for readers embarking upon this journey.

Concluding Comments

It is important to read this book in terms of your major interest in curriculum. The illustrated perspectives included here give an idea of how the chapters can be grouped in various ways. However, the final task of reflection comes back to the reader, who must decide his or her personal priorities.

Part II

Curriculum Planning and Development

3 Curriculum Frameworks

Introduction

Curriculum frameworks can provide an important springboard and focus for teachers in terms of curriculum planning. To a certain extent, they are a tool of control and direction. Yet, they can also be a stimulus for evoking creative ideas and activities.

Many countries are currently involved in developing curriculum frameworks. Some of these are maintaining the status quo while others are very *avant garde*. Various approaches and examples are examined in this chapter.

What Is a Curriculum Framework?

A 'curriculum framework' can be defined as a group of related subjects or themes, which fit together according to a predetermined set of criteria to appropriately cover an area of study. Each curriculum framework has the potential to provide a structure for designing subjects and a rationale and policy context for subsequent curriculum development of these subjects. Examples of school-oriented curriculum frameworks include 'science' (including, for example, biology, chemistry, physics, geology) and 'commerce' (including, for example, accounting, office studies, economics, computing). In the USA the term 'social studies' was first used by the National Education Association in 1894 to describe predominantly history, but also geography, economics, government and civics. However, there have been many other frameworks which have been proposed by educators over the decades, and these are examined next.

Frameworks Produced by Theorists and Educators

Educational theorists over the years have produced their ideal framework groupings. For example, Hirst (1974) has argued convincingly that knowledge can be classified into eight forms, which he labels as:

- mathematics;
- physical sciences;
- human sciences;
- history;

- religion;
- literature and the fine arts;
- philosophy;
- moral knowledge.

Table 3.1 shows a framework based on 'Realms of Meaning'.

As noted by Ribbins (1992), Hirst distinguishes between 'forms' and 'fields' of knowledge, and in some cases there is considerable overlap with school subjects and university disciplines but in other cases very little. Hirst (1967) states:

> I have argued elsewhere that although the domain of human knowledge can be regarded as composed of a number of logically distinct forms of knowledge, we do in fact for many purposes, deliberately and self-consciously organize knowledge into a large variety of fields which often form the units employed in teaching. The problems that arise in teaching such complex fields as ... geography ... are much more difficult to analyse than those arising in such forms as, say, mathematics, physics and history. (Hirst, 1967, p. 44)

Phenix in his work *Realms of Meaning* (1964) maintains that there are six fundamental patterns of meaning that determine the quality of every humanly significant experience (see Table 3.1).

Young (1971) argues that society selects, classifies, distributes, transmits and evaluates educational knowledge. He maintains that academic curricula assume that some kinds and areas of knowledge are much more worthwhile than others. Young argues that frameworks based upon subject-based academic curricula are rarely examined and that they should be seen for what they are – 'no more than historic constructs of a particular time'.

Goodson (1981) is not entirely convinced about the historical basis for the control by dominant groups. Based upon a number of studies he argues that sociologists such as Young have 'raided' history to support their theory:

> Studies develop, so to speak, horizontally working out from theories to social structure and social order. When historical evidence is presented it is provided as a snapshot from the past to prove a contemporary point. (Goodson, 1985, p. 358)

Table 3.1: A framework based on 'Realms of Meaning'

Realm of Meaning	Disciplines
Symbolics	Ordinary language, mathematics, non-discursive symbolic forms
Empirics	Physical sciences, life sciences, psychology, social sciences
Aesthetics	Music, visual arts, arts of movement, literature
Synnoetics	Philosophy, psychology, literature, religion; in their existential aspects
Ethics	The varied special areas of moral and ethical concern
Synoptics	History, religion, philosophy

Lawton (1993) notes that in the United Kingdom conventional subjects that any Member of Parliament could immediately recognize were supported strongly in developing the National Curriculum – any other versions, such as areas of experience (the HMI Entitlement Curriculum Model), were ignored and derided as educational theory; 'an increasingly taboo concept in right-wing circles' (p. 6).

Recent Approaches

Curriculum frameworks developed in the 1990s and twenty-first century are predominantly guides that have been explicitly designed and written to assist school communities of teachers, students and parents in their curriculum 'decision-making' about K-10 programmes (Kerr, 1989). It should be noted that curriculum frameworks can assist in the review and development of curricula by schools *and* system-level personnel. That is, there is an important 'control' element involved too.

Components

A curriculum framework document usually includes:

- a rationale or platform;
- scope and parameters of the curriculum area;
- broad goals and purposes of subjects within the curriculum area;
- guidelines for course design;
- content;
- teaching and learning principles;
- guidelines for evaluation of subjects;
- criteria for accreditation and certification of subjects;
- future developments for the area.

Hardy (1990) argues that the rationale or platform for a curriculum framework is of major importance – a statement of the values, principles and assumptions that have guided those who produced the framework.

Features

A comprehensive and well-developed framework should contain the following features:

- strong links between theory and practice;
- up-to-date and relevant information about pedagogy, learning and resources;
- evocative and inspiring to teachers – they become impressed by its potential as a curriculum area.

Impact upon Teachers

Impact of curriculum frameworks upon teachers:

- frameworks provide greater coherence across subjects and across the grade levels K–12 – they demonstrate the commonalities between subjects within a framework and enable content and skills to be sequenced across grade levels;
- frameworks encourage teachers to evaluate the total learning environment – teachers need to consider the effectiveness of the taught curriculum, and their teaching effectiveness as well as student performances;
- frameworks enable curriculum boundaries to be reconsidered and sometimes redefined – they highlight the changing emphases and the evolving boundaries of subjects;
- frameworks encourage teachers to reconsider their packaging and delivery of subjects – it enables them to develop new emphases (for example, vocational, recreational) and career pathways;
- frameworks enable relatively low-status subjects to be given a more prominent place in the school programme because equal status is given to all frameworks.

Advantages of Using Curriculum Frameworks

The advantages of using curriculum frameworks are:

- students have access to a broader education by being able to select from a number of curriculum frameworks rather than a narrow range of traditional subjects;
- the curriculum will be more coherent and orderly because the framework for each curriculum area is arranged, usually from kindergarten to secondary levels, and priorities are established for each level;
- high-quality curriculum development is likely to occur because planning criteria and standards apply consistently across all curriculum frameworks;
- there are opportunities for curriculum frameworks to include subjects which are highly prescriptive and those that allow considerable flexibility and variation at the school level;
- new content areas and skills can be easily accommodated in curriculum frameworks including various multidisciplinary and interdisciplinary variations;
- curriculum frameworks developed at a state or regional level have the potential to become accepted as national frameworks;
- there are opportunities to incorporate desirable skills into each framework such as communication and language skills, numeracy skills, problem-solving skills.

Disadvantages of Using Curriculum Frameworks

The disadvantages of using curriculum frameworks are:

- if frameworks become too detailed they can become very directive for teachers;
- they can become an instrument of compliance and used as a means of control by central education authorities.

Examples

United Kingdom

In the United Kingdom, a national curriculum framework was established under the Education Reform Act of 1988. It was considered by the Government that 'it is vital to ensure that all pupils between the ages of 5 to 16 study a basic range of subjects – including maths, English and science. In each of these basic subjects syllabuses will be published and attainment targets set so the progress of pupils can be assessed at around ages 7, 11 and 14, and in preparation for the GCSE at 16. Parents, teachers and pupils will then know how well each child is doing' (Conservative Party, 1987).

The National Curriculum consists of three 'core' subjects (mathematics, English and science) and seven 'foundation' subjects (history, geography, technology, music, art, physical education, modern foreign languages). For each subject, programmes of study have been developed that cover a range of knowledge, skills and understandings. Some of the subjects reflect the traditional academic subject boundaries (for example, mathematics) whereas others are used as a broad area or framework (for example, technology). These subjects are intended to comprise 70 per cent of the total school time and students are expected to study all core and foundation subjects.

A tightly prescribed structure has been organized whereby 'attainment targets' (specifying up to ten levels of attainment, covering the ages 5–16) have been established for each subject; assessment activities are for four 'key stages' at ages 5–7, 7–11, 11–14 and 14–16; and 'standard assessment tasks' (SATs) have been designed for each key stage.

There have been major criticisms of the national framework. Goodson (1994) contends that the National Curriculum is a retrogression to the subject-based framework developed in 1904. McCulloch (1998) claims that the implementation of the National Curriculum has proved to be highly bureaucratic and intrusive in its effects.

Ball (1994, p. 46) describes the National Curriculum as 'one which eschews relevance and the present ... Made up of echoes of past voices, the voices of a cultural and political elite; a curriculum which ignores the past of women and the working class and the colonized – a curriculum of the dead'.

Ross (2000) contends that the ten-subject curriculum has an unworkable overload of content and assessment. It produces antagonism from teachers and an alienation of the profession.

Elliott (2002) considers that the National Curriculum in England and Wales is inexorably 'audit-driven', values have been systematically disconnected from the target specifications and the division between core curriculum subjects and foundation subjects creates a lack of balance and a narrowing of the range and variety of learning opportunities for students.

However, there have been some revisions to the National Curriculum since 2000, including reductions in the level of detailed prescription for many subjects and more opportunities for school initiatives at key stages 3 and 4 in the areas of Personal, Social and Health Education and Citizenship Education.

Elliott (2002) contends that the post 2000 reforms are an important shift with their new emphases upon pedagogy and the quality of the learning processes rather than concentrating only upon the content.

Australia

The creation of eight learning areas in Australia in April 1991 has been billed as an innovatory consultative approach to national curriculum development. Although some exploratory mapping of mathematics/numeracy content occurred across all states and territories in 1988, followed by *mapping* of some other areas in 1988–9 (for example, science, technology), a total design was not introduced until several years later by the Australian Education Council (AEC); a new but powerful curriculum player (Grundy, 1994).

At the AEC meeting in April 1991, eight areas of learning were confirmed, namely:

- English;
- science;
- mathematics;
- Languages Other Than English (LOTE);
- technology;
- studies of society and environment;
- the arts;
- health and physical education.

No amplification of these eight areas was produced at this AEC meeting apart from a recognition that a small working group should focus on structures and processes for national collaboration.

Hannan (1992, p. 29), the then Director of Curriculum in Victoria, notes that the creation of the eight learning areas was both pragmatic and conservative – 'this is the break-up nearest to that already in use around the country'.

Of the eight learning areas, four are established subjects, namely English, LOTE, mathematics and science. The remaining four represent collections of subjects or even new studies.

The latter four areas are a curious combination, perhaps reflecting pragmatic decisions and not a little idiosyncratic preference. For example, the inclusion of business studies mainly in studies of society and environment reflects the strongly established grouping of the social sciences and commerce in Victoria. As another example, media studies is included in the arts learning area even though in some states, such as Western Australia, it is incorporated with English at the secondary school level.

For each of the eight learning areas in the framework, national statements and profiles were produced, all within an outcomes-based system. Although Directors-General from each state education system had confirmed in 1992 their strong commitment to implementing national statements and profiles, the political climate had changed a year later (Marsh, 1994). At the AEC meeting in July 1993, state ministers were divided about intentions to implement national statements and profiles, which led to a motion of deferment and subsequent 'posturing' and/or 'killing' of the national curriculum initiative by individual state education systems (Marsh, 1994, p. 164).

Within the following decade, individual state education systems supported to varying degrees the implementation of the national curriculum statements and profiles (Watt, 1998). Although the framework has remained intact in most states, there have been extensive revisions to the structure of each of the eight learning areas, especially the inclusion of more standards-based outcomes (Watt, 2000). In the state of Victoria, the groupings of the eight learning areas have been reviewed, leading to individual subjects being reinstated at secondary school levels. The decision to use syllabuses in the state of New South Wales also led to major variations in that state. Other states, such as South Australia, have recently introduced major variations to the original framework (Blyth, 2002).

As happened in the United Kingdom, there have been criticisms of the national framework in Australia, but the debates have been more muted. Willmott (1994) argues that the eight learning areas of the framework lack a rigorously developed theoretical base – that the division into eight learning areas is a confusing amalgam of traditional subjects and pragmatic expediency.

Reid (1992) argues that there was no research evidence for the profiles approach. He contends that the National Collaborative Curriculum Project 'has been shaped by progressive bureaucrats who are seeking to ward off the worst excesses of the market-driven educational philosophy of the New Right' (p. 15).

Hughes (1990) contends that the professional development implications for teachers are enormous and should not be underrated. Collins (1994b) criticizes the eight areas of knowledge as being 'largely artificial creations with varying degrees of coherence (p. 45)'.

Reflections and Issues

1. 'Frameworks improve the quality of curriculum by assisting in the evaluation of existing curriculum and helping to revise and develop curriculum' (Hardy, 1990, p. 5). In what ways is this likely to occur?
2. 'Schools should operate within the general guidelines of central office personnel – curriculum frameworks enable this to occur.' Discuss.
3. 'Curriculum frameworks provide opportunities for an education system to include new subjects to suit a country's present and future social and economic needs.' To what extent can this occur? Give examples of where such initiatives have been successful.
4. 'The National Curriculum (in the UK) will equip students with the knowledge, skills and understanding that they need for adult life and employment' (Baker, Secretary of State, in Cooper, 1990, p. 144). Do you agree? What have been some of the problems?
5. 'There has been an almost total lack of argument for the National Curriculum (UK), both in general terms and in detail' (Wiegand and Rayner, 1989). Why do you think the foundation subjects were selected for special attention in the framework? What could have been some alternative ways of organizing the curriculum? What opportunities are there for themes and for interdisciplinary work?
6. 'We are left with a curriculum (UK) founded upon a myth about the educational excellence of the old grammar school curriculum. Central to this myth is the idea that the traditional disciplines or subjects encapsulate standards of educational excellence' (Elliott and Chan, 2002, p. 20). Discuss.
7. The national statements and profiles (Australia) reinforce the move towards an outcomes-based education system, in common with many other developed countries. The move towards an outcomes basis is associated with a call for more explicit specification of what should be valued and reported on in schools (Boston, 1994, p. 30). Discuss.
8. The national statements (Australia) represent a summation of the best available knowledge about the content in the eight learning areas. 'It builds upon some of the best of current practice and provides moral support for the continuance of a range of good practices' (Willis 1991, p. 4). Discuss.
9. 'The enthusiasm Australian educational agencies have shown for diverting resources into centrally-driven curriculum development has not translated well into useful products' (Blyth, 2002, p. 21). Discuss.

4 Objectives, Learning Outcomes and Standards

Introduction

Learning within a school environment is typically goal directed. Students are at school because they want to learn certain things, attain specific standards, and perhaps satisfy the requirements for a particular diploma or award. The majority of students are not there, as described mischievously by Postman and Weingartner (1987), to serve out a sentence! Teachers, too, are not serving 'time' in schools but are wanting their students to achieve particular goals or ends.

Objectives provide an answer to what it is that students want to learn and what it is that teachers are trying to teach them. There are many other terms that are used as synonyms, such as 'outcomes', 'goals', 'aims', 'purpose', 'intentions'. Some authors, such as Moore (2001) and Glatthorn and Jailall (2000), make distinctions between some of these terms but, based upon widespread use and application, the major terms are undoubtedly 'objectives', 'outcomes' and 'standards'.

Objectives

Objectives greatly assist the planning process for teachers. The foundation for well-planned teaching is, unquestionably, clearly stated objectives. Some teachers resist using objectives because they consider they are too limiting or are inappropriate for certain content that cannot be specifically defined or evaluated. Yet measurement experts such as Mager (1984) point out that 'if you are teaching things that cannot be evaluated, you are in the awkward position of being unable to demonstrate that you are teaching anything at all. Intangibles are often intangible because we have been too lazy to think about what it is we want students to be able to do' (p. 5).

In terms of the teaching role, objectives provide the opportunity for teachers to formulate and, it is hoped, act upon, clear statements about what students are intended to learn through instruction. We are probably all aware of anecdotes which refer to the guessing games which can occur between a teacher and students. For example: What does our teacher want us to learn? I don't know what he/she wants. Is it to memorize/regurgitate certain content or is it to apply and explain certain content? Objectives, if conveyed to students, can eradicate a lot of these misunderstandings and can lead to a higher level of communication between the teacher and students.

Objectives are also likely to lead to higher levels of achievement by students, but only under certain conditions. For example, objectives can lead to better learning in lessons which are loosely structured, such as research projects or a film. However, for lessons which involve very structured materials, such as a tightly sequenced laboratory experiment or a computer program, objectives seem to be less important (Tobias and Duchastel, 1974). Objectives assist teachers and students to focus upon what will be evaluated. There should be a close relationship between the assignments, tests and checklists used by the teacher and the objectives for the particular teaching unit or lessons. The feedback received by students from particular assessments lets them know whether they are achieving the standards required.

Outcomes

Willis and Kissane (1997) define outcome statements as 'broad descriptions of student competencies which reflect long term learning of significance beyond school, and which are superordinate to the details of any particular curriculum content, sequence or pedagogy' (p. 21).

Outcome statements concentrate upon the outputs rather than the inputs of teaching. Exponents of this approach argue that objectives only concentrate upon the inputs of teaching.

To a certain extent, the approach represents a recycling of earlier movements, especially in the USA, such as mastery learning and competency-based education. Yet, it does not incorporate specific behavioural statements. Rather, the emphasis is upon broad outcome statements to be achieved, eight to twelve statements per learning area (which typically comprises several teaching subjects).

A very successful and leading exponent of outcome-based education in the USA has been William Spady. According to Spady (1993) 'Outcome-based education' means focusing and organizing a school's entire programme and instructional efforts around the clearly defined outcomes we want all students to demonstrate when they leave school (p. ii).

That is, the intended learning results are the start-up points in defining the system (Hansen, 1989). A set of conditions are described that characterize real life and these are used to derive a set of culminatory role performances. Students are required to provide a culminating demonstration – the focus is upon competence as well as content but not on the time needed to reach this standard. Specifically, an outcome is an actual demonstration in an authentic context (Spady, 1993, p. 4).

Moore (2001) notes that in the USA there have been many versions of outcome-based education (OBE) but all of them promote system-level change –

'observable, measurable outcomes; and the belief that all students can learn' (p. 98).

This may have been their major attraction and the cause for their demise; they promised far-reaching reform but could not deliver.

Some states within the USA were enthusiastic about OBE at first, such as the Pennsylvania Department of Education which recommended it be used throughout the state (Glatthorn and Jailall, 2000). However, by the mid-1990s OBE was being widely criticized in terms of:

(a)   its over emphasis on outcomes rather than processes;
(b)   schools inflicting values that conflicted with parental values;
(c)   lack of hard evidence that OBE worked;
(d)   fears that OBE would 'dumb-down' the curriculum and lead to lower standards;
(e)   concerns that content becomes subservient under an OBE approach;
(f)   student outcome statements being difficult and expensive to assess.

As a result, OBE in the USA rapidly declined in the 1990s to be overtaken by standards-based (content standards) and constructivist approaches (Glatthorn and Jailall, 2000).

Standards

The raising of educational standards is a constant cry in educational reform. In the USA there was a major impetus in the 1990s to create 'unified national standards that would ensure consistent delivery and outcomes across diverse state systems and districts via the Educate America Act, 1994' (Blyth, 2002, p. 7).

Knowledge experts in the various subject fields have produced standards for their respective subjects (see Table 4.1). These standards have been taken up by individual states in the USA and incorporated into state curriculum frameworks and mastery tests. According to Arends (2000) 'state frameworks have an important influence on what is taught in schools because mastery tests are usually built around the performance standards identified in the frameworks' (p. 52).

Table 4.1: Examples of subject matter Curriculum Standards (USA)

English	Standards for the Assessment of Reading and Writing
Foreign languages	Standards for Foreign Language Learning
History	US History Standards
Mathematics	Curriculum and Evaluation Standards for Social Mathematics
Science	National Science Education Standards
See also:	http://project2061.aaas.org/
	http://putwest.boces.org/standards.html

A distinction needs to be made between content and performance standards. Content standards declare knowledge to be acquired, whether it is processes or content. Performance standards are tasks to be completed by a student where the knowledge is embedded in the task and where a student has to use the knowledge and skills in a certain way.

Marzano and Kendall (1996) contend that both content and performance standards need to be used. Further, they suggest that the content standards are articulated at a general level but with specific subcomponents at developmental levels or 'benchmarks'. As noted by Blyth (2002) 'benchmarks are essential in describing the developmental components of the general domain identified by a standard.'

Standards seem to be welcomed by many teachers and citizens (see Figure 4.1). Various writers extol the virtues of the new standards – they are a better way to develop conceptual understanding and reasoning (Goldsmith and Mark, 1999).

Rosenholtz (1991) asserts that standards provides a common focus, clarifies understanding, accelerates communication and promotes persistence and collective purpose.

Yet, other educators are more cautious. Schmoker and Marzano (1999) raise the question, will the standards movement endure? They contend that educators have to be very disciplined about writing clear standards and for the standards to be limited in number. Moore (2001) notes that the standards must be carefully linked to assessment. Glatthorn and Jailall (2000) assert that many of the standards are too vague about content.

The Relative Merits of Objectives, Outcomes and Standards

In the 1970s, various educators criticized what they perceived to be undue attention being devoted to objectives in teaching, and especially behavioural objectives. For example, Eisner (1979, p. 103) developed the term *expressive objective* and later *expressive outcome* to demonstrate that not all teaching requires the same degree of certainty.

It is evident that outcome statements together with pointers and work samples do provide considerable guidance for teachers about the standard required in a specific subject or learning area. Whether they are a better planning mechanism than objectives is problematic – there is insufficient empirical evidence available to be categoric about this matter (Ellis and Fouts, 1993). All that we can list at this time are the possible *advantages:*

- they are more explicit statements about what students should be able to do;
- they allow teachers more flexibility in planning their teaching;
- there is less emphasis upon content to be covered and more emphasis upon skills/competencies to be achieved;

- they provide more concrete details about student performance for parents;
- they will enable teachers and school principals to be more accountable about student standards;
- they can address higher-order thinking skills;
- they acknowledge differing learning styles and forms of intelligence.

It should be emphasized that none of these purported advantages has been substantiated in the research literature. Further, educators are still searching for solutions to some major problems such as the following.

- Enormous workloads for teachers (especially primary school teachers) to assess students on outcome statements even when using special computer software such as KIDMAP.
- Providing sufficient professional development training for teachers on the outcomes-based approach. Teachers need substantial training to arrive at a shared commitment to the achievement of a common set of outcome statements (Griffin, 1998).
- Developing outcome statements (and pointers) which are meaningful and assessable. It cannot be assumed that all teachers will interpret them in the same way (Willis and Kissane, 1997).
- Developing an economical system to monitor whether the outcomes have been achieved or not (Brady, 1996).
- Obtaining evidence that an outcomes approach will lead to improved learning (Darling-Hammond, 1994).

Educators reacting to the national profiles in Australia have also been critical of attempts to specify in advance the outcome levels for students. Collins (1994a, p. 14) concludes that the 'profiles are just, quite literally, cultural artefacts ... the levels do not mark a necessary ordering of any developmental sequence (more accurately, we have no evidence that they do), but are simply a setting out of particular, and likely to change, majority cultural patterns.'

It can also be argued that objectives share many of the advantages listed for outcomes without incurring the disadvantages. For example, objectives enable teachers and students to focus upon major concepts, they can be communicated easily to parents and students and they enable assessment procedures to be directly related to the objectives. Furthermore, objectives do not have some of the inherent weaknesses of outcome statements in that there are no assumptions about developmental/growth levels or necessity for semi-arbitrary areas of knowledge to be divided into strands.

Types of Objectives

Objectives can range from the general to the highly specific. It can be argued that the two extremes have relatively little impact upon teachers. General abstract statements about such affairs as intellectual development or citizenship provide little insight for the teacher. On the other hand, objectives that are so tightly focused that they concentrate upon low-level, insignificant facts or processes are also of very limited use to teachers.

Behavioural Objectives

Behavioural objectives are perceived by some educators to be at a middle position between these two extremes. These objectives focus upon observable and measurable changes in students. Typically, adherents of behavioural objectives require three criteria to be met, namely: evidence of achievement, conditions of performance and acceptable levels of performance.

Evidence of Achievement

The performance by learners must be stated as an observable student behaviour. Hence it is suggested that teachers should use terms which are observable, such as:

- List
- Define
- Add
- Calculate
- Demonstrate

Example: Students will *list* the states and territories of Australia.

Conditions of Performance

This criterion requires that the important conditions under which the behaviour is expected to occur must also be specified.

Example: Using a compass and a ruler, construct two tangents to a circle of 6cm diameter from an external point 12cm from the circle centre.

Acceptable Levels of Performance

It is also necessary to state the minimum acceptable levels of performance, or in other words, the criterion for success. It defines the desired performance and may be expressed in terms of speed (amount of time taken), accuracy or quality.

Example: Students must spell accurately 90% of the 15 words presented.

By combining these three criteria, we get detailed behavioural objectives which can be readily observed and measured.

Example: Students will match up accurately 90% of the rivers listed with their location in states of Australia without using their workbooks.

Instructional Objectives

A case can be made for instructional objectives (behavioural or non-behavioural) to be used by teachers to assist with the instructional process. They provide a clearer direction and overcome vague ideas that might not have been fully developed. Further, they assist the teacher in selecting appropriate content, teaching strategies, resources and assessment. Having instructional objectives can also assist the teacher in demonstrating accountability to the principal, to parents, and to the head office education system personnel (Cohen *et al.*, 1998).

For each major unit of instruction it is reasonable and useful for a teacher to develop a number of instructional objectives – for example, two to six. Of course, the teacher will have help in formulating objectives – help from national and state, governmental and professional, local district and school resources. And these objectives should be statements of the major purposes to guide the teacher and the student through the curriculum. As noted earlier, objectives can act like a road map. A road map need not specify every town and creek to be useful. Likewise objectives for a unit of instruction need not specify every change in student behaviour.

Without following the strict criteria described above for behavioural objectives, there are some criteria which enable teachers and curriculum developers to produce effective instructional objectives. These include:

- *scope*: the objectives must be sufficiently broad to include all desirable outcomes, presumably relating to knowledge, skills and values;
- *consistency*: the objectives should be consistent with each other and reflect a similar value orientation;
- *suitability*: the objectives should be relevant and suitable for students at particular grade levels;
- *validity*: the objectives should reflect and state what we want them to mean;
- *feasibility*: the objectives should be attainable by all students;
- *specificity*: the objectives should avoid ambiguity and be phrased precisely.

To follow each of these criteria closely would be an exacting task. Nevertheless, it is important to keep them in mind when devising appropriate instructional objectives.

Classifying Objectives

During the 1970s experts in educational evaluation, led in particular by Benjamin Bloom, began exploring the possibility of classifying objectives in terms of cognitive, affective and psychomotor behaviours. Cognitive objectives deal with intellectual processes such as knowing, perceiving, recognizing and reasoning. Affective objectives deal with feeling, emotion, appreciation and valuing. Psychomotor objectives deal with skilled ways of moving such as throwing a ball, dancing and handwriting. Of course, it is important to remember that in real life, behaviours from these three domains occur simultaneously. Notwithstanding, by focusing upon one domain at a time we can gain important insights about planning lessons.

To celebrate the fortieth anniversary of the publication of *Taxonomy of Educational Objectives, Handbook 1, Cognitive Domain* (Bloom *et al.*, 1956) notable educators in the United Stated produced critiques which were included in the volume edited by Anderson and Sosniak (1994). Some of the conclusions made by these authors are worth noting:

- Teacher educators at universities have used the *Taxonomy* to help teachers plan their lessons, prepare their tests and ask questions.
- Teachers have made little use of the *Taxonomy* because it is too time-consuming, it is not practical to spend time on the higher-order objectives (which takes away time from content), and it is too rational and complex.
- The *Taxonomy* concentrates upon categorizing and does not provide any guidance about how to translate these objectives into teaching programmes – as a result it has had limited impact.
- The major enduring influence of the *Taxonomy* has been to convey the notion of higher- and lower-level cognitive behaviours.
- The *Taxonomy* has been used extensively by experts preparing tests.
- Although the *Taxonomy* purports to be descriptive and neutral, it concentrates upon overt student behaviours only.
- The *Taxonomy* has been a major focus for discussion in most countries of the world; it has forced educators to raise questions as to whether they have varied the cognitive level of tasks, exercises and examinations they propose, and whether they sufficiently stimulate their students to think.

Concluding Comments

Teachers undertake purposeful activities in schools. To give direction to what the teacher and students are doing involves the communication to all parties of particular intents. Over the decades, 'objectives' in their various forms have been used to communicate intent. 'Outcomes' and 'standards' are currently being highlighted as more user-friendly approaches to communicate intent. It is problematic whether their popularity will continue into the next decade (Glatthorn and Fontana, 2002).

Reflections and Issues

1. Instructional objectives can be powerful directives in the teaching process. Discuss.
2. Objectives appear to stand for an excessive interest in efficiency, an undue and misplaced zeal for things rather than process or experience... they seem to portray little heaps of knowledge, rather than an integrating structure or matrix. Critically analyse this statement.
3. To what extent is it possible in practice to devise outcomes for which all students can achieve satisfactory standards? Outline some of the possibilities and problems in achieving this end.
4. Compare and contrast the benefits of 'behavioural' objectives and 'instructional' objectives.
5. Compare the advantages and disadvantages of using an outcome-based and a standards-based approach to curriculum planning.
6. How are the standards established by central policy makers more desirable than the standards currently set by texts and high-status tests?

5 Selecting and Organizing Teaching and Learning Modes

Introduction

The teacher who works at developing a varied combination of instructional modes of teaching is moving strongly to becoming a flexible teacher, and most likely to becoming a very effective one. We tend to prefer particular teaching and learning modes for a variety of reasons. It is less than professional to remain in a state of inertia with regard to a few modes when there are a number of exciting options available. Just some of the possibilities are listed in Table 5.1. Several are described in detail in this chapter.

Matching Teacher and Student Priorities

It might appear to be merely commonsense that teaching styles need to be matched with students' learning styles. We have all experienced at first hand teaching situations where the teacher's style and students' learning styles have been very different, to the extent in some 'war' stories of being diametrically opposed!

Table 5.1: *Overview of eighteen alternative teaching and learning modes*

- constructivist learning
- debates
- demonstrations
- direct instruction
- discussion
- field work
- independent study
- inquiry
- cooperative learning
- learning centres
- lectures and presentations
- mastery learning
- oral reports
- practice drills
- project learning
- small group brainstorming
- questioning
- simulations and role plays

Various authors such as Dunn *et al.* (1989, p. 50) contend that it is crucial for teachers to match their styles with students' learning styles.

Every person has a learning style – it's as individual as a signature. Knowing students' learning styles, we can organize classrooms to respond to their individual needs.

There is significant research evidence to support this stance (Liu and Read, 1994; Witkin *et al.*, 1977). A recent study by Ford and Chen (2001) concluded that students who learned in matched conditions scored significantly higher in conceptual knowledge. However, in their study the males out performed females in matched conditions, so there are other complications to consider such as the role of gender in the interactions between matching/mismatching.

It can be very difficult to diagnose learning styles of students. What criteria do you use? For example, is performance in certain subjects more important than potential? How do you take account of students' needs and interests? Although it might be laudable to argue that you match learning tasks to the needs, interests, abilities and previous experiences of students, how do you do this in practice?

Another element to consider is whether students care about learning. What invites students to learn? Tomlinson (2002) contends that students seek an affirmation that they are significant in the classroom. As a consequence, matching factors should be couched in terms of:

- their acceptance in the classroom;
- making them feel safe – physically, emotionally and intellectually;
- making them consider people care about them and listen to them.

Morrison and Ridley (1988) use a similar argument when they suggest that teachers need to consider the following questions when matching their students.

- How is each students' self concept being developed?
- How is each students' motivation being developed?
- How does a teaching style(s) meet students' individual differences of need, interest, ability and skill?
- How does a teaching style(s) develop individual learning styles and rates of learning?
- How is autonomy being developed in each student?
- How does the organization of the class and school facilities foster security in each student?

The other side of the equation is to consider the teaching styles of teachers, which are often the result of personal attitudes and values, personality, previous experience and availability of resources. Hargreaves (1995) distinguishes between three major teaching styles, which he labels as 'lion tamers' (i.e. firm discipline, teacher as expert); 'entertainers' (i.e. multiple resources, active group work); and 'new normalities' (i.e. negotiated, individualized teaching).

Ryan and Cooper (2000) use the terms 'concrete sequential', 'abstract sequential', 'abstract random' and 'concrete random' to categorize four dominant teaching styles. A 'concrete sequential' teacher relies on hands-on materials, working models and displays to help students learn and tends to use task-oriented lessons. 'Abstract sequential' teachers value depth of knowledge and assist students to think about topics and to generate ideas. 'Abstract random' teachers capitalize on student interest and enthusiasm rather than adhering strictly to a lesson plan. 'Concrete random' teachers rely upon a variety of resources and organize their classes so that students operate independently or cooperatively.

These are just a few of the many groupings and stereotypes which have been produced about teaching styles. The major point to stress is that there are many differences and that we need to be aware that teaching styles will be dependent upon such factors as:

- type of activity in the classroom;
- type of organization of the classroom;
- use of resources;
- grouping and organization of students;
- students' roles in the classroom;
- criteria used for assessing students; and
- nature and amount of student and teacher talk.

Yet it is also important to heed Joyce and Weil's (1986, pp. 433–4) caveats about learning styles, namely:

- It is not possible for teachers to assess the developmental levels of all their students and then create totally personalized curricula exactly matching their levels.
- Students can and will adapt to different teaching styles if we give them the chance.
- The simplest way to discover the environments students progress best in is to provide them with a variety and observe their behaviour.

These authors are emphasizing the adaptability of teachers and by students. No teacher has a fixed style of teaching and no student has a fixed style of learning. In teaching–learning situations it is crucial that participants are flexible and adaptable.

Joyce and Weil (1986) provide additional insights into learning and teaching styles by their use of the term *discomfort*. They argue that a discomfort factor is necessary for teachers and students. If an environment is perfectly matched to the developmental levels of learners, it can be too comfortable and there will be little advance beyond that level. That is, discomfort is a precursor to growth. Teachers need to be constantly trying out new teaching styles even if they are unfamiliar and cause discomfort. For their part, teachers must assist students to acquire the necessary skills to adapt to new, unfamiliar learning styles.

Making Use of Technology

All modes of instruction make use of some form of technology, ranging from chalk to elaborate computer packages. Some forms of technology we take for granted, such as chalk, marker pens and white boards, especially if they do not interfere with a well-proven, traditional mode of instruction. Even the use of slide projectors and overhead projectors causes minimal interference to teacher-directed forms of delivery.

It is when major behavioural changes are called for that teachers espouse concerns about using technology. There may be good reason for this techno-phobia if it involves different grouping patterns of students, if the authority of the teacher role is reduced, or if the teacher has to learn new skills. Fear of using computers in schools, 'cyberphobia' (Russell and Bradley, 1996), may be quite deep seated and may occur in young teachers as well as older, highly experienced teachers.

There are currently many proponents who extol the virtues of incorporating computers into classroom activities – that is, technology-infused instruction. 'It will become as integral a part of the classroom as the whiteboard' (Gardner, 1997, p. 6). 'Multimedia (computers) create rich learning environments where kids really thrive' (Betts, 1997, p. 20).

Within a few short years computer technology for educational use has expanded rapidly. There is now a range of software programs available, which can provide highly sophisticated functions relating to *computer-managed instruction* (CMI) and *computer-assisted instruction* (CAI).

CMI assists teachers with various organizational tasks including recording student activities, resource investigations and presentation, and recording of students assessments.

Instructional opportunities for students (CAI) are forever increasing (Williams, 2000). Norton and Wiburg (2003) include the following examples.

- Skills software for drilling and practising – skills software programs offer interactive experiences, generally with immediate feedback about performance.
- Computer graphics programs enable students to experience the world other than through verbal and print language. According to Norton and Wiburg (2003), 'shape, size, proportion, relationship, scale, surface, texture and rhythm are all expressed more rapidly through image making than through using words' (p. 53).
- Word processors, desktop publishers and web-based editors – word processors are computer programs that allow the student to write, edit, revise, format and print text. Documents can include text and graphics at a standard similar to professional printers. Web-based editors enable students to create Web pages for publication on the Internet.

- Data bases – text-based data bases include only text information; hypermedia data bases provide information with access through links; multimedia data bases include a variety of media forms including pictures, video clips, text and sound.
- Telecommunication opportunities include E-mail messages; listservs distribute a single message to multiple receivers; bulletin boards post a public message to multiple receivers; chat rooms allow online conversations with multiple participants; synchronous communication allows two or more persons to interact at the exact same time.
- Internet-accessing of teaching/learning programs is readily available and fun to use. For example, Jones (2002) refers to 'The Human Race', an interactive Internet site that enables students to enjoy regular physical activity away from their computers.
- Simulations – many educational software publishers produce simulations. 'Students are given the power to "play" with a model of the subject being studied and to experience the effects of changing different variables in the model' (Norton and Wiburg, 2003, p. 57).
- Mathematical devices provide students with the opportunity to explore real-time data. For example, probeware allows students to measure temperature, humidity, distance and many related variables. Large amounts of data can be collected in a class period.
- Assessment of student performance software is increasing rapidly. There are now programs available which create a variety of rubrics (criteria for judging performance); electronic portfolios of work can be created; problem-solving processes of students can be observed and recorded; and a new set of interpretive tools is being created to monitor higher-level thinking and group collaboration.
- On-line courses are being developed at all levels of schooling. Lifter and Adams (1997) describe a Virtual Enrichment Program for primary students living in outback areas of New South Wales, Australia. Secondary students living in small towns and outback areas of Queensland, Australia, are being offered on-line (asynchronous) and real-time (synchronous) forms of instruction (Gibbs and Krause, 2000).

In summary, computer technology enables classroom instruction to be greatly benefited because it:

- provides the flexibility to meet the individual needs and abilities of each student (Norton and Wiburg, 2003);
- provides students with immediate access to rich source materials beyond the school and beyond the nation – that is, it fosters cross-cultural perspectives (Norton and Wiburg, 2003);
- presents information in new, relevant ways;
- encourages students to try out new ideas and to problem-solve (Means, 2000);

- encourages students to design, plan and undertake project-based multi-media learning (Simkins *et al.*, 2002);
- motivates and stimulates learning (Norton and Wiburg, 2003);
- enables students to feel comfortable with the tools of the Information Age.

Yet, it is evident in many schools that modes of instruction have been little affected by computer technology – 'with all of the investment of time and money that has gone into putting the hardware and software in place in schools, students will spend most of their school days as if these tools and information resources had never been invented' (Becker, 1998, p. 24).

Various reasons have been given for the limited amount of take-up in schools, including the following:

- Teachers are unfamiliar with the equipment, and the time and resources are not available for comprehensive, ongoing training.
- There is an insufficient school budget for sufficient numbers of personal computers, software, network wiring or support technicians to be available.
- There is limited pre-service preparation of teachers in the use of computer technology (Norton and Wiburg, 2003) and resultant student teachers' anxiety about using computers (Orlich *et al.*, 1998).
- There is no overwhelming research evidence that teachers can be more effective using computer-based lessons rather than non-computer-based lessons (Russell and Bradley, 1996).
- The problems of equity for poorly funded schools could be heightened.
- Gender problems are caused in that females tend to be portrayed in stereotypical ways. Females still have limited access to computer technology (Norton and Wiburg, 2003).
- Computer-based technology threatens teachers – they are likely to increasingly lose control over the work they do (Bigum, 1997).
- Computer technology is not a neutral force in the classroom. It concentrates upon speed and power and downplays student reflection and ethics (Schwartz, 1996).
- There is increasing evidence that it may discourage social interaction and lead to isolate behaviours.
- There are reports of considerable health risks for teachers (eye strain, wrist and shoulder pain) and students (effects of carrying heavy laptops to and from school) (Norton and Wiburg, 2003).
- There are a growing number of cases of students cheating (Cybercheating) at all levels of teaching (Gardner, 1997; Russell and Bradley, 1996).

Perhaps Means' (2001) warning is timely: 'We should reflect on "Online and offline: Getting the mixture right", or expressed another way "E-world and R-world: Getting the mixture right"' (p. 13).

Phases of Instruction

Before embarking upon a detailed analysis of specific modes of instruction, it is important to note that within each mode there are relatively common phases that tend to occur. All have some introductory phases, a main activity phase, and a concluding or application phase. The amount of emphasis given to each phase will depend upon the orientation/value stance of the mode of instruction.

Various influencing patterns are in operation in every classroom, in activities where the teacher influences students, and in activities where the students influence the teacher. As a result, tactics initially planned by a teacher may need to be aborted, revised or continued as a result of student reactions. Students, in turn, either overtly or covertly accept the mode of instruction, attempt to modify it or, on rare occasions, reject it outright.

Teaching and Learning Modes

Teachers are often urged to use a variety of modes to ensure that diverse student interests and abilities can be accommodated. Yet, teachers are limited in the modes they can use because of:

- restricted student abilities and interests;
- the high number of students in a class;
- the limitations of the teaching room, and/or
- insufficient background or knowledge about a specific instructional mode;
- the type of technology available.

The last point is especially important in that technology has varied application for all modes of instruction. Simplistically, it might be argued that the computer is used as a tutor for teacher-directed lessons (knowledge instruction setting) and as a tool in student-centred lessons (knowledge construction setting) (Galbraith, 1997).

It is evident from Table 5.2 that a wide variety of modes is available and most teachers have the opportunity to expand their repertoire. There is only space to describe two instructional modes below.

Examples of Modes

Directed Questioning

The use of questions to students, both oral and written, is a very common mode of instruction. There are various reasons why teachers use questions and not all are related to student learning! Questions are used to:

- get immediate feedback during a demonstration;
- focus a discussion;
- pose a problem for solution;
- help students sharpen their perceptions;
- attract a student's attention;
- get a particular student to participate;
- diagnose a student's weaknesses;
- allow a student to shine before his or her peers;
- build up a student's security to an extent where the teacher is quite sure the student will respond correctly.

Table 5.2: Teacher-directed (T) and student-centred (S) emphases in lessons

Models of instruction	Introduction	Major activity	Conclusion	Teacher's role	Students' role	Organization mode
Lecturing/ teacher talks	T	T	T	Presents information	Listen and respond	Total class
Practise drills	T	T/S	T	Repeats examples until skill mastered	Respond and practice	Total class/ small groups
Directed questioning	T	T/S	T	Presents questions	Respond with answer, occasional answers	Total class/ small groups/ individual
Direct instruction	T	T/S	T/S	Presents task	Master task	Total class
Demonstration	T	S	T/S	Presents information materials	Observe, listen, practice	Total class/ small groups
Constructivism	T/S	T/S	T/S	Raises issues	Active learning	Total class/ small groups
Discussion	T	T/S	T/S	Questions, listens, responds	Listen, respond, question	Total class/ small groups/ individual
Cooperative learning	T/S	T/S	T/S	Presents goals	Work in groups	Small groups
Problem solving/enquiry	T	S	T/S	Directs activities	Engage in activities	Small groups/ individual
Role playing, simulation games	T	S	T/S	Introduces, monitors	Participate/ act out	Small groups
Project-based learning/ problem-based learning	T	S	T/S	Introduces, monitors	Active learning	Individual or small groups
Independent study	S	S	S	Facilitates, monitors	Initiate, engage in activities	Individual

Questions can be used in rapid-fire succession or they can proceed more slowly with time for thoughtful responses. The types of questions a teacher asks will determine the kind of thinking they want their students to do. Various writers have provided different classifications of questions. Some of these include:

- *high- and low-order questions*
  low-order – mainly recall of facts and specifics
  high-order – mainly application analysis
- *convergent and divergent or closed and open questions*
  convergent/closed – lead to expected answers
  divergent/open – allow new directions in answers
- *what, when, how, who and why*
  a useful range to use which proceeds in sequence from low-order to high-order.

Asking appropriate questions is a difficult task and requires considerable practice. A useful starting point is to choose an appropriate topic and then write down a range of questions which cover the sequences listed above. Ensure that the questions are concise and at an appropriate level of difficulty for students. Eliminate questions that appear to be ambiguous or vague. Table 5.3 provides some useful beginnings for questions based upon the purposes in mind.

It is timely to remember that preparing good questions is only part of the exercise. Knowing how to present the questions to the class and responding to their reactions is of major importance. A basic rule is to ask the question, pause and then call on a specific student by name to respond (Orlich *et al*, 1998). Using eye contact; distributing questions around the room; giving the students plenty of time to answer (wait time of 3–5 seconds); extending thinking by using further probes such as 'Are you sure?', 'Give me an example', are just some of the techniques to ensure successful use of directed questioning.

Moore (2001) has a more detailed list of guidelines to help teachers refine their skill at questioning, namely:

- ask clear questions;
- ask your question before designating a respondent;
- ask questions that match your lesson objectives;

Table 5.3: Some examples of question beginnings

Purpose	Use questions that begin with
To assess knowledge	→ Define, Describe, Tell, List, Who, When, Identify, Where
To check understanding	→ How do you know? Explain, Compare, Contrast
To help analyse problems	→ What causes, How, Why?
To explore values	→ How do you feel? Why do you prefer? Why do you feel?
To encourage creative thinking	→ What if, How else, Just suppose
To evaluate	→ Select, Judge, Evaluate
To apply knowledge	→ Demonstrate, Use the information to construct

- distribute questions about the class fairly;
- ask questions suited to all ability levels in the class;
- ask only one question at a time;
- avoid asking questions too soon;
- pause for at least 3 seconds following each question;
- use questions to help students modify their responses;
- avoid too many questions that give away answers, and avoid one-word-answer questions;
- reinforce student answers sparingly;
- listen carefully to student responses.

Often students are very anxious about teacher questions and, in particular, their answers, because they realize that they will be judged by their peers as well as the teacher. They may be cautious in answering because of a lack of self-confidence. If the climate of the classroom is positive and supportive, students may be more prepared to take personal risks. It is up to the teacher to support students who are not confident about answering questions by rephrasing questions, asking supplementary questions or providing additional information.

Cooperative Learning

Cooperative learning is a form of small-group instruction that has become especially popular with teachers and students. It is advocated as a complement to direct instruction and to teaching which is often highly competitive. Research evidence indicates that students gain considerably from cooperative learning across all grade levels of schooling (Ellis and Fouts, 1993).

A number of different approaches to cooperative learning have been developed but most share the characteristics listed in Table 5.4. Cooperative learning is a technique where a group is given a task to do that includes efforts

Table 5.4: Characteristics of cooperative learning classrooms

- Most classroom activities involve using small groups of three to five students
- Each group is as heterogeneous as possible in terms of gender, ethnicity, and knowledge and ability
- The teacher and students set clear, specific, individual and group goals
- Each student has to achieve certain individual goals as well as being accountable for group success
- The teacher provides worthwhile group rewards on the basis of group members' individual achievements
- Each group divides up group work into individual tasks
- Each group member soon learns that interdependence is needed for the group to function effectively. This involves a considerable amount of face-to-face interaction
- Each group member learns effective listening and communicating skills as well as group-processing skills
- Each group evaluates its level of success

from all students. Students need to interact with and support each other in completing the overall task and the sub-tasks.

According to Cruickshank *et al.* (2003) cooperative learning occurs when learners work together in small groups and are rewarded for their collective accomplishments (see Table 5.5).

Groups or teams of four to six work on particular tasks. The members of the group are selected so that they are heterogeneous in terms of gender, academic ability, race and other traits. The rules of behaviour for participants involve responsibility and accountability to one's self and the team, and a willingness to encourage peer help and cooperate with other team members. The rewards or marks are based on the team's achievement.

A number of different cooperative learning models have been developed and used in school settings. The Jigsaw method involves the following:

- The teacher divides the class into teams of five or six students ensuring that there is a mix of abilities in each team.
- The assigned team activity has subtasks so that there is one task for each team member, which is variously labelled as A, B, etc.
- The persons assigned to do task A in each team come together and form a new team. New teams are also formed for B, etc.
- The newly formed teams (A team, B team, etc.) work on completing their task by discussing issues and then working individually or collectively.
- When the tasks have been completed, the students reassemble in their original teams. Each team member (A, B, etc.) shares his or her information and this is compiled into the overall assignment which is then submitted to the teacher.

Once a teacher has selected a particular approach it is then necessary to undertake the following planning steps:

1. Develop materials – this may involve a mini-lecture to be given by the teacher for the preparation of text, worksheets and study guides for each group to use directly.
2. Plan the tasks and roles for students in each group – students need to have a clear understanding of their roles. It may take several sessions before students are familiar with what to do.
3. Plan for the use of time and space – don't under-estimate the time needed for cooperative learning lessons.

Table 5.5: Benefits of cooperative learning

- Improves learning of academic content
- Improves student strategies for acquiring information
- Develops social skills
- Boosts students' self-esteem
- Allows student decision-making

Once the planning sequence has been completed the steps involved in the actual lessons include:

- Teacher goes over goals for the lesson.
- Teacher presents information to students either verbally or with text.
- Teacher explains to students how to form their learning teams.
- Teacher assists learning teams as they do their work.
- Teacher tests knowledge of learning materials or groups present results of their work.
- Teacher finds ways to recognize both individual and group effort and achievement (Arends, 2000, p. 332).

Not all lessons are conducive to cooperative learning. Ideally, topics are used which require the searching out of answers and the exploration of alternative solutions. The teacher also has to make organizational decisions which may only be possible in certain circumstances – for example, re-arranging the room furniture and organizing materials. There can also be difficulties in groups and personality conflicts still occur. Students may need considerable help in developing problem-solving skills (Barry *et al.*, 1998).

To overcome some of these difficulties, especially with lower grades, it may be necessary for the teacher to assign roles. Chapin and Messick (1999) suggest the following:

- One student as chairperson to organize the group's work.
- One student as recorder or secretary to write down the group's answers.
- One student as check person to check that everyone can explain and agree with completed answers.
- One student as encourager to keep participants interested and excited.

The research evidence on cooperative learning is extremely positive and includes literally hundreds of published studies (see, for example, Ellis and Fouts, 1993; Orlich *et al.*, 1998; Emmer and Gerwell, 1998). Some of the major findings include:

- Achievement effects of cooperation learning are consistently positive – that is, experimental groups have significant positive effects over control groups.
- Positive achievement effects occur across all grade levels from 2 to 12, in all major subjects, and the effects are equally positive for high, average and low achievers.

Concluding Comments

Teachers and students both benefit from initiating/experiencing a range of modes of instruction. How a particular mode of instruction is used in a classroom is dependent upon a number of factors and there will be many variations and hybrids from an idealized mode. Further, it is a learning process for all participants and early experimentations with different instructional modes are likely to cause discomfort – for both the teacher and the students. Yet it is essential that a varied combination of modes are used to ensure that all students are exposed to at least some approaches which are closely amenable to their interests and preferred ways of learning.

Reflections and Issues

1. Reflect upon the modes of instruction you have used/typically use in the classroom. Why do you prefer these approaches? List some possible advantages and disadvantages for each.
2. 'Students are not failing because of the curriculum. Students can learn almost any subject matter when they are taught with methods and approaches responsive to their learning style strengths' (Dunn *et al.*, 1989, p. 15). Do you support the view that students have dominant learning styles? Should students be 'matched' with modes of instructions that suit their learning styles? Give details of how this might be achieved.
3. 'Teaching cannot simply consist of telling. It must enlist the pupils' own active participation since what gets processed gets learned' (Tomlinson and Kalbfleisch, 1998). What modes of instruction can a teacher use to encourage more active pupil participation?
4. Plan a unit that could be taught using cooperative learning. How would the plan differ from other approaches? What might be some possible advantages and disadvantages?
5. Discuss how modern technology can enrich modes of instruction. What are some of the problems for teachers and students in using computers in classrooms? What personal goals do you have for using computers in your various modes of instruction?
6. How do you react to the following statements? 'When I think of using computers in the classroom, I feel anxious.' 'I am unable to evaluate educational software.' (Russell and Bradley, 1996, p. 237). Describe your level of competence and confidence in using computer-based instruction. Are you actively trying to upgrade it? Give details.
7. To what extent is the selection of appropriate study materials crucial to the success of cooperative learning lessons?
8. Teachers should not assume that all their students possess the social skills needed to work effectively in small groups. What can the teacher do to assist students with limited social skills?
9. Middle schooling programmes rely heavily upon cooperative learning strategies. What are the strengths and weaknesses of using this approach with students (Years 5 to 9)?

6 Assessment, Grading and Reporting

Introduction

As noted by Black (2001, p. 80) 'reformers dreaming about changing the education for the better almost always see a need to include assessment and testing in their plans and frequently see them as the main instruments of their reforms'.

Hargreaves *et al.* (2002) argue that assessment-led reform is one of the most favoured strategies to promote higher standards and more powerful learning.

Assessment can take many forms and is certainly much wider than traditional forms of objective tests and essay tests. We should never forget that assessment can have a dramatic effect on the lives of students (Cunningham 1998).

Wherever possible, forms of assessment should be used that raise student's self esteem – learning experiences are needed that enable students to create success criteria and to organize their individual targets (Clarke, 2001).

Some of the newer approaches to assessment such as 'authentic' and 'performance assessment' examined in this chapter may be more inclusive and user-friendly for students than traditional approaches.

Assessment

Assessment is the term typically used to describe the activities undertaken by a teacher to obtain information about the knowledge, skills and attitudes of students. Activities can involve the collection of formal assessment data (e.g. by the use of objective tests) or the use of informal data (e.g. by the use of observation checklists). Teachers typically assign a grade or mark (numerical score, letter, grade, descriptive ranking) for work undertaken by students such as a project or a written test. Some of the basic principles of assessment are listed in Figure 6.1.

Reasons for Assessment

Assessment is usually undertaken for the following reasons:

- diagnosis of learning and monitoring progress;
- grading students;

Figure 6.1: Some basic principles of assessment

---

1. Assessment can only be based on samples of behaviour and therefore inaccuracies will always occur (Salvia and Ysseldyke, 1998)
2. Assessment must communicate to teachers how to make instruction more effective. Assessment is an integral and prominent component of the entire teaching and learning process (McInnis and Devlin, 2002)
3. Assessment of knowledge and skills must be clearly aligned with expected learning outcomes
4. Assessment is not done mainly to grade students but to promote instruction
5. Assessment must be fair to all individuals and groups (Willingham and Cole, 1997)
6. Assessment must measure a broad range of abilities (Darling-Hammond and Falk, 1997)
7. Assessment results should be meaningful to all participants, students, teachers and parents (Wiggins, 1998)

- predicting future achievements;
- motivating students;
- diagnosis of teaching.

Diagnosis of learning that has occurred and monitoring progress is a major reason for assessment (Chase, 1999). This information may be gleaned by a teacher asking questions of individual students or by student comments. The diagnosis should help each student understand his or her weaknesses and it also guides the teacher about where to direct his or her instructional energies.

In most cases, student grades are assigned to indicate achievement at the end of a unit or term, semester or year. Sufficient evidence needs to be collected by a teacher to enable the person to assign accurate grades. Generally, the more frequent and varied the assessments used, the more informed the teacher will be about the grades to assign to students.

Assessment can also be used to predict students' eligibility for selection in future courses. This is usually of importance at upper secondary school levels.

Assessment can often increase the motivation of students even though the teacher may not consciously highlight it as an incentive to work hard! It depends on the individual learner, as some students will be highly motivated by an impending test whereas others might suffer excessive stress and/or be de-motivated.

Assessment data can provide valuable diagnostic information for the teacher – some reasons why lessons fly or flop (Eisner, 1993). It may indicate, for example, that aspects of content or processes were not understood fully by students, or that the material presented was too difficult or too easy for a particular class.

Of course, it is also important to be mindful of the distorting effects of assessment (Gipps and Murphy, 1994). Different forms of assessment will promote particular kinds of learning (e.g. rote learning) and downgrade other kinds, especially if these are difficult to measure (e.g. higher-order thinking).

Assessing for Whom?

There are close links between reasons for assessment and their intended audiences. Possible audiences include the following.

- *Learners*: they should be the main audience but typically they are not given a high priority. They are rarely involved in planning the assessment activities.
- *Teachers*: need feedback about the effectiveness of their teaching. Student assessment data are being used increasingly as a data source for appraising teachers.
- *Parents*: want regular feedback. Media efforts to publicize school results and 'league tables' of schools has led to increased clamourings for assessment information.
- *Tertiary institutions*: universities and Technical and Further Education (TAFE) colleges require specific assessment information from applicants intending to enrol.
- *Employers*: are demanding more specific information, especially in terms of literacy and numeracy and key competencies.

Important Emphases in Assessment

Diagnostic–Formative–Summative

Let us look first at *diagnostic assessment*. Obviously students come into classrooms with varying backgrounds and interests so it is inefficient to start a new teaching unit without checking their knowledge and understandings. Some may lack the prerequisite skills to undertake the lessons required of them and, worse still, others may have certain negative attitudes to the topic, which will provide a major difficulty unless the teacher is aware in advance of these emotional attitudes. On the other hand, if the students already have a number of skills or understandings that the teacher intended to teach them, their interest and enthusiasm would be reduced if the same activities were repeated. Diagnostic evaluation simply reminds teachers that they must start their instruction at the level the students have reached. What is more, the teacher needs to be continually aware of students' levels in their progress through the curriculum unit. In this sense, the teacher is undertaking diagnostic evaluation through all the stages of instruction.

Formative assessment provides data about instructional units in progress and students in action. The data help to develop or form the final curriculum product and help students adjust to their learning tasks through the feedback they receive. Formative evaluation is important, therefore, because it provides data to enable 'on-the-spot' changes to be made where necessary. Students' learning activities can be refocused and redirected and the range and depth of the instructional activities of a curriculum can be revised in 'mid-stream'

(Tunstall and Gipps, 1996). It applies, therefore, to both course improvement and student growth, although some writers tend to concentrate only upon the former (Pryor and Torrance, 1996).

By contrast, Clarke (2001) concentrates very much on the importance of formative assessment to bring about student growth. She cites Black and Williams' (1998) research findings that formative assessment strategies do raise standards of student achievement, especially for children of lower ability.

Summative assessment is the final goal of an educational activity. Eventually, teachers need to know the relative merits and demerits of a curriculum package. Also, they need to have collected appropriate information about the levels of achievement reached by students. Of course, this information may be used in a diagnostic way as a preliminary to further activities, but it must be emphasized that summative evaluation provides the data from which decisions can be made.

Over recent years, related summative assessment terms have become widely used, such as *benchmarking* (the process of measuring standards of actual performance against those achieved by others with broadly similar characteristics) and *value-added* assessment (where raw scores from test results are adjusted to allow for the characteristics of the intake of the school; Clarke, 1998). These forms of summative assessment usually involve 'high stakes' standards and the publication of results for parents and community to make comparisons (Hess, 2003) (see Figure 6.2).

Informal–Formal

Informal assessment is inevitable, ongoing and very useful. Informal observations of natural situations are especially valuable for gaining information about student interactions. The less obvious it is to students that they are being assessed, the more natural will be their behaviour.

Informal assessment is especially important in early childhood and lower primary classes. Teachers use various techniques such as observations, running records, anecdotal records and written notes to assess the development of the whole child (Carr, 2001).

Formal assessment is planned and often an obtrusive activity. Thus any weekly tests and planned assignments could be categorized as formal assessments. There are a number of forms of informal and formal assessments that can be used.

Norm-referenced–Criterion-referenced

Norm-referenced measures are used to compare students' performance in specific tests. These measures simply provide comparative aged-based data on how well certain students perform in a test (e.g. maths or reading). Of course, they are open to misinterpretation. Students who receive special coaching or good teaching are likely to outperform those who do not have these opportunities. Norm-referenced measures provide valuable evaluative data about the performance of students on specific tasks but do not tell us anything about an individual's potential or his or her attitude toward certain subjects.

Criterion-referenced measures avoid the competitive elements of norm-referenced measures because information is obtained about students' performance in terms of their previous performances rather than in relation to the performance of others. Once the skill level for a particular task has been defined (the criterion) then it is presumed that a student will persevere until it is attained. The difficulty lies in defining learning activities in terms of tasks to be mastered. Certain subjects such as mathematics and topics such as motor skills and mapping are particularly amenable to this approach, but it is more difficult to establish criterion-referenced tasks for 'creative writing' or 'art'.

Table 6.2: *Commonly used assessment techniques. Italics refer to the optimal time to use each of the listed techniques. That is, they could be used at diagnostic (early) or formative (middle) or summative (end) levels but some periods are better than others.*

Techniques	Diagnostic	Formative	Summative
Informal observing and recording of student behaviour	Anecdotal records *Case histories* Checklists Rating scales by teacher Unobtrusive techniques	*Anecdotal records* Case histories *Checklists* *Rating scales by teacher* *Unobtrusive techniques*	Anecdotal records Case histories Checklists Rating scales by teacher Unobtrusive techniques
Informal collecting of information from students	*Interest inventories* Rating scales by students Questionnaires Interviews *Sociograms* Self-reports	Interest inventories Rating scales by students Questionnaires Interviews Sociograms *Self-reports*	Interest inventories *Rating scales by students* *Questionnaires* *Interviews* Sociograms Self-reports
Analysis of student work examples	Individual and group projects Content analysis of work book Logbooks and journals Portfolios	Individual and group projects Content analysis of work book Logbooks and journals Portfolios	*Individual and group projects* *Content analysis of work book* *Logbooks and journals* *Portfolios*
Testing of students	Objective test Standardized tests Essay tests Semantic differentials *Attitude scales* *Simulation and role plays* *Projective techniques*	Objective tests Standardized tests Essay tests Semantic differentials Attitude scales Simulation and role plays Projective techniques	*Objective tests* *Standardized tests* *Essay tests* *Semantic differentials* Attitude scales *Simulation and role plays* Projective techniques

Performance-based assessments have gained considerable support over recent years. They can be criterion- or standards-referenced but typically the former. In the USA 34 states are now using tests that include performance tasks (Heck and Crislip, 2001). These performance tests require students to demonstrate their acquisition of problem-solving and critical thinking (Yeh, 2001) or writing skills (Heck and Crislip, 2001). Some writers link these kinds of performance tests with constructivism – the theory that knowledge is constructed by individual human beings and not merely discovered (see, for example, von Glaserfield, 1995; Phillips, 1995).

The intention may be to develop criterion-referenced measures but in many cases they finish up as norm-referenced measures. For example, Elliott and Chan (2002) contend that 'in theory the assessment [for the National Curriculum in England and Wales] was supposed to be criterion-referenced and therefore linked to task specific standards of achievement. However, the standardized tests developed for each key stage have not been able to avoid a considerable element of norm-referencing and are too crude to inform teaching and learning' (p. 8).

Process–Product

Most assessment involves making judgements about *products* such as an assignment, project or object. Products are often perceived to be the major priority of the course. Yet, *processes* such as thinking skills, working cooperatively in groups and problem-solving are very important (Withers and McCurry, 1990).

Payne (2003) contends that assessing processes such as interpersonal relationships and performances are important and that process and product are intimately related. He suggests that if:

- the steps involved in arriving at the product are indeterminate, and
- measuring the processes leading to the product are impractical,

then the emphasis has to be on the product.

Wiggins (1998) considers that although a number of practical techniques are available for assessing processes, this still requires the teacher to make judgements: is the process observed/rated 'exemplary' or 'on course' or 'grounds for concern'?

Notwithstanding, various computer programs are now available whereby multiple process measures can be taken (Asp, 2000).

Learner-judged–Teacher-judged

At most levels of schooling the *teacher* does the judging about standards. Typically, individual teachers set and mark their tests and other forms of assessment. Rarely are students consulted or given responsibility for self-assessment.

Yet there are very promising developments if students are involved (Francis, 2001). Clarke (2001) contends that learners must ultimately be responsible for their learning. She states that the greatest impact on students is an overall rise in their self-esteem, as revealed by such student behaviours as:

- being able to say where they need help without any sense of failure;
- beginning to set their own targets and goals;
- now being able to speak about their learning when they would not have done so before. (Clarke, 2001, p. 44)

Clarke (2001) contends too that learners' self-assessment also gives teachers greater insights into students' learning needs.

Internal–External

Internal assessment involves those directly participating in the teaching–learning process, usually classroom teachers. *External* assessors become involved when 'high status/high stakes' assessments are to occur state-wide or nationally, typically at the completion of senior secondary schooling.

In the USA high stakes, standardized assessments are widely used and have been very popular over recent years in many states because it is argued that they raise academic performances of students and contribute to them earning at least basic educational credentials (Schiller and Muller, 2000).

Yet, there are many critics of high stakes testing. Some of the major concerns include the following.

- Test scores are mainly used for sorting and ranking students – there are serious adverse effects on low-income and minority students (Casas and Meaghan, 2001; Brennan *et al.*, 2001).
- Tests divert valuable instructional time to prepare for testing (Froese-Germain, 2001; Pedulla, 2003; Egan, 2003).

In Australia, with the exception of Queensland and the Australian Capital Territory, all other states and territories use external assessments at Year 12. These are quite evidently high stakes tests – they enjoy considerable public confidence and credibility, despite their limitations.

More recently, tests have been introduced in all states of Australia: literacy and numeracy tests for all students in Years 5 and 7. The attempt by the Federal Government is to develop nationally agreed minimum acceptable standards for literacy and numeracy at a particular year level (Meadmore, 2001). Although it is problematic whether these tests fairly and justly represent the diversity of Australian students, they are likely to be retained as a major, highly visible platform of centralized testing.

Inclusive–Exclusive

The production of forms of assessment should, ideally, provide access to all learners and be *inclusive*, regardless of gender, ethnicity, or disadvantage. Studies have indicated that in many cases assessment is far from inclusive and that it is *exclusive*. Salvia and Ysseldyke (1998) cite examples where minority ethnic groups and females are not given equal opportunities. It is evident that a number of multiple-choice tests tend to be biased against females (Gipps and Murphy, 1994; Willingham and Cole, 1997). Teachers' assessment of ethnic minority students can often be biased, as reported by Cunningham (1998).

Gipps (1994) raises three fundamental questions about inclusivity:

1.   Whose knowledge is taught?
2.   Why is it taught in a particular way to this particular group?
3.   How do we enable the histories and cultures of people of colour, and of women, to be taught in responsible and responsive ways? (p. 151)

Inclusivity also applies to students with special needs. There is a need for all students to have access to appropriate forms of assessment. Kopriva (1999) notes that there has been considerable interest in developing alternative assessments and alternative testing formats for students with special needs.

Technicist–Liberal/Postmodernist

A number of writers argue that traditional forms of assessment are *technicist* and are used to identify and perpetuate the social hierarchy (Blackmore, 1988; Broadfoot, 1979). Many forms of assessment, especially traditional written examinations, concentrate upon a narrow view of student achievement which emphasizes the outcomes of the academic *curriculum*. Hargreaves *et al.* (2002) contend that technological advances in assessment also have this narrow focus – using advanced computer skills to devise and refine valid forms of assessment.

The other option, according to Hargreaves *et al.* (2002) is to consider the postmodern perspective and to highlight uncertainties and diversities. After all, 'human beings are not completely knowable and so no assessment process or system can therefore be fully comprehensive' (Hargreaves *et al.* 2002, p. 83).

Authentic Assessment

Authentic assessment or, sometimes, the assessment of authentic learning are two names that were popularized in the 1990s and continue to be widely used in the assessment literature in the twenty-first century. Authentic assessment encompasses far more than what students learn as measured by standardized tests or even by ordinary teacher-made tests. Authenticity arises from assessing what is most important, not from assessing what is most convenient. Fundamentally, then, there is nothing new about authentic assessment as a reaction against narrowness in education and a return toward the kind of education that connects feeling, thinking and doing as advocated by John Dewey and other progressives early in the twentieth century. Applied to the curriculum, authentic assessment suggests that the curriculum must be directed at learning in the broadest possible sense; hence, the curriculum itself should be evaluated in terms of how well it contributes to students' deep understandings not only of subject matter but also of their own lives. In this sense, the popularization of authentic assessment represents another manifestation of grass-roots, bottom-up approaches to curriculum planning.

Fundamentally, authentic assessment is a way of capturing and somewhat formalizing the myriad things that perceptive teachers have always considered – although often intuitively – about what is happening to their students (Gipps *et al.*, 2000). The advantages of formalizing the process are in making it increasingly accessible to more and more teachers and in keeping it viable as an integral part of flexible curriculum planning and development against the inroads of centralized curriculum control. The basic danger in formalizing the process is that the more widely it is used, the more likely it is to be reduced to a formula co-opted by centralizing influences and thus to lose much of its flexibility and value.

In authentic assessment, therefore, the tasks students undertake are more practical, realistic and challenging than traditional paper-and-pencil tests (Pryor and Torrance, 1996). Students are engaged in more meaningful, context-bound activities, focusing their energies on 'challenging, performance-oriented tasks that require analysis, integration of knowledge, and invention' (Darling-Hammond, Ancess and Falk, 1995, p. 2). Eisner (1993) states that the tasks of authentic assessment are 'more complex, more closely aligned with life than with individual performance measured in an antiseptic context using sanitized instruments that were untouched by human hands' (p. 224). Some general characteristics of authentic assessment are listed in Figure 6.3.

Although there are many enthusiastic supporters of authentic assessment (for example, Wiggins, 1998; McTighe, 1997) there are many accounts of problems in implementing it. Franklin (2002) notes three major difficulties: parental unfamiliarity with the goals of authentic assessment; teacher preferences for traditional methods; and the greater amounts of time required to undertake authentic assessment.

Figure 6.3: Some characteristics of authentic assessment

- Teachers collect evidence from multiple activities
- Assessments reflect the tasks that students will encounter in the world outside schools
- Assessments reveal how students go about solving problems as well as the solutions they formulate
- Procedures for assessments and the contents of assessments are derived from students' everyday learning in schools
- Assessments reflect local values, standards and control; they are not imposed externally
- The tasks students are assessed upon include more than one acceptable solution to each problem and more than one acceptable answer to each question

---

Hargreaves *et al.* (2002) note that teachers have great difficulty in knowing how to measure outcomes, the need to harmonize assessment expectations between home and school and the issue of time and resources.

Hargreaves *et al.* (2002) are also critical on the grounds that from a post-modern perspective, authentic assessment is not knowable – it is contrived – schools are highly artificial places. Meir (1998) considers that 'much of what passes for authentic curriculum and authentic assessment is the jargon of contemporary pedagogy' (p. 598).

Commonly Used Assessment Techniques

A number of assessment techniques are available to teachers and they can be used at various diagnostic, formative and summative stages. On the one hand, it is very desirable for teachers to use a variety of techniques to ensure that the multi-dimensionality of student performance is adequately explored (Haney and Madaus, 1989). But, there is also the danger of over-assessing and collecting vast arrays of data that have limited use.

McMillan *et al.*'s (2002) research study of the assessment practices of over 900 primary school teachers concluded that they use direct observation as a major technique; they only tap students' higher-level thinking skills to a limited extent; and they place greater importance on social behaviour than academic achievement.

Trepanier-Street *et al.* (2001) in their study of 300 lower primary and upper primary teachers discovered that lower primary grade teachers mainly used one-on-one assessment of specific skills, written observational notes, checklists, rating scales and portfolio information. Upper primary grade teachers used more teacher-made tests and published tests from textbooks and reading series.

The examples listed in Figure 6.2 are wide ranging and are repeated in all columns, depending on their applicability at diagnostic, formative and summative stages. They are presented in italics at the perceived ultimate stage of use. Despite the range of informal techniques included in Figure 6.2, it is likely that teachers still tend to use a number of the written tests, such as objective tests and essay tests.

Space precludes a detailed discussion of each of these techniques but the one example given below includes a brief description and a reminder of respective merits and demerits. Every teacher has to make judgements about which techniques to use from a wide selection.

Portfolios

In the USA, student portfolios developed as a major form of assessment in the mid-1990s largely due to the writings and acceptance of cognitive psychologists

– for example, Resnick and Klopfer (1989) and the New Standards Project by Simmons and Resnick (1993).

The use of portfolios of student work has been central to the movement for authentic assessment. Their use has been based on the belief that what is most significant in any educational situation arises from the student's perception of that situation. Thus, authentic assessment emphasizes individual-centred curricula, in which the teacher helps the student identify his or her interests and makes suggestions about how the student can deepen and broaden those interests in ways that lead to a wide variety of worthwhile and concomitant learnings.

Despite the teacher's help, however, authenticity requires the student to take responsibility for what is learned. Only in this way does learning become integrated with the rest of the student's life rather than remaining something apart, as an isolated lesson selected by someone else. Given the responsibility that students must take for their own learnings, it becomes incumbent upon them to demonstrate what they have learned and not simply to wait for their teachers to make these discoveries. Therefore, such use of student-initiated projects is an integral part of authentic assessment, and portfolios of student work are perhaps the most telling form of demonstration.

Portfolios can include any number of things – not only finished work but also notes, drafts, preliminary models and plans, logs, and other records; not only written work but also audiotapes, videotapes, photographs, three-dimensional creations, and other artefacts. Students decide what to create and what to include in their portfolios; hence, the portfolios reveal not only what individual students have done but also the strategies they have used in making their decisions.

Teachers, therefore, can assess not only the finished products portfolios contain but also the processes students have followed in carrying out their projects. What kind of decisions have been made? How wise have they been? Where have they led? What are the alternatives? There may be numerous opportunities as projects unfold for teachers to discuss these questions with students and thus to offer advice and constructive criticism. Much of the authenticity of assessing portfolios is in the opportunities they provide to both teachers and students for considering the development of interests, attitudes and values as well as skills and conventional academic learnings (Lyons, 1999).

Computer-assisted instruction enables students to do a variety of projects (individually or in groups) and these are useful inclusions in portfolios because they provide tangible evidence of a range of problem-solving skills. For example, Lifter and Adams (1997) claim that many of the eight levels of multiple intelligence are incorporated into computer software CD-ROMs. Eisner (1997) argues that computers can now create multimedia displays which capture meanings from alternative forms of data.

Figure 6.4 lists some examples of what can be included in a portfolio, although in practice there is virtually no limit to what a portfolio might contain.

Figure 6.4: Examples of what a student portfolio might contain

- Essays
- Journals
- Summaries
- Records, such as daily logs
- Self-assessments, such as collect-checklists and rating forms
- Experiments
- Demonstration of skills
- Rough drafts and finished products
- Research notes
- Team or group activities
- Creative works
- Major projects or products, such as dioramas, oral history collections, audio- and videotapes, photographs, charts, cards, and timelines
- Tests
- Teacher comments

An increasing number of teachers are exploring the use of portfolios as an important 'authentic' assessment tool because:

- students can reflect on what they have learnt (Calfee and Perfumo, 1996);
- students do the selecting of what to include and have to justify their choices;
- students value the opportunity to assemble their materials;
- students can demonstrate what they have done and, by inference, what they are capable of doing (Salvia and Ysseldyke, 1998);
- students have to demonstrate thinking and expressive skills;
- portfolios provide an equitable and sensitive portrait of what students know and are able to do;
- portfolios enable teachers to focus on important student outcomes;
- portfolios are a tangible way to display and celebrate students' achievements (McTighe, 1997);
- portfolios provide credible evidence of student achievement to parents and the community (Hebert, 1998).

Many states in the USA are now moving toward mandating school systems to use portfolios as a required form of assessment. This will involve some topics being chosen by the district or state, and other quality controls over the criteria to be used for grading the portfolios. These external controls may be necessary to demonstrate the credibility of portfolios to the general public, but some educators have questioned whether the move to state-level acceptance so quickly can be justified. For example, Herman and Winters (1994) note that:

- inter rater agreement on portfolio assessments from state reports is very low;

- portfolio grades have only moderate correlations with other forms of assessment (e.g. a moderate correlation of 0.47 between writing portfolio scores and direct writing assessments);
- portfolios may not represent an individual student's work but the efforts of several supporting peers, teachers or parents;
- teachers' time taken for choosing portfolio tasks, preparing portfolio lessons and assessing portfolios is burdensome;
- there are major costs involved in staff training, development of portfolio specifications, administration of portfolio records and their storage.

Torrance and Pryor (1995), referring to 'authentic' assessment trials in the United Kingdom, also voice caveats about being too ambitious and over-enthusiastic about these approaches because the additional responsibilities for teachers in busy classrooms will be enormous.

Merits

- students find it meaningful and good for their self-esteem.
- students have to justify their choices.

Demerits

- it is very time-consuming to assess portfolios.
- it is difficult to establish appropriate rubrics.

Record-keeping and Reporting

Record-keeping for many teachers might be perceived as a chore but it is impossible to rely on one's memory for details about students' learning and achievements. Record-keeping is typically undertaken because:

- it helps teachers monitor the progress of individual students and to use this as a basis for planning future learning experiences – it serves a formative function;
- parents require detailed reporting of their child's achievements at regular intervals;
- the information can be used for placement of students in subsequent years;
- the information is required by the school or state system or nationally, as an accountability measure (Sutton, 1992).

Record-keeping can be very time-consuming and it is often quite instructive to reflect upon the range and type of record-keeping that is currently used. Some pertinent questions to ask about each item include:

- Why do this?
- Who is it for?

- Does it really match up with the original purpose?
- What happens to the data collected and recorded?
- Who actually uses it and for what purpose?
- Could it be organized more rationally to save time and effort?
- Would computerized records assist?

Many innovatory computer-based packages are already available to assist teachers with the task of assessing and recording students' achievements. Schools have to balance up the cost of these programs versus teachers devoting much of their daily time to assessing, recording and reporting so that their time for teaching is greatly reduced.

Trends in Reporting

Parents have a major role in schools and they have a right to receive regular school reports about the achievements of their children. However, because all parents have experienced schooling in the past, they have expectations about the format of reports and what they consider to be the highest priorities in reporting. There can also be a considerable generation gap between parents' experiences at school and current education provisions.

The new and more complex forms of assessment clearly demand new forms of reporting (Wiggins, 1998). Yet changes to reporting are not welcomed by parents if they create, in turn, further anxieties for them. Most educators agree about basic principles of reporting, namely:

- the process of communication must be fair, timely, confidential and clear (Loyd and Loyd, 1997);
- the basis for comparing students' performance must be made known and be credible;
- the relative weight attached to categories that make up the final grade must be made explicit and kept uniform across students and teachers;
- any summary judgements made in the report must be supported by data (Wiggins, 1998).

A number of schools are now changing the type of communication they send to parents. The mailing to the parents of a single-sheet report form once a term or once a semester as the only form of communication has changed dramatically. Schools now use:

- a variety of written reports;
- parent–teacher meetings/interviews;
- parents information evenings;
- leaflets to explain new curriculum or assessment procedures; and
- newsletters.

New Developments in Assessment and Reporting

Two major factors are currently driving assessment developments: the emphasis upon performance assessment and the priority given to standards and accountability. Recent efforts to develop a comprehensive picture of student learning have involved systematically combining multiple-choice formats and performance formats.

There are many other developments which are likely to make assessment more flexible and tailored to the needs of students and teachers in the future. Asp (2000) lists the following.

- Computer adaptive testing (CAT) – CAT customizes the assessment process so that the computer determines which level of questions to pose to the student. If a student answers a question correctly then he or she receives a more difficult item. Although expensive to develop at present, more customized versions are likely to be developed.
- Large-scale testing can now be done at computerized testing centres – students take their test online and receive their score instantaneously.
- In the classroom (or at home) students can download specific assessment programs and then transmit them to the teacher or computer for scoring.
- Technology will allow a variety of test- and-response formats using the computer's video and audio capabilities. Students will be able to answer orally or by constructing answers on the screen. Computer software will be able to translate items into many languages.
- Automated essay grading has made major advances and prototypes are now available for use on a standard Windows PC (Williams, 2001).
- Much of the paper testing done today will become an anachronism. As students come to do the majority of their learning with technology, they will want the medium of assessment also to be technology (Bennett, 2002).

Concluding Comments

Assessment of students is a constant part of life in schools and a very important element. Although some forms of assessment have stood the test of time and are still used widely (e.g. external examinations), there have been enormous pressures over recent decades to widen the range of assessments and procedures.

It is likely that norm-referenced assessment will decrease as accountability focuses more on what students actually know and can do (Asp, 2000). Performance assessment is likely to become far more prominent in both classrooms and for high stakes testing. Electronic assessment will be integrated into the educational process along with on-line delivery of instruction.

Reflections and Issues

1.   With reference to a specific group of students, reflect upon the assessment techniques you would use. Why do you use these? Which others might you use in the future? Which ones would you not use? Give reasons.

2.   'Assessments should reflect on tasks students will encounter in the world outside schools and not merely those limited to the schools themselves.' (Eisner, 1993, p. 226). How might this be done? Give details of techniques you would use to achieve this end.

3.   What does it mean to be more focused on student performance? Why is this needed? What assessment techniques would facilitate this emphasis?

4.   How can assessment help a student to learn? What information/feedback do they need to have, when and how? Describe an assessment technique that illustrates how assessment can help a student.

5.   'Technology opens up new design choices for assessment so there is great importance on making these wisely. When attention is focused on technology at the expense of thinking through the assessment argument, worse assessment can actually result' (Mislevy, 2002, p. 27). Discuss.

6.   'Technology is becoming a medium for learning and work ... as schools integrate technology into the curriculum, the method of assessment should reflect the tools employed in thinking and learning' (Bennett, 2002, p. 8). Discuss.

7 Curriculum Implementation

Introduction

Curriculum starts as a plan. It only becomes a reality when teachers implement it with real students in a real classroom. Careful planning and development are obviously important, but they count for nothing unless teachers are aware of the product and have the skills to implement the curriculum in their classrooms.

Definitions and Terms

As noted by Fullan (1999) and Scott (1999), a curriculum, however well designed, must be implemented if it is to have any impact on students. Although this is obvious, there are thousands of curriculum documents now gathering dust on storeroom shelves because they were never implemented or because they were implemented unintelligently. The obvious importance of curriculum implementation has not necessarily led to widespread understanding of what it entails or of what is problematic about it.

The term 'implementation' refers to the 'actual use' of a curriculum/syllabus, or what it 'consists of in practice' (Fullan and Pomfret, 1977). It is a critical phase in the cycle of planning and teaching a curriculum. Adoption of a curriculum refers to somebody's intentions to use it, be it a teacher or a head office official, but it does not indicate whether the curriculum is implemented or not.

Implementation refers to actual use, as outlined above, but there is also an important 'attitudinal' element. In education systems where teachers and principals have the opportunity to choose among competing curriculum packages (i.e. acting as 'selectors') then attitudinal dispositions are clearly important. For example, if a teacher perceives that the current curriculum he or she is using is deficient in certain areas, then an alternative will be sought which overcomes these problems. Leithwood (1981) maintains that teachers will only become involved in implementing new curricula if they perceive a dysfunction – they have a desire to reduce the gap between current and preferred practices, with reference to their teaching in a particular subject.

But for many subjects, a revised or new curriculum is produced to be used by teachers in *all* schools in a school district and no choice is available. There is no opportunity for teachers to consider alternatives. Their task is to find out how to use the new curriculum as effectively as possible. In these circum-stances, the dominant implementation questions for the teacher might be:

- How do I do it?
- Will I ever get it to work smoothly?
- To whom can I turn to get assistance?
- Am I doing what the practice requires?
- What is the effect on the learner?

This emphasis on *how* to use a new curriculum is a major concern for teachers because as 'craft specialists' they gain most of their intrinsic satisfac-tion from being successful in using a particular approach and materials with their students. However, the implementation of any new curriculum will take a teacher a considerable period of time as he or she needs to become competent and confident in its use. It is only when a new curriculum is completely accepted by teachers in a school and the activities associated with it are a matter of routine, that the phase 'institutionalization' is said to have been reached.

Nonetheless, some writers (for example, Snyder *et al.*, 1992) argue that the idea of institutionalization unduly implies that the curriculum is some-thing concrete and static. These writers suggest that 'curriculum enactment' is a more useful way of describing the ongoing process of implementation because it emphasizes the educational experiences that students and teachers jointly undergo as they determine what the curriculum will be like in each classroom.

There is also the matter of commitment to change (Cuban, 1992). Not all teachers will automatically accept the notion that a newly proposed curriculum is what they should use, nor will all want to use it with their students (Fullan and Hargreaves, 1991). Most would no doubt welcome the opportunity to choose among several alternatives. In fact, some teachers might be perfectly satisfied with their existing curriculum. In situations where teachers have no choice about whether or not to use a new curriculum, they may embrace the new curriculum with enthusiasm, becoming what is known as 'consonant' users (willing to conform to the new curriculum), or they may be reluctant, making considerable alterations in the curriculum, thus becoming what is known as 'dissonant' users (unwilling to conform). In extreme cases, a dissonant user may erect a façade of compliance while adopting Machiavellian tactics to resist or even to undermine the new curriculum. Again, the attitudes of individual teachers are extremely important in implementation.

Some subjects in schools are considered to be important core areas and are given detailed treatment in syllabus documents. For these subjects, teachers may be expected to cover particular content and to follow a certain instruc-tional sequence. The term used for this adherence to prescribed details is 'fide-lity of use'. Alternatively, there may be other subjects where teachers can exercise their creative flair and implement very special, individual versions of a curriculum. This is then termed 'adaptation' or 'process orientation'.

Factors Affecting Implementation

Several education experts have produced very useful insights about implementation and the relative success of it in schools. In the early 1980s Fullan (1982) produced a list of factors affecting implementation (see Table 7.1) which is frequently quoted in the literature. These factors refer to the attributes of the innovation or change, characteristics of the school district, characteristics of the school as a unit, and factors external to the local school system. A wide-ranging list of factors is provided in Table 7.2 based on the experiences of a project developer (Parsons, 1987).

House (1979) uses three perspectives (technical, political and cultural) to explain how and why certain implementation practices have occurred over the decades. The 'technical' perspective assumes that systematic planning and a rational approach can overcome typical teacher problems of lack of time and expertise. The 'political' perspective recognizes that rational behaviour is limited in practice and that it is the balance of power among parties that determines whether curriculum implementation efforts will be successful or not. The 'cultural' perspective emphasizes cultural transformation as a major factor in determining the success or otherwise of implementation endeavours. It is the deeply ingrained beliefs and values of stakeholders, which are socially shared and shaped, that ultimately affect what happens in classrooms.

Table 7.1:   Factors affecting implementation

A   *Characteristics of the change*

---

    1. Need for and relevance of the change
    2. Clarity
    3. Complexity
    4. Quality and practicality of programme (materials, etc.)

B   *Characteristics at the school district level*

---

    5. The history of innovative attempts
    6. The adoption process
    7. Central administrative support and involvement
    8. Staff development (in-service) and participation
    9. Time-line and information system (evaluation)
  10. Board and community characteristics

C   *Characteristics at the school level*

---

  11. The principal
  12. Teacher–teacher relations
  13. Teacher characteristics and orientations

D   *Characteristics external to the local system*

---

  14. Role of government
  15. External assistance

Source: Fullan (1982, p. 56).

Table 7.2: Some important factors in promoting successful implementation practices

1. Time: to experiment, for attitudes to change
2. A technology for change: a phased plan of action is needed
3. Recognizing school culture: awareness of situational conditions
4. Provision of incentives and rewards: time, resources, materials
5. Sharing of the burden in the workplace: to collaborate and to share
6. Releasing energy for innovation: creating the right conditions
7. A collaborative framework: the value of local collaborative groups
8. Leadership: persons to coordinate and to lead
9. Recognizing system-level culture: awareness of overall policies
10. A political perspective: keeping visible with stakeholders
11. Winning allies: gaining legitimacy and support in a region and within schools
12. Recognizing the role of individuals: commitment and charisma are essential qualities

In a study of implementation practices in seventeen US schools, Corbett and Rossman (1989) noted that there were segments of technical, political and cultural at all sites and that where change strategies addressed all three there was increased implementation success.

McLaughlin (1987) found that the efforts by federal or state officials to promote successful curriculum implementation in local schools depended on what she describes as 'local capacity', 'motivation and commitment', 'internal institutional conditions' and 'balance between pressure and support'. The local capacity to implement an innovation can be improved by increasing financial support and the training of teachers, as long as these increases are significant and continue over a period of years. The motivation and commitment of teachers and administrators is more difficult to improve. Doing so depends on the values of local leaders and their assessment of the relative worth of a particular innovation. However, on some occasions the involvement of local leaders in a project leads directly to greater commitment (Fullan, 1986). McLaughlin (1987) also reported that the structures and policies within schools and the relative stability and support for teachers can have a major effect upon their willingness to implement new curricula. That is, the internal institutional conditions have to be conducive to change. Furthermore, some balance between pressure and support is essential. Pressure is required to focus attention on a specific innovation, and it provides the necessary legitimacy to embark on a new project. But support, whether financial or in the form of expert assistance, is also required to get the project started.

McLaughlin (1987) further argues that implementation is not about transmitting what has previously been agreed, but about bargaining and transformation. Implementation must be framed in terms of individual actors' incentives, beliefs and capacities – a point also confirmed by Werner (1987), Crandall (1988) and Lewis (1988).

Nonetheless, there appears to be a return to a more rigid view of curriculum implementation. The current interest in educational standards and school indicators has seen more explicit listings of requirements for teachers in implementing their respective curricula.

Examples are Porter (1993), who argues for school standards for the delivery of the enacted curriculum and cites the professional standards for teaching mathematics developed by the National Council for Teachers of Mathematics; Blank (1993), who describes indicators based on student outcomes, instructional time, curriculum content, teacher quality, and school conditions and resources; and Schmidt *et al.* (1996), who urge the adoption of a multicategory curriculum framework for measuring the alignment of various elements of implementation.

Problems of Describing/Measuring Implementation

Attempts to describe the implementation of new curricula are fraught with all kinds of difficulties. For example, do you focus upon the curriculum materials, or what the teacher is doing, or what the students are doing? If the intention is to try to do all three things, what criteria do you use to select instances of each, since they are all occurring simultaneously in the classroom? Are there optimal times to examine how a curriculum is being implemented, such as after 6 months of operation, or a year, or even longer?

Trying to measure degrees of implementation is even more difficult than trying to describe it. Decisions have to be made about what kinds of data should be collected, such as observational data, document analysis or self-report data. Measurement data also tend to have a punitive air about them and so this can lead to concerns about who is doing the measuring and who is to receive the results.

Measuring Student Activities and Achievements

A major reason for producing a new curriculum is to provide better learning opportunities for students, such as higher achievement levels in terms of particular understandings, skills and values. Rarely is it possible, however, for measurements to be obtained on student achievements so that it can be stated unequivocally that a new curriculum is superior to the previous one, in terms of particular dimensions. There are so many confounding variables which affect student scores. A single test is unlikely to be suitable for use and to be able to provide valid and reliable comparable data between a new curriculum and the previous one.

Despite the lack of empirical evidence linking testing with student achievement, high stakes testing of students became a political priority in the USA during the 1990s (Nave *et al.*, 2000), and there is pressure from some quarters for a single national test for all students (Porter, 1993). A differing point of view holds that a more promising development is authentic assessment of student learning, such as through the use of portfolios of student work or through increasingly sophisticated ways of measuring problem-solving, reasoning and critical thinking (Resnick and Tucker, 1992).

Measuring Use of Curriculum Materials

In most teaching programmes, curriculum materials figure prominently in the day-to-day activities undertaken by the teacher and students. In fact, surveys have revealed that school students can spend up to 80 per cent of their time engaged with particular curriculum materials (Cornbleth, 1990).

It is clearly important in any study of implementation to gather information about how curriculum materials are used. Some of the curriculum materials analysis schemes developed in the 1970s provide convenient criteria for evaluating curriculum materials (for example, Piper, 1976; Eraut *et al.*, 1975). However, these schemes are often very time-consuming to complete and tend to emphasize the characteristics of the curriculum materials in isolation.

During the 1980s more attention was paid to developing checklists which provide ratings of curriculum materials 'in use' (for example, the Innovations Configuration developed by Hall and Loucks, 1978; and the Practice Profile developed by Loucks and Crandall, 1982).

The Innovations Configuration (IC) describes the different operational forms of an innovation that result as teachers implement it in their classrooms. The checklist can be structured to indicate the variations that are considered to be ideal, acceptable and unacceptable uses of an innovation (Hord and Huling-Austin, 1987).

The rapid growth in the use of the Internet by teachers and students has also spread numerous new ideas about what can be included in checklists of curriculum materials and how they can be used (Means, 2001). In particular, the Internet has become a huge new resource for teachers and students (Molnar, 2000; Schofield and Davidson, 2000).

Measuring Teacher Activities

Various methods have been used over the decades to measure teachers' implementation activities, ranging from formal visitations to observation checklists, questionnaires, interviews and self-report techniques. In the USA, where implementation studies have been very extensively undertaken since the 1970s, observation checklists and rating scales are commonly used. In these studies, particular categories of behaviour are determined in advance and used as the basis for the checklist items and rating scales.

For example, self-report techniques are incorporated into the Stages of Concern (SoC), an instrument developed by Hall *et al.* (1977) and subsequently used widely in many countries. The SoC focuses upon teachers' feelings as they become involved in implementing an innovation. These will vary in both type and intensity. Hall *et al.* argue that there are a definable set of major stages of concern and that as teachers become involved in implementing an innovation they will move developmentally through these stages (see Figure 7.1).

Figure 7.1:   Stages of Concern (SoC)

Stages of Concern	Definitions
6 Refocusing	The focus is on exploration of more universal benefits from the innovation, including the possibility of major changes or replacement with a more powerful alternative. Individual has definite ideas about alternatives to the proposed or existing form of the innovation.
5 Collaboration	The focus is on coordination and cooperation with others regarding use of the innovation.
4 Consequence	Attention focuses on impact of the innovation on student in his/her immediate sphere of influence. The focus is on relevance of the innovation for students, evaluation of student outcomes, including performance and competencies, and changes needed to increase student outcomes.
3 Management	Attention is focused on the processes and tasks of using the innovation and the best use of information and resources. Issues related to efficiency, organizing, managing, scheduling and time demands are utmost.
2 Personal	Individual is uncertain about the demands of the innovation, his/her inadequacy to meet those demands, and his/her role with the innovation. This includes analysis of his/her role in relation to the reward structure of the organization, decision making, and consideration of potential conflicts with existing structures or personal commitment. Financial or status implications of the programme for self and colleagues may also be reflected.
1 Informational	A general awareness of the innovation and interest in learning more detail about it is indicated. The person seems to be unworried about himself/herself in relation to the innovation. He/she is interested in substantive aspects of the innovation in a selfless manner such as general characteristics, effects and requirements for use.
0 Awareness	Little concern about or involvement with the innovation is indicated.

The left margin labels IMPACT (stages 6, 5, 4), TASK (stage 3), and SELF (stages 2, 1, 0).

Source: Hall *et al.* (1979); Hall and Hord (1987).

The SoC has been widely used in a number of countries, as noted in studies by Wells and Anderson (1997), Bailey and Palsha (1992) and Guan (2000). Of special interest is a confirmatory study by Marsh and Penn (1988), who found that the concerns of students engaged in a remedial reading programme progressed in a sequence similar to the SoC.

Second-generation research in Belgium and the Netherlands (Vandenberghe, 1983; Van den Berg, 1993; Van der Vegt and Vandenberghe, 1992) has produced an alternative version of the SoC that includes an increased number of self-oriented concerns.

Van den Berg (2002) highlights the major impact of concerns theory on the professional development of teachers and the extent to which concerns-based instruments, such as the SoC, have been used to examine levels of curriculum implementation in a variety of subjects, including new innovations such as School Net technology.

Nonetheless, weaknesses in the SoC have also been uncovered. One major weakness is that the fixed stages do not discriminate completely between how different teachers in different schools might implement a new curriculum.

Examples

Hong Kong

The coordinated and concerted effort to reform the education system in the Hong Kong Special Administration Region is an interesting example. In 2000, the Curriculum Development Council produced a major reform document 'Learning to Learn'. The components of 'Learning to Learn' were not dissimilar to many others introduced in industrialized countries. They included:

- eight key learning areas within a curriculum framework;
- a number of generic skills (for example, communication skills);
- changes in assessment with a greater emphasis upon formative assessment;
- diversified learning and teaching materials;
- life-long learning;
- whole-person development;

What is very different is the commitment of the education department to ensure that the new curriculum is implemented effectively. Some of the implementation strategies include:

- A major emphasis on teacher development. Each year approximately 100 teachers are selected to become 'seed teachers' who work full time developing materials, giving workshops to teachers in schools and generally acting as change agents.
- Creation of a new promotional position in all primary schools, 'Curriculum Development' leader, who acts as a catalyst and curriculum leader in each primary school.
- Provision of research projects and light-house schools, which experiment with new student-centred approaches to individual differences.
- Provision of a range of workshops and courses for school principals and vice-principals.
- Creation of Web pages providing teachers with a wealth of practical examples.
- Hiring of a large number of overseas experts to give presentations and workshops to teachers and principals.
- Provision of information sessions and materials for parents.

Above all, the education department wisely decided upon a long lead time for implementing the new curriculum, and targets for different elements of curriculum reform are moderate and achievable.

The progress to date is most impressive. There is evidence that a number of schools are developing very well with their implementation targets (Marsh, 2002).

United Kingdom

The Blair government's education reforms after taking office in 1997 focused especially on higher standards for all students. The White Paper 'Excellence in Schools' set out specific details, especially with regard to literacy and numeracy, namely:

- the introduction of a National Literacy Strategy into every primary school from September 1998;
- the introduction of a National Numeracy Strategy into every primary school from September 1999;
- the setting of numerical targets for pupils' attainments in every school, linked to the government's pledge to increase pupil's scores in national assessment tests by the year 2002 (Southworth, 2000).

Again, what is especially interesting is the implementation strategies used to bring about these reforms. Fullan and Earl (2002) describe the strategies as an effective combination of accountability mechanisms and capacity-building strategies. They include:

- ambitious standards (high standards and tests);
- devolved responsibility (the school and especially the school head as the unit of accountability);
- good data/clear targets (benchmark data for every school, results shared annually);
- access to Best Practice and Quality Professional Development (professional development for all; leadership development through the National College for School Leadership: Mackay, 2002);
- accountability (through national inspections by the Office for Standards in Education (OFSTED) and publication of results in the media);
- intervention in inverse proportion to success (rewards are given to successful schools, schools with poor results are supported in the first instance, or closed: Fullan and Earl, 2002).

Fullan and Earl (2002) contend that in terms of literacy and numeracy gains from the base years, the implementation strategies have been very successful (18 per cent increase in achievement levels in literacy, 17 per cent increase in achievement levels in numeracy). However, Fullan and Earl

(2002) caution the government about a continuance of such a strong centre-directed approach. Although this top-down initiative may have been required at the beginning, there now needs to be a greater 'investment in local capacity-building, followed in turn by greater attention to local creativity, reflection and networking' (Fullan and Earl, 2002, p. 4).

Concluding Comments

How a planned curriculum is implemented as the enacted curriculum in any school is a complex process that can vary enormously from school to school. The only certainty about curriculum implementation is that there is no one right way of going about it for all teachers in all schools. The ongoing issues concerning curriculum implementation are not likely to be resolved, but in recent years there has been growing awareness of the complexity of the process, and hence more reason for both caution and guarded optimism.

Reflections and Issues

1. Some common implementation problems according to Clough *et al.* (1989) include the following:
    *   too little time for teachers to plan and learn new skills and practices;
    *   too many competing demands make successful implementation impossible;
    *   failure to understand and take into account site-specific differences among schools.
    Explain why these could be major problems. What solutions would you offer?
2. 'For a new curriculum project to be fully implemented there are four core changes required of a teacher – changes in class groupings and organization, materials, practices and behaviours, and in beliefs and understandings' (Fullan, 1989, p. 8). Do you agree with these four core changes? Give examples to illustrate their importance. Alternatively, put forward other more important factors.
3. 'Because implementation takes place in a fluid setting, implementation problems are never "solved". Rather they evolve ... new issues, new requirements, new considerations emerge as the process unfolds' (McLaughlin, 1987, p. 174). What are the implications of this statement for implementing new curricula in schools? What implementation elements can or cannot be planned in advance What contingency plans should be developed?
4. 'Successful implementation is an individual development process within certain organizational conditions and strategies' (Fullan, 1989, p. 24). To what extent are individual development factors (for example, commitment, skills, willingness to experiment) important? What are some important organizational conditions?
5. 'Testing certain content in certain ways will result in an alignment of classroom practices with the official view of what and how subjects should be taught' (Matheison, 1991, p. 201). Does testing ensure that fidelity of use implementation occurs? What are some problems associated with curriculum controlled by testing?

6. Pressure and support are both needed to ensure that implementation occurs. Do you agree? How might pressure and support occur simultaneously within your school or school district?

Part III

Curriculum Management

8 Innovation and Planned Change

Introduction

We live in an era in which change has become a familiar term. In fact, one frequently used phrase implies that the only permanent feature of our time is change. There is hardly any social institution which escapes the process of change, and education is no exception. Formal education in schools of the last five decades has been marked by significant and frequent changes in its aims and objectives, its content, teaching strategies, methods of student assessment, provisions, and the levels of funding.

Glatthorn and Jailall (2000) use a 'streams' metaphor to explain all the changes which are ongoing in educational systems – some streams ebb, some gather strength, sometimes the streams are widely separated, at other times they flow together.

Not always have the changes led to something better – some innovations have been disappointing and brought about yet another turn in the search for the 'best' education.

Fullan (1993) contends that the major problem in education is that educational systems are fundamentally conservative – they want to retain the status quo – and when change is attempted 'it results in defensiveness, superficiality or at best short-lived pockets of success' (p. 3).

Yet, there is a moral purpose for education (Fullan, 2001). Teachers and schools should be making a difference to the lives of students – 'they are in the business of *making improvements*, and to make improvements in an ever changing world is to contend with and manage the forces on an ongoing basis' (Fullan, 1993, p. 4).

Developing a new mindset for teachers is indeed a major challenge (Spillane *et al.*, 2002). Some educators contend that 'teachers have the reputation of being inherently and universally stubborn when facing change' (Corbett and Rossman, 1989, p. 36). Much of this purported stubbornness could be attributed to the selection process in recruiting teachers and the socialization process experienced by teachers.

On the other hand, it might be argued that the problem lies with the naivete of educational leaders and their inept ways of bringing about change. Some leaders simply assume teachers will carry out their proposals; others use regulations and mandates to enforce change. Too many leaders focus upon change as a product and overlook the processes – the human face of change (House, 1996).

Then again perhaps educators underestimate what it takes to make fundamental changes in an organization. Hatch (2002) contends that the private sector will use up to 20 per cent of their resources to make substantive changes to their organization whereas in education we rarely spend more than 1 per cent on change efforts. Staff members are often expected to donate their time. Expecting change at bargain basement rates is unlikely to be successful.

Some Basic Terms

'Change' is a generic term which subsumes a whole family of concepts such as 'innovation', 'development' and 'adoption'. It can be either planned or unplanned (unintentional, spontaneous, accidental movements or shifts). The literature tends to focus upon 'planned change', which, for Fullan (1991) is multidimensional involving possible changes in goals, skills, philosophy or beliefs, and behaviour, but above all is change in practice.

Poppleton (2000) notes that planned change can refer to innovations at classroom or school level as well as to reforms and reconstructions of the whole or parts of the educational system of a country.

The term 'innovation' may mean either a new object, idea or practice, or the process by which a new object, idea or project comes to be adopted by an individual group or organization. Early studies in the curriculum literature tended to view innovations as objects or events, similar to a new item of machinery for farmers or a new apothecary line. Much more emphasis is now placed upon innovation as a process. A working definition of innovation is the planned application of ends or means, new or different from those which exist currently in the classroom, school or system, and intended to improve effectiveness for the stakeholders.

This definition, with its emphasis upon 'intention' and 'application', is indicating that the innovation process is not only an awareness but a definite intention to implement one or more of the alternatives. Many early studies of innovations tended to focus upon knowledge, awareness and adoption decisions, but few penetrated the crucial area of implementation, to find out how teachers were actually using an innovation.

The definition also directs attention to 'improving' effectiveness for the stakeholders. Educators do not always agree with the contention that a change has to be an improvement to quality to be classed as an 'innovation'. Whether an innovation is regarded as an improvement or not depends of course upon the judgement of the adopting agency or individual, as they will perceive an innovation in terms of their past experiences and aspirations. If it is 'new' to them, and different to what they have done before, then they will probably choose it because it is considered likely to bring about an improvement. Innovations are not objective and unchanging, but are constantly being changed and redefined as a result of experience. In other words, the initial perception of an innovation by teachers and other individuals or agencies may be that it is 'new' and an 'improvement' to what they were doing, but the final judgement of worth cannot really be known until some time later when they have become fully conversant with the innovation and how it might be applied to their situation (Poppleton, 2000).

The inclusion of the attribute 'improvement' in the concept of an innovative process emphasizes the political nature of curriculum innovations. Whilst other educational terms such as 'child development' or 'age grading' tend to be analysed and discussed by educationalists as important concepts and ends in themselves, 'innovations' are initiated in school situations because certain authorities are not satisfied with particular directions or levels of learning and want to do something different (Soder, 1999).

There is no doubt that politicians are taking a leading role in determining directions for innovations (Angus, 1995; Peddie, 1995; Sarason, 1990). Caldwell (1993) suggests that governments are adopting a more powerful and focused role in terms of setting goals, establishing priorities and building frameworks for accountability.

Yet, the literature is also replete with examples to demonstrate that many current reforms and innovations are contradictory and illogical. Post-modernists contend that many of the assumptions about Western society need to be dismantled and exposed. Many of the policies of politicians and bureaucrats need to be challenged (Giroux, 1992; Glatthorn and Jailall, 2000).

Teachers need to enter into dialogue about the uncertainties, the concerns, doubts and questions about teaching and so-called improvement projects. It is a challenge for teachers to transcend traditional, positivist approaches – it can indeed be emancipatory for them even if the context of schooling appears to be constraining and antagonistic (Ball, 1994; Day and Roberts-Holmes, 1998).

The Process of Educational Change

A number of writers have coined phrases to describe the process of educational change. Fullan (2001) on many occasions in his writings has produced interesting phrases to 'capture' the spirit of the change process. He lists the five components as:

1. The goal is not to innovate the most.
2. It is not enough to have the best idea.
3. Appreciate the implementation dip.
4. Redefine resistance.
5. Reculturing is the name of the game.
6. Never a checklist, always complexity (p. 34).

A more traditional approach to educational change processes is to separate out the phases involved:

1. Orientation/needs phase

Dissatisfaction, concern, or need is felt and expressed by one or more individuals who seek answers to such dominant questions as:
- What is the problem that is concerning me (us)?
- How and why has it arisen?
- Is it important enough to rectify?
- Do I (we) want to take the necessary steps to overcome the problem?

2. Initiation/adoption phase
A person (or a group of persons) initiates and promotes a certain programme or activity. Dominant questions of this phase are:
- What should I (we) do?
- What will it look like?
- What will it mean for me (us)?

3. Implementation/initial use phase
Attempts are made by teachers to use the programme or activity and this can have varied results from a success to a disastrous failure. Dominant questions for the teacher at this phase include:
- How do I do it?
- Will I ever get it to work smoothly?
- To whom can I turn to get assistance?
- Am I doing what the practice requires?
- What is the effect on the learner?

4. Institutionalization/continuation phase
The emphasis here is to ensure that structures and patterns of behaviour are established so that the use of the innovation will be maintained over time. The dominant questions for the school are:
- How do I (we) make sure that the innovation will continue?
- Who will take responsibilities to ensure the adequate operation of it?

Although these four phases can be separated for purposes of analysis, in practice they will merge imperceptibly into each other. There can be forward and backward modifications between the phases (as indicated by the two-way arrows in Figure 8.1), and the time periods for each phase can vary tremendously.

The 'initiation/adoption' phase is often termed 'the front end' of an innovation. This is the period when basic decisions are made by external agencies and publishers for whom numbers of adopters (and therefore sales) are of crucial importance. They can expect that schools and teachers will adopt a curriculum package only if it fulfils a special need for them, although there are other factors which can influence their decision. Fullan (1991) listed a number of factors which co-determine adoption rates, including existence and quality of related innovations, access to information, advocacy from central administrators, change agents, availability of federal or state funds, community pressures, and decrees by state governments.

Figure 8.1: Educational change process

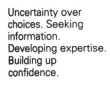
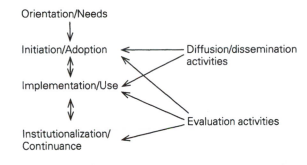

Uncertainty over choices. Seeking information. Developing expertise. Building up confidence.

Building up resource base. Building support role.

Orientation/Needs
↓
Initiation/Adoption ← Diffusion/dissemination activities
↕
Implementation/Use
↕
Institutionalization/ Continuance
Evaluation activities

Source: Fullan (1982)

The 'implementation phase' has been defined as 'what an innovation consists of in practice' (Fullan and Pomfret, 1977). But this simple statement does not reveal the complex realities and problems associated with the phase. Leithwood's (1981) definition raises some of the complexities: 'Implementation is a reduction in the gap between current and preferred status'.

Whilst the answer to the question of whether an innovation has been adopted can be simply 'yes' or 'no', the same cannot apply to implementation. There is a continuum of degrees of implementation ranging from major to minor adaptations through to high fidelity of use level. The only definite point on the continuum is for non-implementation (see also Chapter 7).

'Institutionalization' occurs when an innovation is supported in schools after an initial period of use (usually 2–5 years). The real test for continuance or disappearance of an innovation comes after external funds have been terminated or after consultant assistance has stopped. It can be argued that institutionalization has to be reached before it is possible to judge the outcomes or effects of an innovation since otherwise an adverse evaluation would lead to the removal of the innovation. Institutionalization is facilitated by such factors as administrative commitment, pressures and support (Scott, 1999). It is weakened by staff mobility and changing student populations.

The above phases are useful in establishing likely stages in the change process but they ignore the 'emotional' work of change (Hargreaves *et al.*, 2001) or the 'personality of change' (Goodson, 2001b). Goodson maintains that a teacher's personal beliefs and missions are a crucial building block in the change process.

Carless (2004) reminds us that frontline teachers are faced with multiple innovations and they have to juggle with a variety of commitments. Hargreaves (1997) suggests that 'the chaos of multiple innovations and intensified reform efforts is often a sign of governments in panic' (p. 62).

Churchill and Williamson (1999) conclude from their study that teachers' experiences with previous educational changes affect their receptivity to future changes. Those teachers who had a high level of commitment to a recent change are more likely to adopt a positive approach to future innovations. Those who played resistant roles previously are likely to respond negatively in the future.

Change Leaders

There can be a number of change leaders within a school or agency. According to Binney and Williams (1995) 'they are clear about what they want to change and they are responsive to others' views and concerns' (p. 52). They need not be senior-level teachers or administrators. Any person who helps other teachers with the curriculum (both content and processes of teaching), or who helps teachers identify problems and search our resources and linkage groups, is a change leader.

According to Scott (1999) an effective change leader:

1. gives positive support and doesn't put people down;
2. is enthusiastic and cares about education;
3. is committed to doing things well;
4. can tolerate ambiguity;
5. accepts change as inevitable;
6. is action-oriented;
7. possesses a wide repertoire of communication skills;
8. understands and can work with the dynamics of change.

Fullan (2002) focuses especially upon school principals – 'only principals who are equipped to handle a complex, rapidly changing environment can implement the reforms that lead to sustained improvement in student achievement' (p. 16). He suggests that 'the principal of the future – the Cultural Change Principal – must be attuned to the big picture ... Cultural Change Principals display palpable energy, enthusiasm and hope' (p. 17).

Sulla (1998) notes that change leaders external to the school are often a crucial element in ensuring that an educational change is implemented successfully. She maintains that external change leaders are better placed to take into account the local context, and to help teachers engage in reflective inquiry.

Diffusion and Dissemination

'Diffusion and dissemination' activities are crucial for an understanding of how innovations are communicated. Rogers (1983) defines 'diffusion' as 'the spontaneous, unplanned spread of new ideas'. It involves a special type of communication between individuals and groups because the messages are concerned with 'new' ideas. Groups and individuals will often seek out further information about an innovation before they make a decision to adopt it or not. If they are unable to decide between several alternatives, the diffusion of information enables them to make an informed choice.

Information transfer is rarely a one-way process: most frequently it is effected by an exchange of ideas and information between individuals. Diffusion activities typically involve a two-way communication of information. Information about an innovation can of course be diffused by different communication channels, from mass media to face-to-face exchange.

The term 'dissemination' is often used synonymously with diffusion but it really has a narrower focus and applies to the specific procedures used to inform individuals or groups about an innovation and to gain their interest in it (Coulby, 2000). The emphasis is upon goal-directed activities and upon the arousing of interest in the innovation among potential clients. Some writers (for example, Zaltman *et al.*, 1977; and Rosenau, 1973) see dissemination very much like marketing activities and provide detailed guidelines about how a range of tactics such as direct mail, workshops, visits or telephone calls can be used in certain educational situations. They analyse each of these tactics according to various criteria such as relative cost, coverage, impact and user convenience.

For other writers (Simpson, 1990; Sarason, 1990), curriculum dissemination occurs within a cultural framework. They maintain that change agents need to be aware of a school system's attitudes and administrative structure and to use only those dissemination activities which are suited to these prevailing norms.

Change Strategies and Tactics

'Strategy' in the area of educational change means, reduced to its simplest form, a plan for replacing an existing programme by an innovation. Several such strategies have been proposed by education writers. The difficulty with some of them is that they have been devised for curriculum change in quite specific educational settings at a particular point in time. The latter (the temporal factor) is understandable as strategies suggested for the 1960s would necessarily differ from those for the 2000s with their different sets of relationships. Nevertheless they are helpful for the purposes of analysis.

Major strategies have been classified in the typology by Bennis *et al.* (1976), who allocated each of them to one of three groups which they labelled as 'power-coercive', 'normative/re-educative' and 'empirical-rational'.

'Power-coercive' strategies are based on the control of rewards and punishments and are relatively easy to apply. The recipients simply have to comply if they want to obtain the rewards offered. The motivation for complying is of course not meaningfully related to the innovation. That is, it is extrinsic in nature, and teachers on the receiving side will have no inner self-generated need for accepting and implementing an innovation (intrinsic motivation).

'Normative/re-educative' strategies refer to actions intended to manipulate recipients so that they see the situation differently. This can be achieved by biased messages, persuasive communication and training workshops. The recipients are trained or re-educated to appreciate the beneficial aspects of a particular innovation.

'Empirical-rational' strategies rely upon the recipients realizing that they should change to the new innovation in their best interests. The strategies rely upon providing detailed knowledge about the innovation by holding workshops, seminars and demonstrations.

It is not difficult to identify any of these strategies included in educational changes which have occurred in the past. All education systems will on occasions use a 'power-coercive' strategy if a major change is envisaged and it is seen to be necessary for all students (for example, a new core area in computing). But there will also be occasions when the authorities will be less coercive and they will appeal to teachers' rational judgements or, if this fails, they may try to re-educate teachers to their point of view. All three strategies may be used concurrently and at different levels with different groups of teachers and administrators (Hess, 2003).

The particular strategies used will vary from situation to situation, but to maximize their effect, certain 'tactics' will tend to be associated with them. A change agent may not systematically plan to use particular tactics but some tactics can clearly reinforce or reduce the potential impact of specific strategies. Examples of the wide range of tactics available, including personal contact, user involvement, information distribution and training/installation tactics, are shown in Table 8.1.

At different times particular tactics might appear to be the most appropriate. For example, a busy school principal might prefer to send a general e-mail/memo (impersonal information) to all staff because of the time saved (relative cost). However, the impact on the teachers is likely to be far less than if the principal had called a meeting or met up with key teachers (personal) (see Table 8.1).

The categories included in Table 8.1 have a distinct marketing orientation. This is deliberate because it is argued that educators can gain important insights from how commercial businesses embark upon change.

Contexts of Innovations

Schools in which innovations are implemented can vary enormously in terms of staff interest and expertise, organizational structures, and resources. The staff will have their own special identity based upon their attributes, informal and formal values and norms, leadership traits and organizational climate. Students at a particular school will have certain characteristics in terms of socio-economic status, social orientation, norms, values and skills (Wideen, 1994).

Table 8.1: Dissemination tactics and their effects

	Rel. Cost of Imp.	Rel. Coverage	Relative Impact	User Convenience	Feedback	Ideal for	Unsuited to	Incentives Required
IMPERSONAL Information								
Direct Mail	L	H	L	H	H	Installing or replacing visible, low-risk, familiar innovations	Complex innovations	Low price, ease of ordering, guarantee, bonus, etc.
Mass Media	L	H	L	M	L	Awareness, arousal	Complex, high-cost innovations	Stimulus to act on information (limited time, special introductory offer, etc.)
Printed Matter	L	M	L	H	L	Awareness, interest	Complex innovations requiring hands-on trial	Stimulus to act on information
Professional Association	L	M	M	M	M	Awareness of innovations, data on trials	Mass-market adoptions	Professional membership status, interaction with peers, prepaid travel to meetings
PERSONAL Demonstration								
On-Site	M	L	M	H	H	Trial of high-risk innovations in large LEAs	Low-risk routine adoptions	Released time for observation testimonials
Visitation	H	M	M	L	M	Demonstration of complex, high-risk innovations	Low cost, routine adoptions	Released time, prepaid travel, materials to take home, testimonials
Workshop	M	L	L	M	M	Hands-on trial	Persuasion of university personnel	Free registration, credit, materials to take home, snacks
INTERPERSONAL Field Agents								
Non-Commercial	H	M	M	H	H	Implementing high-risk, unfamiliar, complex training or organizational innovations	Mass-market adoptions	Free consultation, technical assistance, targeted information retrieval system, etc.
Commercial	H	H	H	H	H	Installing high mark-up, low-risk, consumable innovations	Low mark-up, complex innovations	Free samples, entertainment, volume discounts, special deals, etc.

L = low   M = medium   H = high

Persons in the local community may have interests that can affect, or be affected by, their school (Prawat, 2000). Parents and community groups may develop a number of initiatives about the type of curriculum they wish to have taught at their school, but the teachers may then respond differently and try to influence their students and, indirectly, the parents. Differing points of view represented by the numerous 'cultures' of a school (parents, teachers, head office bureaucracy) may then create tensions on particular curriculum issues.

Because of these differences it is not possible to predict in advance how participants at a specific school will react to a proposal to implement an innovation (Scott, 1999). Readiness for change is clearly a major factor, but this will depend in turn on such aspects as advocacy from central administrators; access to information; teacher pressure and support; community pressure, support, opposition or apathy; availability of external funds; and new legislation or policy. In many cases, innovative successful schools lose their creativity and atrophy as a result of loss of leadership, and internal divisions and conflicts (Azzara, 2000).

Models of Change

Various education writers have outlined models of change that they contend have been successful in particular contexts. In general terms we can classify them as either being 'external' to the school or 'internal' to a school (see Table 8.2). The external model typically relies upon authority to exercise influence over people, processes and the use of resources (Desimone, 2002). The internal model relies upon interaction, group processes and consensus.

There are, of course, many other variations that might be located at different points on the continuum depicted in Table 8.2. Sometimes top-down, external models are effective but on many occasions they are not. Furthermore, not all internal, school-focused models are successful.

Some writings on educational change tend to differ from model-building assertions but the principles they espouse have a particular value-orientation.

Table 8.2: Categories of models of change

External to school	Internal to school	External/ internal/ personal	External
High control	Interactive	Interactive	Research-based
Example: Research Development and Diffusion (Clark and Guba, 1965) Authority Model	*Example*: Concerns Based Adoption Model (Hall *et al.*, 1979)	*Example*: Goodson's Model (2000)	*Example*: Comprehensive school reform programmes (Education Commission of the States, 1998)

Take, for example, Fullan's (1993) 'eight basic lessons about change', as depicted in Table 8.3.

It is evident from these lessons or principles that Fullan is espousing a process-oriented model with an emphasis upon individual and organization variables.

Principals also have to make some difficult decisions relating to a proposed innovation too (Southworth, 2000). They may not have any choice if the change is a system-wide one (Male, 1998). The proposed innovation may be at a considerable personal cost to them if they have to find the time to lead it, along with other responsibilities such as managing the academic performance of students, curriculum and instruction, professional performance of staff, administrative organization, school facilities and external relations.

As noted by Murphy and Rodi (2000), principals develop different coping strategies and some might have a well-developed resistance to any changes which threaten to undermine the present organizational pattern and behaviours at their school. Other principals may not be confident with initiating change, preferring to have an orderly well-organized approach and established procedures for all routine tasks.

Which Innovations Last?

A simple answer to the above question is 'not many'! Many traditional school practices continue to endure, despite attempts over the decades to bring about change. At different periods particular innovations appear to be the catchcry

Table 8.3: *Eight basic lessons of the new paradigm of change*

Lesson One:	You can't mandate what matters
	(The more complex the change the less you can force it)
Lesson Two:	Change is a journey not a blueprint
	(Change is non-linear, loaded with uncertainty and excitement and sometimes perverse)
Lesson Three:	Problems are our friends
	(Problems are inevitable and you can't learn without them)
Lesson Four:	Vision and strategic planning come later
	(Premature visions and planning blind)
Lesson Five:	Individualism and collectivism must have equal power
	(There are no one-sided solutions to isolation and group think)
Lesson Six:	Neither centralization nor decentralization works
	(Both top-down and bottom-up strategies are necessary)
Lesson Seven:	Connection with the wider environment is critical for success
	(The best organizations learn externally as well as internally)
Lesson Eight:	Every person is a change agent
	(Change is too important to leave to the experts, personal mind set and mastery is the ultimate protection)

Source: Fullan (1993, pp. 21–2).

Table 8.4: The longevity of innovations

Innovations that have lasted
• Teacher aides
• Cooperative learning
• Whole language learning
• Site-based management

Innovations that have not lasted
• Homogeneous grouping
• Merit pay
• 8mm projectors

for all stakeholders, only to fall into oblivion a few years later (Rosenshine, 1995).

Cuban (1988) reminds us that innovations keep on appearing. There may be all sorts of reasons for this, such as previous practices failing to remove the problems they were intended to solve; or because the politics of the problem were emphasized rather than the problem itself. He suggests that few educational innovations make it past the schoolroom door permanently.

The two lists included in Table 8.4 reveal that there are a number of innovations which were widely used in earlier decades that are no longer in use today. Some are products while others are processes. Those that have survived appear to have done so because they have had a relative advantage, were easily managed and stimulated active involvement by teachers (Vanterpool, 1990).

Teachers have a number of responsibilities including providing a stable, supportive learning environment for their students. Some innovations and changes have the potential to bring about valued school improvement but no educational change is simple or without cost. Stakeholders have to make informed choices about whether to become involved in an innovation or not. As concluded by Ellis and Fouts (1993), some of the innovations that sweep through the school scene are nothing more than fads, while some have greater staying power. We have a responsibility to take change seriously, to be aware of the motivations and pressures for change and the implications and demands on all stakeholders (Chatterji, 2002).

Reflections and Issues

1. Examine an innovation in education that occurred recently and with which you are quite familiar. Who initiated it? What steps were taken to implement it? How were impediments overcome? Is it still being used in schools? If not, when did it cease and why?
2. Compare and contrast the following statements using examples from schools with which you are familiar:

- 'Most innovations that have lasted began with teachers involved in the planning.' (Vanterpool, 1990, p. 39)
- 'Teachers are not willing to explore innovations because they guard jealously the privacy of their own classroom and their established procedures.' (Marsh, 1997, p. 24)

3. 'Real change is always personal, organizational change is always painstaking. Success will require both high strivings and realistic acceptance – and authentic leaders who keep a steady focus on the human face of reform' (Ross, 2000). Discuss.

4. School reform has failed because we have focused too narrowly on academic achievement. Give some examples to support or refute this statement.

5. 'Sustaining school-wide reform programs past the initial stage of enthusiasm is one of the biggest problems that schools face.' (McChesney and Hertling, 2000, p. 14). How might a principal sustain a high level of enthusiasm? What would be the incentives for teachers?

6. 'The essential nature of an innovation can be eroded with small, almost imperceptible alterations so that the school "tames" it' (Jansen and Van der Vegt, 1991, p. 33). To what extent should adaptation be permitted in school settings? Is it necessary for all of a planned innovation to be maintained? Can strict fidelity of use be maintained without violating the autonomy of teachers and students?

9 Leadership and the School Principal

Introduction

At whatever level you consider it, school heads/principals have a major role to play. At the level of an individual school, few would deny that students learning depends upon good school leadership.

In terms of large-scale education reform, school principals also have a key role to play (Fullan, 2002).

Despite the acknowledged importance of school principals and their leadership role there is far from consensus on the goals of principals and leadership styles. Some recent conceptions involve performance outcomes, instructional leadership, moral leadership, managerial leadership and transformational leadership. A number of these approaches are considered below.

Expectations about the Role of Principal

The position of school principal is certainly an exciting one to uphold. So many different groups and individuals have expectations about what the school principal should do and should achieve:

- Parents and community members expect a public-minded, highly principled person who is open to outside initiatives and who will communicate information regularly to them.
- Teachers expect their school principal to be an instructional leader and a supporter of curriculum initiatives and to be very visible and active around the school buildings.
- Students expect a sympathetic counsellor and the final arbiter on matters of justice, discipline and penalties, but above all, an inspirational, charismatic figurehead.
- State department officials and senior regional officers expect school principals to be thorough, reliable and efficient and capable of implementing and monitoring departmental policies and not to be overly influenced by vocal minority groups.

The expectations in total are overwhelming and, in most cases, quite unrealistic (Grace, 1995). Copland (2001) contends that expectations for the principalship in the USA have steadily expanded, always adding to and never subtracting from the job description. Because of these additional expectations, the principal's role has come under ever closer scrutiny – it is increasingly difficult to recruit 'quality' principals. According to Copland (2001) 'we have reached the point where aggregate expectations for the principalship are so exorbitant that they exceed the limits of what might reasonably be expected from one person' (p. 529).

Woods (2000), in describing the scene in the United Kingdom, argues that it is not only the additional expectations but the enhanced emphasis upon market and public regulatory mechanisms. School principals have to demonstrate performativity – 'to amend their identity nearer to innovative, enterprising, competitive entrepreneurs modelled on the private sector' (Woods, 2000, p. 15)''. Male (1998) refers also to the marketplace environment and a move to individuality and isolation for head teachers.

There is a further complication in that many of the expectations described above are based on 'dated' stereotypes. For example, there is the expectation that effective school principals are males and as a result females are in the minority in positions of authority even though women are in the majority in the teaching service (Porter, 1994). Lee *et al.* (1993) refer to a recent empirical study which revealed that male teachers assess the leadership of female principals they work for as relatively ineffective even though measures of self-efficacy and staff influence demonstrated higher results for both male and female teachers working for female rather than male principals!

Leadership and School Principals

The role of the school principal contains many conflicts and ambiguities. The principal leads a communication network – a two-way flow of information between schools and head office and community agencies and individuals.

Functions/Standards

Leadership responsibilities can be analysed in terms of 'functions' and standards or in terms of special 'qualities'. A typical listing of functions or domains is provided in Table 9.1. These are major areas but of course in daily activities they merge imperceptibly with each other.

A similar approach is to use competency frameworks to describe standards of principals' work. For example, in the United Kingdom, the National College for School Leadership has produced national standards for new head teachers comprising a set of key areas and a set of skills and abilities. Candidates have to demonstrate competence to obtain the National Professional Qualification for Headship (Louden and Wildy, 1997).

In the USA a number of frameworks are available such as the standards framework produced by the Interstate School Leaders Licensure Consortium (Council of Chief State School Officers, 1996).

Table 9.1: Domains in which the principal is expected to demonstrate leadership

Curriculum and instruction
- reviewing or revising an existing subject
- influencing specific teaching methods
- introducing new subjects/units

Academic performance of students
- influencing achievement standards in all subjects
- encouraging high attainments by students in accordance with their abilities
- monitoring tests and examinations in specific subjects

Non-academic development of students
- managing or controlling student behaviour
- influencing student welfare/attitudes
- influencing students' extracurricular activities

Professional/personal performance of staff
- influencing the performance of teachers
- influencing the performance of administrators
- influencing induction of newly graduated teachers
- influencing the performance of student teachers
- supporting teacher welfare and their personal development

Administration/organization
- influencing schedule of teaching
- influencing student enrolment priorities
- influencing student decisions
- influencing operational efficiency

School facilities
- managing use of buildings, grounds and furnishings
- initiating changes to improve instruction
- initiating changes to improve aesthetics

External relations
- maintaining regular communication with school board members
- maintaining regular communication with regional and state education department officials
- providing positive public relations with the local community

Louden and Wildy (1997) contend that these competency/standards frameworks have limited value because:

- they divide complex professional performances into hierarchical lists, i.e. they fragment professional performance;
- they separate the performance from the contexts where it occurs;
- they apply a degree of precision which does not reflect the real professional contexts.

An alternative to standards frameworks is proposed by Louden and Wildy (1997) based upon a probabilistic framework, utilizing written case studies and Rasch modelling. Performance of principals is located on a set of continua, offers only an estimate of performance, and describes what normally can be expected rather than judging mastery of a skill.

Qualities

Fullan (2002) refers to essential qualities that he considers are needed for the principal of the future – the Cultural Change Principal, namely:

- moral purpose: the school principal treats students, teachers and parents well – the principal seeks to make a difference in the lives of students;
- understanding change: the school principal helps others find collective meaning – works on transforming the culture;
- improving relationships: the school principal builds relationships with diverse people and groups – the principal tries to motivate and energize disaffected teachers;
- knowledge creation and sharing: the principal is the lead learner and shares with others;
- coherence making: the principal concentrates on student learning as the central focus and then brings together other elements to facilitate this – the principal does not take on too many projects for the sake of it.

Leadership Style

The reality of the school day, with its constant interruptions, can put a principal under considerable stress. Typically, a principal will adopt a particular 'leadership style' which emphasizes certain priorities and limits others. This is his or her coping mechanism and it is quite understandable.

A leadership style commonly listed is instructional leadership (Lezotte, 1997). This emphasis was a development of the effective schools movement and it involved principals actively participating in the instructional process – collecting weekly lesson plans from teachers, reading about different instructional strategies, undertaking the clinical supervision process (pre-observation conferences, classroom observations, post-observation conferences) (Du Four, 2002).

A leadership style which has been championed in the 1990s and the 2000s is transformational school leadership. Bass and Avolio (1994) developed a model of transformational leadership which they considered was exemplified by the four I's:

- idealized influence – being a role model for their followers;
- inspirational motivation – motivating and inspiring followers;
- intellectual stimulation – stimulating followers to be innovative and creative;
- individualized consideration – paying special attention to each individual's needs.

Leithwood *et al.* (1996) have identified specific dimensions of transformational school leadership as well as behaviours associated with each of the dimensions. Their dimensions include:

- charisma/inspiration/vision;
- individual consideration;
- intellectual stimulation;
- structuring;
- culture building;
- high performance expectations;
- modelling.

This leadership style focuses especially on visionary concerns while largely ignoring routine managerial concerns. It emphasizes the significance of the person and personal traits in bringing about social and cultural change (Crowther *et al.*, 2000).

Although transformational leadership has had a major influence some educators argue that it overstates the importance of individuals. For example, Gronn (2000) criticizes transformational leadership because it exaggerates the sense of agency attributed to leaders – naïve realism, the belief in the power of one.

Yet, shaping of the school culture seems to be a major leadership element whether or not it can be encapsulated as transformational style.

Lucas and Valentine (2002) argue that creating a school culture that accepts and encourages experimentation, risk-taking and open dialogue is likely to be successful.

If these different leadership styles are considered en masse rather than separately, it may be the case that additional understandings are grafted onto a comprehensive definition of the principal's role and in turn lead to even further overwhelming expectations for principals (Copland, 2001).

Concluding Comments

Capable principals are critically needed in schools to provide leadership. Each school has its own culture and each school principal has to develop coping strategies (Fullan, 2001). Principals need help if they are to cope with unrealistic expectations from school communities and the general public.

A transformational approach to leadership has the potential of developing a school culture with vision, intellectual stimulation and high expectations, but many impediments can occur using the individualistic style.

Reflections and Issues

1. Principals as dynamic change agents are still very rare – probably fewer than one in ten. 'Is this simply a function of training, selection and support on the job or do we have the wrong conception of the role of the principal?' (Fullan, 1988, pp. 708). Discuss.

2. 'Women have always been real leaders in education. It is time for their skills and values to be recognised in formal positions as well as informal roles' (Porter, 1994, p.21). Are there empirical data on the role of women as school principals? What evidence do you have about the effectiveness of female principals?

3. 'Whether by choice or circumstance, a significant dimension of the school princi-palship in the 1990s necessarily involves school law' (Hartmeister, 1995, p. 5). What are some legal matters that cause problems for school principals? Are they increasing? What kinds of training are needed by principals to cope with these matters?

4. 'We need to move away from the notion of how the principal can become master implementer of multiple policies and programmes. What is needed is to reframe the question: What does a reasonable leader do, faced with impossible tasks?' (Fullan, 1988, p. 12). Is it more productive to consider schools as operating in a non-rational world – with complex, contradictory happenings occurring daily? What realistic priorities should a 'reasonable' leader select?

5. 'Women principals are found to act in a more democratic and participative style, whereas male principals are more directive and autocratic' (Lee *et al.*, 1993, p. 156). Discuss.

6. 'Leadership is and must be oriented toward social change, change which is trans-formative in degree' (Foster, 1989, p. 52). To what extent is this a major concern for school principals? What impediments may limit this as an option?

7. 'Principals, as middle managers, must simultaneously manage at least four sets of relationships: upward with their superiors; downward with subordinates; laterally with other principals; and externally with parents and other community and business groups. Managing one set of relationships successfully may interfere with or hinder another set of relationships' (Goldring, 1993, p. 95). Explain this management problem giving examples.

8. 'A leader in the postmodern world needs a clear sense that nothing is guaranteed; that nothing, certainly, will be easy' (Starratt, 1993, p. 157). Discuss with refer-ence to the school principal as leader.

10 School-based Management

Introduction

Many countries and states have introduced systems of school self-management. Different titles are often used such as 'school-based management' (SBM) and 'site-based management' but they are all pursuing similar goals – to decentralize certain areas of authority, responsibility and resources down to the school level.

Where self-managing school systems have been developed there have been examples of good practices but also a number of failures. Questions are often raised about whose interests are being served by these systems of decentralization.

Some Basic Terms

Although it is difficult to define precisely what is meant by 'self-managing schools' it is important to exclude what is not. As noted by Caldwell and Spinks (1998) 'a self-managing school is not an autonomous school nor is it a self-governing school, for each of these kinds of schools involve a degree of independence that is not provided in a centrally determined framework' (p. 15).

Caldwell links the emergence and popularity of SBM with decentralized tendencies in business. In terms of business and industry, 'responsibility, authority and accountability are being shifted to the level of the operational unit' (Caldwell, 1993, p. 1).

Within the education sector, a similar major push toward management at the school level has been occurring and continues to gain momentum. Regardless of the philosophies of different governments, the trend seems to be irreversible and is characterized by:

- centrally determined frameworks;
- a leaner bureaucracy;
- the shift of responsibility, authority and accountability to schools;
- a better-informed community exercising more choice in schooling;
- empowered leadership, especially for school principals/heads. (Caldwell, 1995, p. 1)

However, these changes to the management of schools do not necessarily generate better-quality curricula, teaching and learning (Dimmock, 1993). As noted by Burrow (1994), the shifting of responsibility to the local level has occurred for other than pedagogical reasons. Smyth (1994, p. 2) argues that the concept of the self-managing school is deceptive in that:

- the rhetoric of devolution is really about recentralization of education;
- it is closely linked to structural changes in the economy;
- the trends are not emancipatory or liberating for teachers.

Research on SBM

Studies undertaken in the USA in the 1990s have not shown positive impacts of SBM.

For example, Taylor and Teddlie (1992) examined 33 schools, of which 16 had established SBM programmes and 17 served as a control group. The authors concluded that teachers in their study did not alter their practice and did not collaborate with their colleagues.

Rossi and Freeman's (1993) study of SBM in 12 high schools in 11 states in the USA (half selected because they had implemented SBM while the other half had traditional-led school principals) found that schools implementing SBM did not pay any more attention to issues of curriculum, pedagogical issues and student concerns than the traditionally managed schools.

Leithwood and Menzies' (1999) review of 83 empirical studies of SBM found little evidence for or against. Their overall conclusion was that 'there is virtually no firm, research-based knowledge about the direct or indirect effects of SBM on students ... There is an awesome gap between the rhetoric and the reality of SBM's contribution to student growth' (p. 34).

By contrast, Caldwell (2002a) contends that the connection between SBM and improved student learning is now becoming clear and that Wee (1999) at the University of Melbourne is mapping the links. Caldwell (2002) cites a UNESCO forum held in February 2001 at which participants 'shared international experience of success with strategies that linked SBM, enhanced professional development for teachers, community support for schools and making learning for students more active and joyful' (p. 9).

Many education systems operating in the twenty-first century are maintaining some centralized control mechanisms such as by the use of centrally determined frameworks and centrally determined funding mechanisms.

Fullan and Watson (2000) assert that the use of 'decentralization' is a misnomer because key aspects of authority are retained at the control level.

A number of descriptive accounts have been published about the benefits of self-managing schools or SBM. Yet despite the positive rhetoric it is difficult to find any research-based evidence on the direct or indirect benefits of SBM.

SBM Characteristics

For SBM to work in practice, people in legal authority over a school must exercise restraint in exerting their control over the curriculum and must demonstrate leadership in promoting harmonious curriculum deliberations among those who work within the school (Price and Vallie, 2000). This mixture of restraint and leadership is a form of administration that is basically antithetical to the familiar staff-and-line arrangement, in which all members of an organization are ranked within a hierarchy in which people of higher rank give directives to those of lower rank.

Seen in this light, an administrator is a facilitator of an organization's work, just as a teacher can be a facilitator of student learning.

Applied to a school, this form of administration acknowledges teachers as the people who do the substantive work. The school principal, however, may help teachers consider what the curriculum should be and how it might fit with the curricula of other schools. In addition, the principal should provide both material and psychological support to the teachers in their deliberations and should be prepared to explain to the community what they are doing while deliberations are in progress and what they have accomplished when any new curriculum has been developed. In this sense, the principal is not the instructional leader of the school, but the leader of instructors.

In SBM, each school plans and implements its own curriculum; however, these curricula are not necessarily out of touch with each other. The idea behind SBM is not individualism for the sake of individualism. State systems may provide general guidelines, the understanding of subject matter of the teachers of one school may parallel that of teachers in another school, consultants may offer similar advice, teachers may face common classroom problems, and the characteristics of the community in which a school exists may be similar to those of other communities (Watson *et al.*, 2000). The idea behind SBM is that students benefit because the curricula they are taught are developed specifically for them, based on a close assessment of their individual characteristics and needs and of the available resources in the school and the community. Teachers benefit because they do most of the assessing and develop specific curricula that they believe will lead to the greatest benefit for the students. Hence, teachers exercise professional judgements and develop some sense of personal commitment to the curricula they create.

SBM is not a panacea. Many on-site conflicts and problems can and do arise. Some scholars, such as Davies and Ellison (2000), argue that a rigorous theoretical framework for understanding how SBM can be optimized is still lacking. Nonetheless, SBM clearly encourages the development of a professional culture within a school in which teachers, other personnel and members of the community work collaboratively in ongoing cycles of curriculum development and improvement.

It is instructive to examine SBM more closely in the United Kingdom, Australia and the USA.

Examples

United Kingdom

The 1988 Education Act provided specifically for the Local Management of Schools (LMS) whereby each school was given responsibility for school-level planning including the selection and removal of staff. In addition, schools were encouraged to opt out of local education authorities and become Grant-Maintained Schools (GMS) and receive their resources direct from the national body, the Department of Education and Science.

According to Davies and Ellison (2000) different stakeholders offered various reasons for these changes, including:

- philosophical – a belief that teachers and parents should be involved in decisions that affect them;
- pragmatic – an organization is too big to run effectively from the centre;
- financial – financial delegation to schools is good management.

Currently, each school receives a minimum of 90 per cent of its potential, student-related budget as a direct grant. The responsible body for each school is the governing body of up to 19 people. The governing body is responsible and accountable for the administration of the funds (Male, 1998).

These measures were intended to allow for market forces – to free schools from local authority control and to give increased parental choice of schools. Yet, Davies and Ellison (2000) contend that market forces do not operate because there is not effective choice, it is not easy for new educational providers to be allowed entry, there are restrictive government regulations and there is no price mechanism operating between schools.

Helsby (1995) considers that a pronounced scientific management approach is operating in UK schools. Quality is now defined in quantifiable terms of student attainment in examinations and National Curriculum tests – 'assessment and increased accountability are seen as the real keys to quality assurance and improvement' (p. 5). Further, Helsby (1995) argues that teachers are being viewed as 'technical workers whose performance is to be inspected and rigorously judged, rather than responsible professionals' (p. 5).

Woods (2000) maintains that market and public regulatory mechanisms have changed the operation of schools – performativity has become a culture and a mode of regulation.

Initiatives by the Blair government include incentives for the 'best' schools to be granted greater autonomy. The White Paper 'Education and Skills, Investment for Reform' (Department for Education and Skills, 2002) focuses upon transforming secondary education. Details of further devolution and delegation by the introduction of community development plans, 300 Advanced Schools by 2006 and 48 Networked Learning Communities involving over 600 schools are included in the paper.

Australia

School restructuring occurs and re-occurs constantly in many state education systems within Australia. According to Grundy and Bonser (1997) many of the features of restructuring include devolution of responsibility to schools and lean head-office management. Yet, the restructuring actually occurring, as noted by Grundy and Bonser (1997), is replete with tensions and contradictions.

Solutions to these tensions have been attempted in the different states and territories to provide for a coexistence of central directions and maximum school-level autonomy (Angus, 1998). Examples include: 'Schools of the Future', 'Schools of the Third Millennium', 'Self-Governing Schools' (in Victoria), 'Leading Schools' (in Queensland) and 'Directions in Education' (in Tasmania) (Caldwell and Spinks, 1998). A number of educators argue for autonomy at the school level; that school-based management by teachers, students and parents is important because many key decisions have to be made at the local, school level; that school-based management is consistent with trends in modern business management; and that it activates all the stakeholders (Beare, 1995; Boyd, 1990; Watson *et al.*, 2000).

Caldwell (1993, pp. 16–18) focuses upon the inevitability of forces bringing about self-managing schools, such as:

- effects of recession and financial crises that have led to drastic cuts in head office personnel and resources;
- choice and market forces: an assumption that competition and the influence of the market will lead to an improvement in the quality of education;
- empowerment of teachers and parents; especially as a result of Commonwealth Schools Commission initiatives;
- politics of education; for example, attempts to reduce the influence of teachers' unions in Victoria;
- a national imperative: an emerging national framework, based upon economic considerations, to guide school-based activities.

By contrast, M. Angus (1995) asserts that SBM schools have not been successful to date because:

- some schools take unlimited autonomy without regard to system-wide requirements;
- the status of school principals is ambiguous: are they the leader of a self-determining school or an end-of-line manager?
- intensive and bitter campaigns by the teachers' union.

L. Angus (1994), however, argues that the managed education occurring in several state education systems devalues 'the notion of teachers as professionals, as quality performers and valued resources in the process of teaching' (p. 152). Brennan (1994) argues that local decision-making in Victoria has been frustrated by corporate managerial approaches and that only a few school communities have been able 'to develop networks, share knowledge and develop educative organisational strategies without centralised steering' (p. 96).

Caldwell (2002b) asserts that self-management of schools has now become an international phenomenon and that major transformations are imminent. Further, he asserts that technology will enrich and support the work of teachers and, in many situations, liberate them from present demands. He maintains that evidence from the Schools of the Future reform in Victoria indicates 'that teachers' knowledge about learning and teaching has been enhanced through school self-management' (Caldwell, 2002a, p. 73).

Boyle's (2000) study of school principals in the Australian Capital Territory (ACT) noted that in general 'principals viewed SBM more as an additional administrative function than as an opportunity to engage in restructuring the school for the needs of the new millennium' (p. 7).

USA

Although there are a range of practices occurring in the USA, SBM is a major emphasis in reforms associated with the programmes 'America 2000' and 'Goals 2000', but there are also centralizing forces such as the new National Goals and state curriculum frameworks.

There are also initiatives to develop stronger school–business partnerships and local community links. In turn, this has brought about new tensions and political concerns such as conflicts over 'official knowledge' and differences of opinion between local school consumers of education and new central control officials (Klein, 1991).

Anderson and Dixon (1994) contend that SBM has been strong on rhetoric but limited in action – 'what is believed to be devolution of power to parents and teachers becomes shared power among already empowered individuals over less influential groups' (p. 59).

A promising development over the last decade in the USA is an interesting variation of SBM: charter schools. Charter schools are schools of choice for the parents, students and teachers involved in them, and are conducive to on-site curriculum decision-making. Although laws differ from state to state, in general, charters for such schools may be granted to local school districts, to groups of parents or teachers, even to business organizations. In 1998, California had the highest number of students in the nation enrolled in its 130 charter schools (Wells, 1999). By 2000 charter laws were in place in 36 states, and national enrolment had swelled to some 350,000 students (Manno *et al.*, 2000).

The boards that govern charter schools usually are small and composed of persons directly involved in running the schools. The schools themselves are typically small, with only 150 to 250 students, and encourage parents and teachers to work together to provide their own unique educational programmes.

Manno *et al.* (2000) describe charter schools as independent public schools of choice, open to all who wish to attend, freed from some regulations and pursuing their own programmes (and in this respect similar to private schools), but paid for with tax dollars and responsible to the public. Charter schools have emerged with strong bipartisan support at the federal level as well as at state level. Good and Braden (2000) contend that they have been created because there is a widespread belief that a market-driven organization will outperform a traditional bureaucratic model. This view assumes that teachers in public schools neither work hard enough nor are sufficiently sensitive to the needs of students, and that competition from charter schools will increase innovation and improve learning in ordinary public schools. Despite the negative image of teachers that this view entails, teachers' organizations have been cautiously supportive of charter schools, but with the proviso that charter schools, as public schools, should be staffed by licenced teachers.

Some studies suggest that, in a number of cases, charter schools have been extremely popular. Wells (1999) reports that she met hundreds of satisfied charter school educators and parents, and concludes: 'people who work in and send their children to charter schools are incredibly committed to these schools and their purposes' (p. 312). According to Gresham *et al.* (2000), teachers in Arizona's charter elementary schools experienced a sense of empowerment.

Yet, in practice, charter schools have not lived up to all the glowing rhetoric. Good and Braden (2000) contend that charter schools:

- have not served as locations for experimentation and innovation, many having taken a traditional approach to classroom instruction;
- have not spent an increased proportion of their budgets on direct classroom instruction;
- have not improved access and equity for students, having instead further segregated students by ethnicity, income level, and special needs;
- have not provided reasonable physical environments for students, many charter schools occupying unstimulating, unattractive, and – in some cases – unsafe buildings.

Mickelson (1999) notes that one of the most serious problems about business intervention into charter schools is that the strategic self-interest that guides business practices can often predominate over the altruism that the public expects schools to instil. A few charter schools have been closed because of financial mismanagement.

Concluding Comments

Fullan and Watson (2000) conclude that SBM is not an end in itself – 'rather it is a means of altering the capacity of the school and community to make improvements; it is something that requires training, support and other aspects of capacity – building over a period of time' (p. 472).

Reflections and Issues

1. 'Successful management of the curriculum depends upon the principal's capacity to maintain a purposeful concentration on the tasks in hand while at the same time providing sensitive and encouraging support to individuals' (Day *et al.*, 1985, p. 122). What are some problems in trying to achieve these ends?

2. Smyth (1994) argues that the 'self-managing school is not fundamentally about "choice", "grassroots democracy" or "parent participation" – it is a cruel hoax' (p. 4). Explain this statement. What are the real priorities? How can self-managing schools achieve democratic goals?

3. 'The key problem is how the existing practices and cultures in many schools can be transformed into realising the potential benefits offered by school-based management' (Dimmock, 1993, p. 8). What are some of the potential benefits? Describe some approaches which can be used.

4. 'School-based management stems from a belief in the individual school as the fundamental decision-making unit within the educational system' (Guthrie, 1986, p. 306). Do you agree that the individual school should be considered as the management base? What are some problems in making this assumption?

5. 'In many schools the professional staff appear to go through the motions of collegiate management without integrating the full implications of the approach into everyday practice – a situation of innovation without change' (Wallace, 1990, p. 110). Is this a common occurrence in your experience?

6. 'A change to school-based management implies greater flexibility of decision-making, changes in role accountability (particularly for the principal) and the potential enhancement of school productivity' (Brown, 1990, p. vii). Do you consider that these are the major changes resulting from school-based management?

7. 'Public schools around the world are moving from a state a dependency on others toward greater responsibility through self-management and self-government, while remaining part of a system of public education' (Caldwell, 1994a). Is site-based management having an impact on schools? What are the implications for school principals?

---

11 School Evaluations/Reviews

Introduction

Financial pressures in the 1980s and early 1990s led to system-wide evaluations by administrators and consultants who were especially concerned about cost-effective achievements in schools. These pressures were very evident for both public and private schools. There have also been increasing concerns about student performance in core subject areas and this has led to system-level evaluations. Performance testing in literacy at specific age levels as well as testing in core subjects is now common in many countries. In most countries individual schools receive details of their students' results and so school-level evaluative data are also available.

The development of curriculum frameworks and standards, couched largely as outcome statements, provides a major opportunity for systems to evaluate the performance of their respective schools. Thus, in many systems annual reports have to be submitted by individual schools together with external evaluations over longer periods, usually triennial. It is in the self-interest of many schools to undertake their own school-level evaluations and to use the results to target their market share of students.

School-level evaluation, whether defined in terms of accountability or standards of performance, is a major focus for schools in the twenty-first century.

Some Basic Terms

'Evaluation' is a process of collecting and communicating information and evidence for the purpose of informing judgement and ascribing value to a particular programme (Simons, 1987). It can refer to small-scale activities involving a very limited number of clients (such as a teacher and his or her class) or to massive large-scale studies involving many schools and teachers (and other interested parties such as parents and community members).

Neve (2001) examines the relative advantages of external school evaluation (for example by OFSTED inspectors in the United Kingdom) where the emphasis is upon accountability, setting standards and benchmarks, and internal school evaluations where the emphasis is upon self-evaluation, empowerment evaluation, reflection and the professionalization of teachers.

He argues the case for a combination of external and internal evaluation. Specifically, external evaluation can:

- stimulate internal evaluation – to motivate persons and organizations to do internal evaluation;
- expand the scope of internal evaluation – by providing benchmarks and comparative data;
- legitimize the validity of internal evaluations.

Further, internal evaluations can benefit external evaluations by:

- expanding the scope and examining unique elements;
- improving the interpretation of findings;
- increasing the utilization of the evaluation results.

McGehee and Griffith (2001) and Visscher (2001) acknowledge that large-scale evaluations are becoming an important part of the education culture. Fullan and Earl (2002) undertook a large-scale evaluation of the National Literacy and Numeracy Strategy in the United Kingdom and noted that it is a prime example of the intricacies of national reform. Ainley *et al.* (2002) noted the renewed interest in large-scale evaluation in Australia with regard to literacy and numeracy.

School-level evaluation as part of the general field of evaluation can be undertaken as a small-scale or large-scale activity. Skilbeck (1982) supports the use of small-scale activities rather than elaborate, comprehensive, managerial evaluations, and suggests that they should be at the level of 'intelligent forms of reflection on experience, self-appraisal and forward thinking'. In his opinion, educators often amass vast quantities of unmanageable data, and this should be avoided by being quite clear about such questions as:

> What do I need to know about this activity?
> How can I most economically find out?
> How can I use what I know?
> What do I need to make known to others?

School evaluation differs from other kinds of educational evaluation in that it focuses upon how teachers and students interact over a particular curriculum or syllabus at one school site. It is not just an analysis of how students perform in a teaching/learning unit, nor is it just an analysis of the lesson plans which teachers use in instruction. Rather, school evaluation involves an examination of the goals, rationale and structure of teachers' curricula, a study of the context in which the interaction with students occurs (including parent and community inputs) and an analysis of the interests, motivations and achievements of the students' experiences.

School evaluations also focus on the needs and interests of the constituent groups involved in the school community. Particular interest groups operating at the school level, mainly teachers, administrators, students and parents, may have very different views about the purposes of schooling. Consequently, evaluation studies have to reflect different orientations and not give undue emphasis to single dimensions such as the behaviour of individuals (students), an analysis of materials, or the behaviours of a school as a social institution.

Rogers and Badham (1992) suggest that school evaluation is about *accountability* and *development*. Accountability is crucial to prove quality – to ensure that standards in a school are rising. Development is also most important because it establishes a positive staff climate – staff are more aware of the data that needs to be collected as an aid to certain developmental goals.

Wilcox (1992) emphasizes the developmental aspect also (see Figure 11.1), along with four other important aspects of curriculum evaluation:

1. It is based on evidence which is systematically collected.
2. The evidence is seldom unambiguous and therefore needs to be interpreted.
3. Judgements of value are made about the entity being evaluated and its effects.
4. It is action oriented, intended to lead to better practices and policies.

Purposes

The two fundamental questions to be answered before considering any evaluation are:

1. Why do you want to evaluate?
2. What do you want to evaluate?

In large-scale studies, the purposes of evaluation are usually related to policy concerns at the head offices about the widespread implementation of programmes into an entire school system.

At the local school level, evaluation activities may be undertaken for a multitude of highly personal reasons. These could include:

- concerns about providing better teaching and learning for students within a particular school community;
- the need to examine the impact of a new programme or organizational processes;

Figure 11.1: *Elements of school-level evaluation*

- collecting and presenting information from teachers and administrators, students and parents
- analysis of information collected and making judgements
- strategic planning
- development – improving quality
- accountability – proving quality

- the need to substantiate the value of a particular programme or organizational structure to parents and/or to local business;
- response to dissatisfaction expressed by individual teachers or a group/
  association.

When establishing purposes of evaluation at the school level it must be realized that any teaching situation brings about some unintended outcomes. Any comprehensive evaluation study must therefore provide for the collection of data on side effects and unintended learnings.

Because evaluations at the school level rely upon conviviality and coop-eration, it is essential that disparate motivations such as those listed above are discussed by staff who, in a series of informal and formal meetings, may come to a consensus about what are the most important purposes for them in doing the evaluation (Thornton, 2001). Simons (1987) argues that one of the best ways to develop effective curriculum practices is to grant schools the authority to formally evaluate in addition to external agencies. However, in many cases individual schools cannot avoid external accountability forces – they are the driving force above and beyond the personal needs of a school community.

As an example, all government primary schools operating in Western Australia are required, under the School Accountability Framework:

- to produce, in partnership with their school community, a school plan
  setting out their objectives, priorities, major initiatives and evaluation
  measures;
- to assess their performance in terms of standards of student achievement and the effectiveness of the school;
- to make available to the public and to the District Director a School
  Report that describes the school's performance;
- to be accountable for the performance of the school – school staff to the
  principal and school principals to the District Director (Department of
  Education, 2002a, p. 5).

Yet, the accompanying documents for schools are couched in the language of 'self-assessment' and schools are encouraged 'to see this document as a resource to augment their existing self-assessment practice' (Department of Education 2002b, p. 8). Further, there is some scope for schools to select particular themes and a choice of tools.

What to Evaluate

In the terms of Schwab (1969) these factors are 'commonplaces' of curriculum and consist of 'learner', 'teacher', 'subject matter' (curriculum) and 'milieu'. Any evaluation activity must necessarily examine the impact and interaction of these elements.

The sources of information about these four commonplaces can vary considerably. For example, information about the school milieu might be obtained from parents, community members and employers; information about the subjects taught at school might come from school administrators, external subject specialists, publishers, superintendents and parents. The range and choice of sources of data relates back to the purposes of the evaluation, the scale of the activity, the time and funds available.

Once the focus of an evaluation has been determined, it is then possible to plan the kinds of information needed. For example, the evaluators may decide that information about students should include data about their previous academic levels, ongoing information about their class performance and interactions with the teacher, and information about their achievements. This type of information is obviously collected at different time periods and the examples listed above refer to all three types of data: that is, diagnostic data collected prior to the beginning of a curriculum unit to find out interests and achievement levels of students; formative data collected during the teaching of a unit to pinpoint aspects of the teaching that are mismatched and not being successfully implemented; and summative data, which are collected at the completion of a unit and focus upon specific student outcomes and achievement levels.

Techniques that can be used to collect diagnostic, formative and summative data about students are included in Figure 11.2. Similar techniques can be used for collecting information about teachers and teacher–student interactions, as depicted in Figure 11.3.

Figure 11.2: Techniques for collecting data at different phases of implementing new programmes

	Early planning discussions	Working party meetings	Documents produced	Materials provided	Implementation phases
Colleague evaluation checklists					
Rating scales					
Anecdotal reports					
Observation category systems					
Interviews					
Questionnaires					
Self-evaluation checklists					
Diary entries					
Questionnaires					
Student evaluation checklists					
Rating scales					
Interest inventories					
Attitude scales					
Questionnaires					
Objective tests					
Essay tests					
Standardized tests					
Interviews					
Photographs					

Figure 11.3: Techniques used to obtain evaluative data about teacher–student interactions (processes)

Informal observing and recording	Audiotaping and videotaping
	Observation
	Category systems
	Unobtrusive techniques
	Colleague observation
Informal collection of information from students	Interviews
	Questionnaires
	Rating scales
	Group discussions
Formal visits by senior supervisors (superintendents, inspectors, principal education officers)	Combination of observations and check lists

Collecting evaluative data about teachers requires considerable support and goodwill. George *et al.* (1998) highlight some of the problems and issues. They suggest that the ideal situation is for teachers to work in peer panels comprising three to five teachers. The important considerations are that:

- they choose each other and there are no superordinate–subordinate relationships;
- matters that are discussed are private to them but generally focus upon skill development;
- they agree to meet regularly, ideally once a week;
- they give low-inference feedback to each other (observe/record/report).

They do not make high-inference judgements as this would interfere with their peer relationships.

As depicted in Figure 11.3 teaching-partner observer or peer panels can use a variety of techniques to collect useful data over the various phases, ranging from informal observations to rating systems to the use of interviews and questionnaires.

Self-reflection and analysis are extremely valuable activities for all teachers and especially important for school-level evaluation (Wroe and Halsall, 2001). Schon (1987) refers to the need for teachers to be reflective practitioners. He focuses specifically upon how and why teachers should reflect upon their experiences.

The evaluative techniques listed in Figure 11.2 can be used both in terms of self-evaluation and using a teaching-partner or peer panel. However, the most common techniques include some form of written recording sheet (e.g. keeping a diary) and a variety of observational techniques. Diaries represent a 'shorthand' method of recording the significant happenings of a teacher's day. It is recommended that diaries should concentrate on one or two aspects that are considered most important. Points that may be useful as foci for diary entries include such questions:

- Is my teaching behaviour having the desired effect in classroom management?
- Has a particular seating arrangement encouraged the desired behaviour from the students concerned?
- Has a particular teaching strategy improved the performance of a specific group of students?
- Is a special project being positively accepted by the class or is there a lack of interest?

Observation is a direct, systematic way of determining what is happening in the classroom. Observations of classrooms can often be very revealing! For example, the literature contains examples of teachers who have complained that certain students in their class do not contribute to their lessons. However, observations by colleagues revealed that these same teachers did not encourage the students in question to participate and in some instances prevented their interaction with other students. There are often massive discrepancies between what teachers state they are teaching compared with what actually occurs in classrooms.

Several alternatives are available for the classroom teacher who wishes to collect his or her own observational data. These include using audiotaping or, if resources are available, videotaping. Student observations can also be sought via informal discussions and interviews or by the use of checklists and questionnaires.

It should be clear that self-evaluation techniques for the teacher are fairly limited, and that far more data, including important additional perspectives, are available if colleagues on a school staff assist each other cooperatively with their evaluation activities. However, this requires colleagues to collect data about each other and to submit themselves to self-reflective activities, as listed in Figure 11.2. The challenge may be troublesome for some teachers unless peer panels (as described above) or similar pairings are organized. It is suggested that if teachers are willing from the outset to collect evaluative data about their own activities and their colleagues, then the feedback they obtain will enable them to be more successful and presumably more fulfilled.

There are, of course, many hidden assumptions involved in all this. Not all colleagues will want to submit themselves to all of the types of data collection listed in Figure 11.2 and to peer and panel procedures. Teachers in a planning group have to be sufficiently empathic toward each other to accept feedback even if it is low-inference feedback.

The kinds of evaluative activities, therefore, have to be carefully negotiated with the individuals concerned. Some readers might consider that the types of self-evaluation listed in Figure 11.2 are too superficial and are likely to lead to over-concentration upon the frequency of occurrence of activities rather than the quality of the actions. Also, time constraints are often so pressing that it is not always feasible to undertake many, if any, of these evaluative activities.

A combined qualitative/quantitative technique, which is widely used in the USA, in the United Kingdom and in other European countries (Visscher, 2001) is the performance indicator (see Figure 11.4). These can be directed specifically at teacher performance (especially teacher competence tests in the USA), at student performance (e.g. the General Achievement Test in Victoria, Australia) or at school-wide issues.

Performance indicators are linked directly to specific objectives or goals for a school programme and are intended to indicate the extent of progress made towards a specific objective. Rogers and Badham (1992) suggest that performance indicators should be capable of being collected on several occasions over a period of time.

As examples, three objectives for a school are listed in Figure 11.4 along with possible performance indicators. It is evident that performance indicators should not be used in isolation but they can add an important perspective to an evaluation.

Persons Involved

Depending upon the size and scope of school-level evaluation, persons involved may be a team of one or two external experts, the entire school staff (together with selected school council members) or just one classroom teacher taking up the role of an evaluator. The US evaluation scene is normally dominated by the experts who are hired as consultants to evaluate school district programmes and similar large-scale activities. The literature on evaluation contains numerous references to the characteristics of 'good' evaluators (Simons, 1987; Popham, 1995; Wood, 1991) and includes such attributes as technical competence, personal integrity and objectivity.

External, full-time professional evaluators are not very evident on the Australian scene. External evaluators, as members of a team to undertake

Figure 11.4: School objectives and performance indicators

School objectives	Performance indicators
1. The school provides students with suitable opportunities to learn domains of knowledge and skills	−Student attendance rates −Destinations of students after leaving school −Survey of students
2. The school encourages hard work and achievement from its students	−Attitude survey of students −Parent questionnaire
3. The teachers at the school create and implement effective programmes of learning	−Teacher time for planning per week −Administrative and clerical support time per week

school evaluations, are found in all states but they are mostly experienced teachers and school principals who serve on evaluation panels for short periods of time, including site visits of one or two days.

In the United Kingdom, the Office for Standards in Education (OFSTED) has recruited a wide range of registered inspectors and inspection contractors who are in turn subject to inspection quality audits (OFSTED, 1997).

Internal evaluators, by contrast, are persons who are involved in, and responsible for, duties in a specific school. A pair of teachers in a primary school or a small team of teachers from within a subject department at the secondary school level, might undertake small-scale evaluation activities. These individuals may turn to external experts for particular forms of assistance – for instance, in designing the appropriate data-gathering instruments, or in developing appropriate criteria for validating the evidence. On occasions, school staff may be able to obtain small grants to employ external consultants for particular tasks, such as initiating the evaluation exercise, coordinating the diverse activities or collecting some of the data (e.g. observing teachers in the classrooms). Checklists of specific questions are a very useful way of providing evaluators (individual evaluator or a team) with the necessary guidelines.

Concluding Comments

The management of schools, system wide or individually, brings attention to bear on performance issues and matters of evaluation. Various stakeholders want information about achievements (especially in terms of the students, teachers, subject matter and milieu) to justify the substantial financial expenses. In addition to accountability reasons, participants in a school community need to 'sample the temperature' of what is going on so that development plans can be targeted to areas of need.

There are a range of techniques available for obtaining evaluative data about teachers, students and the milieu. However, if participants at a school are not committed to regular evaluation activities and are not willing to produce developmental, strategic plans based upon evidence obtained from these evaluations, little can be achieved.

Reflections and Issues

1. 'Evaluations are designed increasingly to be *used*, to accompany or initiate changes in schools and central offices' (Rogers and Badham, 1992). Do you agree? If this is the case what are the implications for the time taken and who initiates the evaluation?

2. '"Value-added" measures indicate the educational value that a school adds over and above that which could be predicted given the backgrounds and prior attainments of the students within the school' (Hill, 1995, p. 6). What are some exam-

ples of value-added measures? Comment on their potential successes and problems.

3. 'In the last ten years we have witnessed a rapid growth in school self-evaluation models and practices ... What is least clear and most controversial in this range of activity is who has control of the process, who has access to any product that emerges and whose interests are served' (Simons, 1987, pp. 319–20). What groups do you consider are controlling school evaluation processes? Are you aware of successful evaluation efforts? What do you consider are some of the major inhibiting factors?

4. 'Evaluation can be a constructive process leading to stronger professionalism, but only if teachers grasp the opportunity for reflection and growth that it presents.' (Granheim, 1990, p.1). Do the evaluation approaches with which you are familiar allow teachers to 'reflect and grow'? What are some important safeguards you would propose to allow this to happen?

5. 'In the final analysis the evaluator's role is to assess the educational quality of the curriculum policy or program. But (s)he can still do this democratically through dialogue and discussion with a variety of interest groups, including practitioners. Through such dialogue an evaluator can deepen and extend his or her own understanding of the nature of educational values and how they can be best realised in particular contests' (Elliott, 1991, p. 231). How important is the dialogue and discussion between interest groups in a school evaluation? What techniques can be used to achieve it? Elaborate upon some of the restrictions.

6. 'Evaluation is a form of inquiry whose end product is information. Information is power, and evaluation is powerful.' (Guba and Lincoln, 1989, p. 56). Can school evaluations be powerful? Which stakeholders are most affected by school evaluations? How can their needs be communicated and respected? Use examples to illustrate your point of view.

7. The UK Education acts legislate for the local management of schools. 'Any school which seeks to use management information effectively for planning purposes will need to devise systems for integrating a review of:
   • curriculum delivery and pupil outcomes;
   • staff appraisal and development;
   • use of finance and other material resources (Rogers and Badham, 1992, p. 85). Describe how you would plan an integrated evaluation of these elements. What might be some potential constraints?

12   Curriculum Reform

Introduction

Proposals for reforms in education appear frequently in the literature and especially proposals for curriculum reform. Presumably this means that there are problems to be solved. Because of the frequency of reform proposals this would seem to indicate that previous reforms did not remove the problems they were intended to solve.

Curriculum reforms continue to bombard us every few years. Educators, and especially politicians with an eye to their respective electorates, exhort us about reforms that we have to have (Glatthorn and Jailall, 2000; Hargreaves, Earl *et al.*, 2001).

What is Curriculum Reform?

Bourke (1994) notes that the term 'reform' is typically used to refer to changes instituted from above – 'the implication in much of the rhetoric is that only government decision-making can reform education' (p. 1). He questions whether governments are always able to reform (to make better) – on many occasions the changes implemented by a government are worse for at least some groups.

Kennedy (1995) asserts that curriculum reform is really about changes to the content and organization of what is taught, within the constraints of social, economic and political contexts. Curriculum content and organization is of central importance but unless a reform effort is consistent with the values of the wider society it is unlikely to be successful.

Glatthorn and Jailall (2000) consider that curriculum reform not only involves content and organization but that it is mainly directed at students and teachers.

As far as student learning is concerned, we continue to seek out improvements in excellence and equity for our schools. The twenty-first century has the same strong emphasis that we experienced in the previous century.

Reforms are also targeted at the quality of the teaching force. There are concerns about the old norms of individualism, isolationism and privatism (Lortie, 1975) and that teachers should be addressing the new social realities of teaching (Lieberman and Miller, 2000).

Hargreaves (1995) takes the issue further and notes the interconnectedness of curriculum reform in terms of societal change. For example, he argues that secondary schools are the prime symbols and symptoms of 'modernity' (for example, bureaucratic complexity, inflexibility) and that 'postmodern' conditions of the 1990s (and beyond into the twenty-first century) require very different principles.

Ideology and Reform

Kennedy (1995) refers to the similarities in reform efforts occurring in the United Kingdom, the USA and Australia. He concurs with Coombs (1985) that in all these countries there has been 'a crisis of confidence in education itself' (p. 9). No longer is curriculum decision-making the preserve of professional educators – governments are now playing a central role in terms of broad social, political and economic agendas.

In the United Kingdom, the National Curriculum introduced in 1988 was based on the Right ideology of a market economy and a consumer-oriented emphasis. A number of schools have opted out of local education authority control, supposedly to allow parents more choice. A policy of open enrolment and local management of schools is now in place. The Left ideology since 1997 (New Labour government) has been conservative and pragmatic and focused squarely on literacy and numeracy standards for students (Crump 1998).

In Australia in the 1990s an attempt to develop a national, outcomes-based curriculum using curriculum statements and profiles almost succeeded but was jettisoned due to the active opposition from several states. Since then slightly modified 'state versions' of outcomes-based approaches have been implemented (Watt, 2000). The ideology behind this is largely economics-driven, with emphasis on higher-order skills and standards (Marsh and Willis, 2003).

In New Zealand a massive restructuring of the education system occurred in the late 1980s. According to Peters (1995) the ideology for these reforms was based on neo-liberal principles of individualism, deregulation and privatization.

There is currently in the USA a strong interest in national standards and the need to develop a core of knowledge and skills that all students should be taught. However, the underlying ideology is about state-led standards and common practices for all students.

The ideology supports standard practices and uniform goals and tends to minimize the importance of equity issues and reduces the impact of local initiatives. Apple (1988) argues that reforms should concentrate on the relationship between schooling and the larger society and on the structure of inequalities in society – the deskilling of jobs, and the lowering of wages and benefits.

Categories of Reforms

In the USA over the last decade, various reforms have been advocated via official reports but also through state legislation. Not all reforms are integrated into one major reform policy, and in fact, some authors such as Cibulka (1990) argue that some of the reform proposals are not consistent and are even contradictory. Cibulka suggests that there are some major or 'core' proposals which have occurred in most states (for example, state mandates) and 'ancillary' proposals (for example, greater choice of schools) which have been advocated by some pressure groups in some states.

These proposals represent a 'pluralist' approach to reform and because of the inconsistencies between different policies there is little shared consensus over ends or means. These pluralist bargaining games may create a lot of media publicity but the lack of unity could mean limited chances of success. By contrast, reforms in the United Kingdom have 'coherence' and were implemented as a total package of reform, despite widespread criticism. The ruling Conservative party under the leadership of the then Prime Minister Margaret Thatcher produced reforms that were aimed at raising standards of all students. The creation of core and foundation subjects, key stages, attainment targets and standard assessment tasks were carefully orchestrated to achieve this end. Notwithstanding, it is far from clear whether these reforms were accepted and implemented appropriately by teachers.

Plank (1988) suggests that there are four main types of reform, which he categorizes as 'additive' reforms, 'external' reforms, 'regulatory' reforms and 'structural' reforms (see Table 12.1). By far the most difficult to achieve are the structural reforms.

'Additive' reforms are relatively easy to implement because they involve additional resources and do not affect the organizational character of schools. An example would be a fully funded computer literacy programme.

'External' reforms also have little effect on the structure of schools, as they concentrate upon teachers entering the system or students leaving the system.

Table 12.1: Types of curriculum reforms and examples

Additive	External	Regulatory	Structural
• increased salaries • pre-school initiatives • computer literacy programme	• pre-service teacher tests • new high school graduation requirements • certification changes	• longer school day • longer school year • more basic skills • state-wide assessment	• smaller classes • vouchers/tax credits • merit pay plans • competency tests for teachers

Source: Plank (1988).

Examples include higher tests for pre-service teachers or more stringent requirements for high school graduation. These types of reforms are typically welcomed by school boards and teachers' unions.

'Regulatory' reforms seek changes in schools but do not necessarily affect the basic structure. The emphasis is upon more time and effort to achieve higher student achievements. Examples include longer school days and school years, core curriculum, statewide testing.

'Structural' reforms require alterations to the structure and operation of schools. They question current school structures and have the potential to be extremely disruptive to teachers and students. Examples include merit pay plans and voucher systems for parents to use at schools of their choice.

Reform Reports

Reform reports are often a popular means of bringing a purported problem to the consciousness of the public. The reports tend to focus on one or two key elements, often dramatizing the problems so as to elicit the solutions. Examples include:

USA

National Commission on Excellence in Education (1983) *A Nation at Risk: The Imperative for Educational Reform.* Washington, DC: US Department of Education.

National Council of Teachers of Mathematics *(1991)* Professional Standards for Teaching Mathematics. *Virginia: NCTM.*

National Center on Education and The Economy (1997) *New Standards: Performance standards: English Language Arts, Mathematics, Science, and Applied Learning. Vol. 1: Elementary School; Vol. 2: Middle School; Vol. 3: High School.* Washington, DC: NCEE.

United Kingdom

Department for Education and Skills (1997) *White Paper, 'Excellence in Schools'.* London: HMSO.

Department for Education and Skills (2001) *Education and Skills: Investment for Reform.* London: HMSO.

Examples

United Kingdom

Fullan and Earl (2002) refer to the national literacy and numeracy strategies in the United Kingdom as 'large-scale reform'.

Commencing in 1997, when they came to power, the Labour government established literacy and numeracy as their first-order priorities. They used 1996 as the base line to check on the targets achieved by 11-year-olds in literacy and numeracy. The results in 2001 were impressive: 75% of children achieved the desired target for literacy (compared with 57% in 1996) and 71% of children achieved the desired target for numeracy (compared with 54% in 1996).

It has been a heavily directed top-down approach to reform (Fullan and Earl, 2002). Some critics consider that the costs to teachers have been very high. For example, Furlong (2002) criticizes the rigorous forms of quality control and inspections carried out by the Office for Standards in Education (OFSTED) inspectors.

Brown *et al.* (2002) note the amount of teacher stress, and teacher burn-out for primary school teachers. Southworth (2000) contends that recent central initiatives by the government have added to the power of primary school heads and that the emphasis upon the head as chief executive has increased their authoritarian power and limited any democratic sharing by teachers.

The central government's *Education and Skills: Investment for Reform*, published in 2001, is an attempt to reform and transform secondary education by driving school leadership, school structures, teaching and learning, and partnerships beyond the classroom. The emphasis is upon recognizing and rewarding advanced schools (high-performing schools with particular expertise) and using them to drive reforms in secondary education.

USA

Standards-based approaches are currently strongly supported in the USA. The majority of the standards are subject-based and have been developed by the major professional subject associations, such as the National Council of Teachers of Mathematics.

Standards-based approaches call for high standards for all students oriented around challenging subject matter, acquisition of higher-order thinking skills, and the application of abstract knowledge to solve real-world problems (McLaughlin and Shepard, 1995).

More importantly there are various reinforcing processes (or drivers) to ensure that standards are introduced, namely:

- curriculum frameworks that state the academic content to be covered;
- provision of curriculum materials to support teachers;
- professional development to ensure that teachers have the requisite content knowledge and instructional abilities;
- assessment and accountability systems to monitor student progress;
- leadership and support by discipline-based professional organizations;
- states requirements for all schools including:
  - content standards that all students should learn,
  - performance standards – levels of mastery required,

- aligned assessments – state-wide testing of students,
- training and certification requirements for all teachers (Swanson and Stevenson 2002).

However, there are critics of standards-based reform in the USA. Donmoyer (1998) argues that standards-based reform is largely rhetoric and myths about what politicians and educators 'believe' will happen.

In a similar vein, Chatterji (2002) concludes that there has been little coherence in the way in which reforms have filtered down to districts, schools and classrooms.

Levin (1998) contends that standards-based reform has been formulated to create economic benefits, yet there is little evidence to demonstrate any marked improvements in worker productivity. Lea and Fradd (1998) argue that high standards for all is creating problems for students from non-English-language backgrounds because the new academic curriculum does not have the flexibility to accommodate students' different cultural experiences.

It is evident that there are a number of issues still to be resolved with standards-based reform. To a certain extent, the reform uses a 'big stick' approach to wake up and challenge unmotivated students and unmotivated teachers (Nave *et al.*, 2000).

Yet, it is more than this. It does provide detailed curriculum support for teachers so that they can inspire their students to achieve at higher levels. Professional associations are providing strong collaborative support to schools. Despite the fiery opposition to this powerful, nation-wide movement (Thompson, 2001) it is proving to be a very durable reform (Sirotnik and Kimball, 1999).

Concluding Comments

The first decade of the twenty-first century is revealing some perennial challenges in terms of curriculum reform but also some promising developments. A number of reforms are cyclical – at certain periods they have strong support while at other times they can be quite minimal.

The strength and influence of standards-based reforms in several countries is impressive. It is interesting to ponder on which are the main factors driving it – is it a general world view and the economic status of the society, is it due to the recommendations of prestigious committees; or is it due to the emergence of new technology (Glatthorn and Jailall, 2000)?

Despite the enthusiasm that can be generated by new reforms it is important to remember that making reform proposals is only part of the process and that there are many problems in getting reforms implemented. The factors affecting innovation and change, and implementation, as noted in Chapters 8 and 7 respectively, are most pertinent.

Reflections and Issues

1. 'Educational reform cannot progress without financial resources. People, time and materials are necessary costs that are not considered to any great degree in most reform reports' (Presseisen, 1989, p. 135). Why is it that reform reports rarely include detailed budgets? Who should determine priorities for finance for reform proposals?

2. Some of the most difficult dilemmas we face currently have been around for a long time. Give examples of reforms that have been proposed over the decades to solve a particular curriculum problem. Have any proposals been more successful than others? Give reasons.

3. 'Do schools exist to increase the nation's productivity or for other equally important personal and social goals?' (Passow, 1988, p. 254). What is your stance on this matter?

4. The reform proposals in the USA reflect and help perpetuate practices that are at odds with equity goals. Why do you consider that equity goals which were being advanced in the 1960s and 1970s are not being given a high priority in the twenty-first century? Are equity and excellence diametrically opposed goals?

5. 'Schools and especially classrooms, are remarkably resistant to change, much to the consternation of politicians, policy-makers and innovators ... Professional and institutional structures are resilient. They withstand many an assault and have powerful capacities to maintain and reproduce themselves despite surface changes' (Hargreaves, 1994). Can this claim be substantiated? Give examples to support your response.

6. 'English education has a history of power domination rather than power sharing. The recent and current reforms in English education ensure that schools endure as organised hierarchies' (Southworth, 2000, p. 14). What are the implications for the success of transformational reform if such hierarchies exist?

Part IV

Teaching Perspectives

13 Learning Environments

Introduction

The classroom environment is an integral part of the learning process and no teacher or student can be unaffected by it. It is the learning environment for both the teacher and their students (Emmer *et al.*, 2000).

In any school, the class teachers and students have to adjust to the building architecture – the overall space, the position and number of doors and windows, the height of the ceiling and the insulation qualities of the walls. Yet, as Bennett (1981) reminds us: 'This does not indicate architectural determination. Architecture can certainly modify the teaching environment, but teachers determine the curriculum and organization' (Bennett, 1981, p. 24).

Teachers and students have the opportunity to 'express their "personalities" through the arrangement and décor of the environment and the arrangement of space' (Ross, 1982, pp. 1–2). However, creative arrangements need to be undertaken in the knowledge that specific physical conditions and space allocations can have important consequences on the attitudes, behaviours and even the achievements of students.

Classroom Settings

How an area of space is used in a teaching/learning situation is clearly important, but often taken for granted. The particular pattern of juxtaposing furniture and spaces within the confines of a classroom (or open teaching area) is done for a variety of purposes. In some instances, the teacher arranges a particular pattern because he or she is convinced that this configuration aids learning. As examples, single rows of desks might be considered to be most useful for students listening to an expository, teacher-directed science lesson; a grouping of desks in clusters of four might be far better for sharing materials in an art lesson; and a circle of chairs with the desks pushed to the sides might be the most appropriate for a literature lesson.

However, the teacher may have other reasons in mind that explain a particular pattern. Perhaps the teacher is concerned about a general atmosphere of restlessness in the class and wants convenient aisles and spaces so that 'seat work' can be continuously surveyed. In this case, the classroom spaces take on a greater significance than the furniture, because the opportunities for supervising are uppermost in the teacher's mind. It is impossible to separate these 'emotional climate' needs from the physical setting (Konza *et al.*, 2001).

Room Arrangement Principles

The following guidelines may be helpful in making decisions about the class-room – the teacher's special learning environment along with thirty or more students!

First, *use a room arrangement that facilitates a teaching and learning style and does not impede it.* The classroom teacher needs to be aware of whether the physical environment he or she has provided facilitates the student behaviours desired. That is, unless the two are interrelated or congruent (the technical term is *synomorphic*), then undesirable effects are likely to occur.

In broad terms, a teacher may desire to organize the class on the basis of *territory* or by *function*; the former focuses on a teacher-dominated purpose while the latter emphasizes a resource specialization, student-initiated focus.

In classrooms organized by territory, the major decision is how to allocate and arrange student desks and chairs. It is assumed that each student has his or her own domain or work space and that this is the basis for considering how certain learning activities will occur.

Classrooms organized on the basis of function enable students to engage in generative learning (Harris and Bell, 1990). They are commonly found in junior grades in primary schools in specialist subject areas (e.g. media or science) and subjects using computer-based projects (Anderson-Inman and Horney, 1993) in many secondary schools. In this case, the allocation of space is based upon what specialist material/activities can be accommodated in a given area, and the matter of the location of desks is only of minor consideration.

Second, *ensure that high-traffic areas are open and not congested.* There are always high-traffic areas such as around doorways, the pencil-sharpener, computers, certain bookshelves and the teacher's desk. According to Emmer *et al.* (2000), high-traffic areas should be kept away from each other, have plenty of space, and be easily accessible.

Floor Space

There are numerous classroom shapes and sizes but it is possible to highlight the common elements of classrooms. The typical classroom is 12 metres long and 8 metres wide and is designed to accommodate approximately 30 students. One wall is typically taken up with blackboards or whiteboards and another wall often contains several pinboards. The teacher's table is usually at the front of the room and students' desks are arranged in four rows of seven or eight.

In this relatively formal classroom situation it is likely that the 'action zone' (Brophy, 1981) for interaction between the teacher and students will be found in the front and centre. That is, students seated near the front and centre desks facing the teacher are more likely to be the focus of the teacher's attention, rather than the students seated on the margins or at the rear of the room.

Many teachers are able to devise very different, creative patterns of use within the confines of the standard classroom (Cohen *et al.*, 1998). Small-group activities are facilitated by clusters of desks. A common area formed by the combination of five or six desks may be ideal for spreading out documents and charts as well as providing close physical contact between a small group of students. The desks can still be oriented towards the blackboard and the teacher or they can be located at points in the room which maximize space between groups.

Arrangement of Student Desks

Depending on space available, many different arrangements are possible. In devising the location of students' desks it is important to remember their needs, including:

1. a need to be seated at points in the classroom where they can comfortably undertake the learning activities;
2. a need for them to be located at desks or tables adjacent to peers with whom they have a close and mutually positive relationship;
3. a need for them to have access to the teacher and to resources in the room.

Arrangement of Furniture and Equipment

Large items of furniture such as cupboards can be used as dividers within a room. Pieces of pegboard can be used to cover the sides of a cupboard and thereby provide additional display space. It is also helpful to have one or two large tables in a classroom even though they take up a lot of space. These tables can be used for a multitude of purposes including storing audiovisual materials, storing unfinished work or for displays of completed projects/units.

The placement of computers in the room is an additional complication. A single computer might be located in any convenient corner but a pod of five or more computers can cause difficulties in an already crowded room. Some primary schools have all their computers located in a separate computer laboratory.

Learning Stations and Work Centres

Learning stations and work centres are areas where a small number of students come to work on a special activity. These areas need to be located so that they do not distract from major learning activities.

Learning stations are examples of functional areas which are often established in primary schools. A learning station is simply an area in a room where a group of students can work together at well-defined tasks. Usually, all resource materials are provided at the one location and tasks are included on colour-coded cards so that individuals or groups can involve themselves with minimal supervision by the teacher.

In addition to the traditional specialist rooms in secondary schools such as manual arts centres, home economics and science laboratories, it is interesting to note how this has been extended over the last decade to include sophisticated language laboratories, media centres and micro-computer laboratories (Cohen *et al.*, 1998; de Castell, 2000).

Pin-up Boards and Bulletin Boards

Pin-up boards are a major element in any classroom because they can be used to display various items of interest such as student work, charts, posters, class rules and routines.

Primary school students might have class banners, class photographs, birthday charts and monitor charts (Konza *et al.*, 2001). Secondary school students might prefer posters on media topics, environment and sporting figures (Glickman, 2003).

Special Items

Plants can add a very positive effect to a classroom and of course students learn to be responsible for their watering.

At primary school level, various animals may be kept such as fish, birds, tadpoles and mice. They add novelty and colour and are further opportunities for students to develop responsibilities for the animals' safety and welfare. The task for each teacher is to work out how to make the best use of available furniture and facilities. It is often amazing how the rearrangement of particular desks or cupboards leads to unforeseen increases in space/access. Mezzanine floors suspended above the tables and chairs, withdrawal areas complete with lounge chairs and occasional tables, are just some of the more adventurous schemes which have been implemented by some teachers. The checklist included in Figure 13.1 provides useful reminders about space utilization.

Other Physical and Psychological Factors in the Classroom

Winston Churchill once remarked: 'We shape our buildings, and afterwards our buildings shape us'. This statement underlines the importance of the physical buildings in which we work and play, and especially the environments in

Figure 13.1   Checklist to evaluate the use of classroom space

1. Is there too much furniture?
2. Is the best use made of the whole space of the school?
3. How does the use of space reflect the range and nature of different activities?
4. How effectively is shared space used?
5. How attractive and stimulating is the space?
6. How does the grouping of tables and work areas reflect the needs of the students and the tasks, especially computer-based tasks?
7. How well do students understand the classroom organization?
8. How appropriately and effectively are the resources deployed?
9. How accessible are resources and spaces?
10. How easy is pupil and teacher movement?
11. How effectively does the organization of space promote pupil interaction?

which school children spend at least 12 years of their lives. However, Churchill also appears to be attributing a considerable degree of determinism to the physical buildings, and it is far from clear whether this stance can be supported.

Research evidence indicates that relationships between the physical environment and students are far from clear. There are some patterns emerging related to crowding, privacy and territoriality, but few conclusive studies relating to specific physical environment factors. In fact, it is very difficult to disentangle the physical from the psychological factors. The research studies that have provided conclusive results are those that have demonstrated particular interrelationships between the two, such as the density of students in a classroom with student attitudes of dissatisfaction. The examples which follow indicate the interrelationships between physical environment factors and affective states of students rather than direct influences on achievement measures.

Colour

The communications media are very aware of the use of colour and it is little wonder that colour television, colour inserts in daily newspapers, glossy colour magazines and full-colour computer games and graphics are so popular (Cohen *et al.*, 1998).

So it is in classrooms. The list of items that can add colour to a classroom are endless and not limited to those listed above. Newspaper clippings, pamphlets and photographs are an integral part of many classrooms and they can add to the visual impact. So, too, can three-dimensional models (e.g. of landscapes, buildings and animals) and dioramas. Personal computer nooks and cubicles found in many classrooms add to the diversity of colours. However, a variegated assortment of colours, vying for students' attention in a classroom, needs to be considered in terms of educational purposes (Emmer *et al.*, 2000). Colours may be used by the teacher to gain students' attention and motivation, but they are also included to provide satisfaction and 'belongingness' to the student members of each classroom (Konza *et al.*, 2001). As Field (1980, p. 197) notes, 'classrooms belong to the children, and teachers need to help them identify with it more readily'. If students are involved in the planning of materials to be displayed and in the regular changing of them, then it is likely that they will identify far more readily with their teacher and the classroom endeavours he or she is trying to pursue.

Despite the many assertions from education writers about the value of colour in classroom environments, there is little research evidence to support or refute its use.

At the primary school level, Santrock (1976) studied first- and second-grade children in a specially designed room, which was decorated alternately with happy, sad and neutral coloured pictures. The results indicated that the type of pictures in the room had a strong influence on the children and that they worked longer at a task when they were in the setting with the happy pictures.

Related to colour is the amount of natural light available to students in a classroom. Rosenfeld's (1999) research demonstrated that primary school students in Seattle, Washington who studied in light-filled schools scored higher in maths and reading tests than those students working in classrooms with least light.

Noise

Sounds are all around us but when certain sounds are unwanted it is generally termed 'noise'. Bell *et al.* (1976) make this point when emphasizing that noise involves a physical component (by the ear and higher brain structures) but also a psychological component when it is evaluated as unwanted.

As far as the classroom in concerned, it is important that the physical environment provides acoustics which enable participants to hold discussions in a normal conversational voice. The level of desirable noise will vary in different settings, such as a manual arts workshop with noisy lathes and electric drills to an extremely quiet library. Each instructional setting has its own noise level requirements to the extent that each person can hear clearly what is needed to be heard and not to be distracted by other noises (Eriksen and Wintermute, 1983).

Research studies on the effects of noise in classrooms have been considerable over the last six decades, but the results are inconclusive and often contradictory. Some of these studies have examined short-term exposure of students to noise within the school while others have monitored long-term exposure to severe noise from external sources.

As an example of the former, Slater (1968) examined seventh-grade primary school children's performance on a standardized reading test under three conditions. The first classroom of students was isolated from surrounding background noise, the second had normal background neighbouring noise of 55–79 decibels (dB), and in the third room additional noise sources were used (lawn mower tape recordings) to maintain a background noise level of 75–90 dB. The results indicated that the students' performance on the reading test was not affected either positively or negatively by the different levels of noise. In another study of primary school students, Weinstein and Weinstein (1979) compared the reading performance of fourth grade students under quiet (47 dB) and normal background noise (60 dB) and also found that there were no significant differences in performance.

Noise affects all teachers and students but the problem is compounded for students with hearing problems (Anderson, 2001). Ray (1992) noted in his study that 20 to 43 per cent of primary school students had minimal degrees of permanent or fluctuating hearing impairment that could adversely affect listening and learning. The problem is especially acute with special education students, many of whom have significant histories of hearing loss (Reichman and Healey, 1993).

Temperature

Common sense would indicate that there is a fairly limited temperature range in which school students might be expected to work at their best. High temperatures will tend to make some students irritable and uncomfortable. In extreme cases students can become lethargic and even nauseous. Then again, cold temperatures seem to bring out aggression and negative behaviour in some students.

Judgements about temperature control in schools are typically made at head office, in that decisions about the architectural design of schools and the use of specific building materials are made at this level. The use of particular designs, the siting of buildings and the use of insulating material will clearly affect maximum and minimum temperatures.

Seating Comfort

Having comfortable seating in classrooms is of major importance. If students are confined to uncomfortable seats for extended periods of time they become distracted from the learning task (Gay, 1986). Uncomfortable seating may also lead to negative attitudes about the teacher (Tessmer and Richey, 1997). Mann (1997) reports on a study where students were given modular, modern furniture and noted major changes in attitude.

Lieble (1980, p. 22) states the problem succinctly: 'the mind can only absorb what the seat can endure'.

Class Size

Of course, interactions between the teacher and students can be increased when class numbers are small. It results in less desk space and therefore more free space is available for informal activities or for specialist equipment.

However, research evidence is contradictory on whether class size affects student achievement. For example, Murphy and Rosenberg (1998) and Finn *et al.* (2001) contend that there is compelling evidence that reducing class size, especially for younger children, will have a positive effect on student achievement. By contrast, Rees and Johnson (2000) and Galton *et al.* (2003) conclude that there is no evidence that smaller class sizes alone lead to higher student achievement. O'Donnell (2000), commenting on the funding resources in Australian education systems, notes the reluctance of governments to make significant reductions in class size.

Biddle and Berliner (2002, p. 20), in a major synthesis of research studies, form several conclusions:

- Small classes in the early grades generate substantial gains for the students and those extra gains are greater the longer the students are exposed to those classes.
- Extra gains from small classes in the early grades are larger when the class has fewer than 20 students.
- Students who have traditionally been disadvantaged in education carry gains forward into the upper grades.
- The extra gains appear to apply equally to boys and girls.
- Evidence for the possible advantages of small classes in the upper grades and high school is inconclusive.

Psychosocial Environment

A number of studies have been done on students' perceptions to obtain information on a better person–environment fit in classrooms (Fraser and Walberg, 1991). At the primary and secondary school levels, students can be surveyed to obtain data on their present levels of personal satisfaction and adjustment, and their respective teachers can then use this information to make changes where appropriate (Griffith, 1997).

A number of student inventories have been developed which provide this information. The *Classroom Environment Scale* (Moos and Trickett, 1974) has been widely used in the USA. This instrument measures nine different dimensions of the classroom environment including students' interpersonal relationships, personal growth, and teacher control.

My Class Inventory is an instrument developed by the Australian researchers, Fisher and Fraser (1981), and is used to gain information about primary school students' perceptions of classroom goals and value orientation. The items require students to make ratings on actual classroom environments as well as preferred environments. This information can be of great interest to class teachers who are concerned about providing instructional environments which are more in accord with those preferred by students.

More recently, a questionnaire instrument was developed by Fraser *et al.* (1996), *What is Happening in this Class*, to measure students' perceptions of their classroom environment. Items are included which provide data on seven dimensions of student cohesiveness, extent of teacher support, extent of student involvement, investigative activities, task orientation, cooperation and equity.

Other Learning Settings

The school is not the only learning environment for young and older children. There are other non-formal agencies such as the church and youth groups that provide organized, systematic and educational activities. Informal education is a lifelong process by which every individual accumulates knowledge, skills, attitudes and thoughts from a variety of learning environments – from family, friends, travel, reading, listening and viewing (Tuijnman and Bostrom, 2002).

Service learning has become an important priority in recent years, whereby students visit other environments (for example senior citizen homes, hostels for disabled persons) and provide caring services to others in need. Doing these community services gives students an opportunity to reflect on their own development (Dinkelman, 2001).

Participation in these community activities enables students to realize the value of life skills – they develop self-confidence and understand more about personal dependability (McLaughan, 2001).

Full service youth and community centres provide additional learning environments apart from classrooms. They have family resource centres, health care suite, preschool, before and after school child care, and auditoriums. These sites are open day and night and do capture the spirit of a community school (Dryfoos, 2000).

Concluding Comments

Descriptions of classroom environments run the full gamut from invective criticism:

> Judging from what is said and from what is available as a measuring stick, schools are architecturally and environmentally sterile ... Their structure is insipid, cavernous and regimented. They are only now and then really creature-comfortable. Their designs maximize economy, surveillance, safety and 'maybe' efficiency. (George and McKinley, 1974, p. 141)

to unbridled praise:

[Open planned classroom environments] are a liberatory measure capable of emancipating children from the authority of teachers. (Cooper, 1982, p. 168)

In this chapter an attempt was made to place judgements about classroom environments on a more substantial footing and not to subscribe to either extreme view. Classroom instruction is affected by different uses of space and physical conditions. It is not possible to have knowledge of all the inter-relationships but it would be less than professional to ignore the evidence that is available. Creative arranging of the classroom is one thing, but it must be tempered by careful consideration of the effects of the classroom environment in all its complexities.

Reflections and Issues

1. 'In my space there must be a wide range of ways to succeed, multiple interests to pursue, a variety of possible contributions to make. This means the room is decentralized and characterised by lively work stations or interest areas, rather than by straight rows' (Ayers, 1993, p. 60). How achievable is this? Describe how you have developed classrooms in terms of multiple interests.
2. To what extent is it possible to cater for students' individual learning styles in terms of environmental elements such as noise, temperature and colour? Give examples from your classroom experiences or from classes you have visited.
3. 'A certain level of adequacy must be attained in seating, acoustics, temperature and lighting for high level learning to occur' (Tessmer and Richey, 1997). Explain, giving examples from your classroom experiences.
4. 'Machines change relations within the traditional classroom. Film, video, computer software and web sites act as teachers and partially displace the human teacher' (De Vaney, 1998, p. 3). Discuss.
5. 'School is diffusing spatially, merging into the physical backdrop of society. Schools are losing their architectural individuality, becoming increasingly difficult to recognize as places of learning' (Hopmann and Kunzli, 1997, p. 262). What are other places of learning? Are schools losing their individuality? If so, what will the impact be in the short and medium term?
6. 'Children's attitude and behaviour is determined, to a considerable extent, by the design of school grounds' (Titman, 1997, p. 2). What messages do school grounds convey to school children? What are positive and negative elements of school grounds for children? How might this affect their behaviour in and out of the classroom?
7. 'Teachers have little training in how to arrange a room. Perhaps every new teacher should receive an empty classroom and then plan what they want to do in it and how they want to operate'. If you were given an empty room explain how you would arrange it.
8. 'The classroom environment is such a potent determinant of student outcomes that it should not be ignored by those wishing to improve the effectiveness of schools' (Fraser, 1986, p. 1). In what ways does the classroom environment

determine student outcomes? What can a class teacher do to maximize the positive elements of a classroom environment?

9. According to Evans (1990), a school is both the temple and the exhibition hall of the modern world. Brightly coloured curtains and carpets are part of the intentions to display desired features to the public. But important aspects of teaching and administration remain hidden. In fact, care is often taken to indicate the 'official' way into the school. Do you agree with this statement? To what extent do the physical forms of schools give out messages to the public?

14   Teacher Appraisal

Introduction

The education of students is becoming increasingly results-driven, and as a result, attention is focused on the quality of teachers and how they perform in teaching students.

It seems that many stakeholders want to measure/appraise the quality of teaching which occurs in schools. According to Burnett and Meacham (2002) the stakeholders 'range from governments who are keen to dispel beliefs concerning the decline in the quality of public instruction, school administrators wishing to derive maximum benefit from their staffing dollar, professional teaching bodies looking to enhance the professional status of their members, individual teachers desiring job security and promotion on merit, and parents wanting the best for their children, to the children themselves' (p. 141).

As professionals, teachers are constantly monitoring their work and that of colleagues working at the same school. In some schools, site-based initiatives have involved more formal monitoring of teachers' contributions. Whether all states and territory systems move to formal teacher appraisal schemes in the near future is uncertain but highly likely, given their prominence in the United Kingdom and the USA. A number of educators argue that teacher appraisal schemes have the potential to improve teaching, but there are many traps for the unwary, given recent experiences (Down *et al.*, 2000).

Some Basic Terms

How persons define teacher appraisal will depend on their attitudes and values. Parents at local social events often swap war stories about 'good' and 'bad' teachers. They apparently have criteria for making these judgements and see appraisal as a means of getting rid of the 'bad' teachers who teach their children.

In private industry and increasingly in the public service, 'performance appraisal' activities are commonly undertaken. These involve managers and staff in planning particular targets. Criteria are used to judge levels of performance of staff in achieving or working towards these targets. In these situations the targets are clearly defined and so the measurement of achievement or lack of achievement is usually easily prescribed. Wragg (1987) argues that an interpolation of 'performance appraisal' to teaching is very problematic because do we really know what effective teaching is and can we recognize it when we see it?

L. Bell (1988) argues that teachers attach different meanings to staff appraisal, namely:

- to identify incompetent teachers;
- to improve pay and promotion;
- to provide external accountability;
- to improve teacher performance;
- to provide effective management of teachers;
- to provide professional development.

This wide listing of meanings by a UK educator needs to be contrasted with that provided by a US educator (Danielson, 2001) who contends that teacher appraisal (in the USA the term is typically 'teacher evaluation') has only one major purpose and that is quality assurance – 'As trustees of public funds who are responsible for educating a community's young people, educators in public schools must ensure that each classroom is in the care of a competent teacher. Most educators recognize that teaching is a complex activity and that a simple, brief observation of a teacher in the classroom is not enough. An evaluation system should recognize, cultivate and develop good teaching (p. 13)'.

The weeding out of incompetent teachers is of course a less than helpful reason for implementing teacher appraisals but it is cited regularly in education documents, and given great prominence in the media. For example, Tucker (2001), citing empirical research in the USA, states that 5 to 15 per cent of the 2.7 million teachers in public school classrooms perform at incompetent levels. She provides details of assistance plans that have been used in some public schools in the USA and notes that 'the remediation requires a substantial investment of effort by both the teacher and the administrator, but has the potential to yield substantial benefits for all concerned parties, especially students' (p. 55).

A more positive meaning is to link appraisal to improving pay and promotion. In most states, advanced teacher status positions are now available to teachers who can demonstrate that they have high-quality classroom skills. This approach to appraisal is promoted by Ingvarson and Chadbourne (1994) in terms of a career development model. Yet there have been difficulties in establishing criteria and operationalizing the concept of an Advanced Skills Teacher (AST), or Level 3 teachers, in Western Australia (Louden, 2000).

For many interest groups, teacher appraisal is needed to provide accountability to a range of external parties, but especially to parents and employers. This point of view seems to indicate that there is considerable room for improvement within the teaching profession – there are deficits to be overcome. School councils could be appropriate groups to initiate these accountability measures.

It is also argued that teacher appraisal schemes are a powerful way of motivating teachers to perform better. Again this appears to be based on a deficit model that teachers need assistance in refining their strengths and overcoming their weaknesses.

Another view is that teacher appraisal is needed because management in schools by principals, deputy-principals and senior teachers relies on effective deployment of staff – they need to know more about the skills and competencies of individual teachers.

A less threatening view of teacher appraisal is to perceive it as a basis for professional development. Systematic assessment of each teacher's performance provides the information needed for designing appropriate staff development activities (Hannay and Seller, 1998). It provides for professional enhancement because it pinpoints areas where a teacher can obtain specific in-service or related assistance. Some would argue that this is the major meaning that should be attributable to teacher appraisal – it would increase job satisfaction and benefit the school as a whole (Darling-Hammond, 1998).

This preliminary analysis of meanings of teacher appraisal reveals that it is a very slippery term! Depending upon how the term is interpreted there is likely to be opposition and rejection or support. The degree of support or opposition is also dependent upon the historical contexts and these matters are explored in the next section.

Teacher Appraisal Developments

United Kingdom

In the United Kingdom, the Education Act of 1986 enabled local education authorities to consider teacher appraisal schemes for their respective schools. In due course, various pilot schemes were introduced.

According to Bennett (1992) the pilot schemes were influenced by two conflicting models: a control model and a staff development model. The control model had its antecedents in the 'great debate' era of the 1970s with the emphasis upon efficient and effective use of resources and parent-power, governor-power and national intervention. The staff development model can be traced to the James Report (James, 1972) and its emphasis upon the in-service needs of teachers, the prioritizing of these needs and the provision of appropriate resources to service them.

The directors of the pilot schemes, coordinated under the School Teacher Appraisal Pilot Study, eventually accepted the staff development model as the basis for their activities after some initial disagreements. Each of the pilot schemes trialled procedures involving teacher self-appraisals and designed targets to improve performance.

When the Education Regulations for School Teacher Appraisal were passed by Parliament in mid-1991, appraisal became a requirement for all teachers. The government declared that all teachers would be appraised by the end of 1995. Unfortunately, government priorities changed the staff development emphasis quite considerably and more of a control emphasis slipped into the regulations.

The election of the Blair government in 1997 brought with it a new goal of raising educational standards. The school inspectors (OFSTED) and the new bureaucracy (DFEE) were garnered together in a new partnership to improve school management and leadership through school targets (Crump, 1998). A National Teacher Education Board was created and this is charged with bringing about workplace reform. The National College for School Leadership is well funded to provide leaderships for school heads, who are deemed to be the major catalysts for change. The government also established an Innovations Unit to stimulate new teaching ideas (Mackay, 2002).

Not surprisingly, work-related stress for teachers has increased dramatically (Brown *et al.*, 2002). The drive to raise standards and managerialism has caused major problems of stress for teachers and head teachers (McMahon, 2000). It appears that the government has concentrated predominantly on central management and incentives for producing higher student standards, with only limited interest in the professional development and needs of teachers.

USA

In the USA, teacher appraisal (termed teacher evaluation) has always been given a high priority but the schemes used have varied in emphasis over the decades.

In keeping with the USA's penchant for testing, it is not surprising that the schemes have largely depended upon assessment instruments to measure teacher performance. Most states have introduced legislation requiring assessment of all beginning teachers and in some cases for principals, superintendents and continuing teachers. The assessment instruments tend to be standardized tests which either are low inference (relatively objective counts of behaviours) such as direct instruction behaviours or high inference (more subjective, professional judgements) ones dealing with descriptions of classroom behaviour (Porter *et al.*, 2000).

Teacher knowledge continues to be an important focus. Darling-Hammond (1997) argues that teacher knowledge and teacher expertise are significant influences on student learning. This was one of the major findings of the National Commission on Teaching and America's Future (1997).

An interesting perspective on teacher knowledge by Heibert *et al.* (2002) places the emphasis upon practitioner knowledge – knowledge that is integrated and organized around problems of practice. In-service programmes on 'lesson study' approaches focus upon developing practitioner knowledge, building upon lesson study research in Japan (Fernandez *et al.*, 2003).

The other ongoing scheme, and one that has major support currently at all levels, is the focus upon teacher professional standards. According to Delandshere and Arens (2001) the professional standards for teachers approach parallels the movement towards developing curriculum standards for students. National organizations have been working together to 'strengthen the teaching profession and raise its standards – eventually enhancing the quality of student learning – by redesigning teacher licensing and accountability requirements for teacher education programs, and engaging teachers in ongoing professional development' (p. 548).

The standards-based professional learning system generated by the National Board for Professional Teaching Standards (NBPTS) has been extremely influential. It assesses teacher performance within the context of specific subjects at different levels of schooling. 'Teachers undertake two types of task. One asks them to prepare a portfolio with four entries: one based on documented contributions to the school and professional community. The other uses an examination format to assess subject-specific pedagogical knowledge over one half day' (Ingvarson, 2002, pp. 14–15).

Recent research studies support the validity of the NBPTS standards and methods for assessing teacher performance (for example, Guskey, 2002). Strongly supportive accounts of NBPTS standards at specific schools are appearing in the literature (for example, Howard and McColskey, 2001).

As noted by Ingvarson (2002), NBPTS certification is gaining in credibility and, as a consequence, governments and education Authorities are creating a market for National Board Certified Teachers. Forty-four states now recognize this award and provide tangible rewards such as salary increases.

Despite these impressive developments, it should be noted that these schemes cannot address all the issues which confront teachers. The schemes focus upon major aspects of what it means to be a knowledgeable and reflective practitioner but other elements are omitted. For example, they do not appear to give attention to the 'teacher as activist, the skilled change agent with moral purpose, who will make a difference in the lives of students from all backgrounds' (Cochran-Smith, 2001a,b).

Australia

In Australia, teacher appraisal is evolving on a number of fronts but is still embryonic in terms of major developments.

There has been a quickening in the pace recently. Four of the largest teacher professional associations have entered into partnerships with universities to develop subject-specific sets of professional standards in English and Literacy, Mathematics and Science. It should be noted that these standards appear to be modelled on those developed by the NBPTS in the USA; the standards are higher than those developed in the first wave of competencies and standards in the 1990s and they have been developed without input from employers or teachers' unions

(Louden, 2000). It is highly likely that subject-based standards will be developed in quick succession by other subject associations.

National standards of teaching and teacher professional development are still evolving despite numerous national meetings of educators. Ingvarson (2002) contends that 'we are close to creating a national alliance of interested parties who could make a standards-based professional learning system a reality' (p. 18).

It would seem logical for a national standards framework for teachers to mirror the curriculum frameworks of outcomes/standards.

What is certain is that if new methods of performance assessment for certification are developed nationally, it will be a powerful incentive for teachers to engage in the programmes. It is highly likely that employing authorities will give recognition (and financial rewards) to teachers who obtain the certification, as noted above with regard to US teachers gaining NBPTS awards.

Why Do Teacher Appraisals?

From the outset, it is important to note that in everyday teaching teachers continually get informal and formal feedback about their actions. Teacher appraisal schemes are only part of this continual process of feedback, along with regular meetings, informal talks and staffroom and corridor conversations. Miles (1984) asserts that teacher appraisal should never become a substitute for frequent, informal feedback, nor should it be conducted in ways that cause a deterioration of professional relationships with other teachers.

Teacher appraisals enable balanced critiques of performance, which can include congratulations and recognition – a powerful motivator for teachers. As noted by Samuel (1987, p. 69) 'indeed at times it can provide the opportunity for that measured congratulation that so many of us are too mealy-mouthed to express on the informal occasion'. Teacher appraisals can produce a considerable amount of praise and can provide opportunities to celebrate good practice.

Shulman, as interviewed by Tell (2001), contends that many teachers in the USA preparing for NBPTS certification do so 'for the chance to demonstrate to themselves and to others that they are really, really good at what they do' (p. 10).

Another important reason is that teacher appraisal enables more detailed and, it is to be hoped, objective, information to be made available to each teacher (Preiss, 1992). There are several elements of this point to be considered. Few would argue that in a busy day of teaching the teacher can never be aware of all the things that are happening. He or she will know a lot of what is happening, but not all. Research studies of teachers in action often provide surprising results for the teachers being observed. Teacher's self-descriptions can often be very different from the independently observed data.

Yet, it must also be added that additional information obtained about teachers comes at a cost. In many cases fellow-teachers at the school may be required to undertake the observations, thus creating yet another time-consuming burden. Also, observers have their own agenda about what is significant and what is not. Data about a teacher's behaviour are provided with an end always in mind – to encourage changes and progress toward particular, desired goals.

There is also the matter of curriculum planning and implementation. Curriculum planning done at the school level may appear to be very appropriate, but until it is implemented in the classroom and evaluated it is not possible to know what the outcomes will be. Appraisals of how curricula are used – either by individual teachers, or by the school as a whole – provide important feedback for future curriculum planning.

Iwanicki (2001) argues that teacher appraisal (evaluation) should improve student learning in the classroom: 'In today's world we should not build professional employee appraisal systems to fire people. We should build systems to help them develop and increase the productivity of their organizations. In education, productivity means improved teaching and student learning' (p. 59).

The same can be said for general school planning. For a school to know whether it is achieving its goals requires systematic feedback, part of which is detailed information about teachers' contributions. There are time limitations regarding how frequently this information can be collected. A solution practised in many schools is for a smaller number of activities/functions to be evaluated each year.

The opportunity for professional development of teachers is a major reason and a central focus for many of the appraisal schemes. The improvement of teaching is not just the arrival at a reasonable standard for the initial few years (probationary period) of teaching, but steady progress as a life-long process. The appraisal process can enable a teacher to become increasingly effective in his or her present role, to make better use of strengths, and provide further opportunities at a school or elsewhere in terms of career advancement. Professional development is also about dovetailing the professional needs of individual teachers into the needs of the school as a whole.

Ingvarson (2002) argues for elaborate forms of professional development for teachers but cautions that not all forms of appraisal are effective for professional development. In the United Kingdom, Haynes *et al.* (2001) surveyed English teachers who had prepared for the threshold promotion (97 per cent passed over the threshold and were then placed on a new salary scale). Their research indicated that 98 per cent of the teachers reported that the experience had not had a positive experience on their practice, and in general had been detrimental to their morale.

Teaching Portfolios

Shulman (1994) introduced the idea of using portfolios in teacher assessment in the early 1990s. He claims that a portfolio is a theoretical act – 'it is a broad metaphor that comes alive as you begin to formulate the theoretical orientation to teaching that is most valuable to you. Your theory of teaching will determine a reasonable portfolio entry' (Shulman, 1994, p. 5).

Teaching portfolios have been promoted, especially in the USA, as a valuable method of appraising teachers at all levels from beginning teacher to master teacher (Lyons, 1999; Van Wagenen and Hibbard, 1998).

Hurst *et al.* (1998) contend that professional teaching portfolios are especially useful for teachers because:

- they are reflective compendiums – representations of teachers professional and personal lives;
- they are representations of teaching credentials and competencies – an organized collection of documents, letters, papers and photographs that lauds a teacher's personal and professional achievements in a compact, concrete way;
- they provide holistic views of teachers – they give teachers the opportunity to show not only their teaching strengths but also their heart and soul and passion for teaching;
- they provide documentation for strengthening interviews – it gives teachers applying for positions increased confidence and a competitive edge.

A teaching portfolio is likely to contain:

- carefully selected items about an appraisee's teaching and learning over a period of time;
- items that represent examples of best work;
- some examples of student work; and
- reflective commentaries by the appraisee.

Painter (2001) makes the distinction between folios and portfolios. A teaching folio is just a collection of a teacher's artefacts. A portfolio must contain reflections about their teaching in terms of the standards or rubrics required. Portfolios must provide details of a teacher's intellectual and professional ideas – 'thoughtful reflection, not a colour printer, is the key to portfolio success' (Painter, 2001, p. 92).

Problems and Issues

Experiences in the United Kingdom, USA and Australia indicate that a number of teachers are finding appraisals to be a valuable experience even though some were apprehensive about it initially – the first time for many teachers when they have been able to have a serious professional discussion about their work (McMahon, 1994). Case study accounts from various Australian states also provide confirmatory support for appraisals (e.g. Richards 1994; Billing 1994).

If appraisals are organized and planned just within a school, then a problem is finding the scarce resources required in terms of time and of money. As noted by L. Bell (1988), it is unrealistic to involve peers as appraisers and expect that they will do all their appraising outside of normal working hours. Yet to free up teachers to be involved in interviews and class observations during the school day would require substantial payments for relief teachers.

Other problems relate to the need for training of appraisers and the overcoming of suspicion and lack of trust by various interest groups. Some positive and negative elements of teacher appraisal are included in Figure 14.1.

If teacher appraisals are organized through national organizations, such as the NBPTS in the USA, it is a voluntary decision by teachers and they make their own arrangements about when and where they will submit themselves to the certification process. Similar arrangements are being trialled in Australia using the NBPTS portfolios adapted to the Australian context, using the standards developed by the Australian Science Teachers Association (Ingvarson, 2002).

It is highly likely that further trials will occur shortly in Australia using standards developed for English and Literacy and Mathematics and, in time, other subjects.

Figure 14.1: *Benefits and problems of teacher appraisal*

Difficulties / disadvantages	Advantages and rewards
Difficulties	
Suspicion	Leads to the identification of clear aims and
Concern	objectives
Lack of experience (in self-appraisal and appraising others)	Improves relationships
Training may be required	Provides opportunity for honest
Opposition of significant groups	communication, understanding, training
	and development
Disadvantages	
Appraisal requires:	Displays concern and commitment
time and commitment, especially from senior staff	Generates motivation
honesty from all involved	It is open and seen to be open
the need for discipline	
It can provoke conflict	Reduces subjectivity in assessment
	Provides permanent (and available) records
	Provides opportunity to praise
	Person being reviewed has an ownership in the process, which leads to clearer understanding of expectations, responsibilities and aspirations

Source: Based on L. Bell (1988).

Concluding Comments

There are various interpretations of teacher appraisal, ranging from 'a chimera, looming threateningly and foully over our shoulders; for others it is a fantasy that cannot come to pass; and for some it is a practical part of institutional autonomy and individual professionalism' (Clandinin, 1986, p. 3).

In this chapter the latter stance is taken. Given initiatives with teacher appraisals in the United Kingdom, the USA and Australia and the potential they have for improving schooling, it is extremely likely that teacher appraisals will become more widespread in the twenty-first century.

It is therefore of importance to all teachers to be aware of why appraisals are undertaken, who appraises and the methods commonly used. The practical examples included in this chapter should enable teachers at all levels to relate to important issues about teacher appraisals.

Reflections and Issues

1. 'Traditionally appraisal was what was done to teachers. The new approaches to teacher appraisal place teachers in more active and professional roles' (Danielson, 2001, p. 14). Is this what is really occurring? Discuss.
2. Smyth and Shacklock (1998) consider that teachers at a school should use collegial processes to appraise their own teaching rather than having experts undertake it and thereby disempower teachers. He uses the term 'clinical supervision' to describe the face-to-face dialogue between classroom teachers. Take a stance for or against this argument.
3. There are numerous examples in industry where annual appraisals of staff are undertaken. Consider arguments for or against the assertion that education is an industry too and should use similar appraisal schemes.
4. Is it possible to develop a system of learning in the teaching profession that engages all teachers? Should it be developed at a local level or at a national level?
5. According to Wragg (1987) the major emphasis for teacher appraisals should be to improve the quality of teaching rather than increasing bureaucracy or power. Do you agree? Which methods of appraisal have the potential to improve the quality of teaching?
6. We should not forget that appraisal is about recognizing effort and achievement and praising the commitment of teachers. Bennett (1992, p. 129) states that it 'must not be allowed to become a grand biennial ritual to be endured and ultimately ignored'. Discuss.
7. Why is a national professional body needed in Australia? Is it appropriate and realistic for such a body to develop standards and responsibility for ensuring the system for assessing teacher performance against those standards is rigorous?

Part V

Collaborative Involvement in Curriculum

15 Collaborative Teacher Planning and Empowerment

Introduction

Lieberman and Miller (1990) lament that 'the greatest tragedy of teaching is that so much is carried on in self-imposed and professionally sanctioned isolation' (p. 160). Nevertheless, there are growing initiatives and developments with collaborative activities between teachers, which are gradually breaking down the traditional culture of individualism.

Self-managed schools can maximize the opportunities for collaborative teacher planning and empowerment, but whether this really happens or not will depend upon whether central control is retained. For teacher empowerment to occur the sphere of decision-making must be broad.

Some Basic Terms

Many definitions of 'collaborative teams' and 'collaborative schools' are exhortative. For example, schools are collaborative and inclusive when they use diverse perspectives to frame problems and craft workable solutions – they use cooperative rather than controlling power – vision building and action is used to motivate and energize others (Cavanagh and MacNeil, 2002). Heller (1993) defines a collaborative school as a school that values educational improvement – 'teachers are encouraged and supported, to engage in positive dialogue about teaching as it relates to current research and practice' (p. 96). There appears to be implicit in these definitions a common understanding of terms, but is this likely to be the case? For example, what does it mean to say that teachers should 'work together'? Does it mean informal interactions or delegated meetings?

Weaver *et al.* (1987) provide the caveat that collaborative work is not just doing something with friends – 'collaboration in curriculum development involves working with friends while cavorting with the enemy' (p. 2). In any collaborative activity differences of perspective can lead to suspicion and disrespect. As Sarason (1990) notes, as collaboration gets played out, politics, personalities and financial constraints may dampen the enthusiasm for collaborative projects.

Hayes and Kelly (2000) note that not all teachers find collaborative activities attractive. For some teachers, opportunities for cooperative decision-making are unwanted and rejected. Lortie (1975) has written extensively about this: 'teachers prefer classroom tasks over organizational tasks and classroom claims over organizational initiatives' (p. 164).

Riordan (2001) also focuses on this issue by considering teacher collaboration as a continuum from independence to interdependence. Teacher individualism occurs when a teacher considers that his or her teaching is an individual responsibility and a private matter. If a teacher starts to move towards the other end of the continuum then he or she starts to interact more with others, undertakes peer consultation and mentorship. Teacher collaboration, according to Riordan (2001), 'denotes joint work, shared responsibility and the existence of high levels of trust, respect and mutuality' (p. 6).

The term 'teacher empowerment' has various meanings associated with it in the education literature. Examples include a slogan for class struggle; a term to connote collegial learning with students; and a term for connoting increased expertise due to technological advances.

Empowerment assumes that persons holding power (for example, state or local managers or school principals) give the power to someone else (for example, teachers or students) in the interests of improving schools (Elmore, 1988). However, it is not always clear who has the power and how it might be transferred. Then there is the matter of responsibility. If persons are empowered, to whom are they responsible: To parents and students? To the community? To the teaching profession?

'Power' can be defined as control, but in terms of educational settings it is more useful to consider power as 'doing or acting'. Opportunities for teachers to try out new approaches, to problem-solve and to enquire, assist them in becoming 'empowered'. Empowerment of teachers (and students) occurs when they have opportunities to create meaning in their respective schools. By contrast, 'disempowered' teachers are those who teach defensively and control knowledge in order to control students (McNeil, 1988). In these situations schooling becomes an empty ritual, unrelated to personal or cultural knowledge.

Teacher empowerment is seen by writers such as Giroux (1992) as a significant concept in understanding the complex relations between schools and the dominant society. He argues that teachers and students need empowerment to resist and to struggle against the domination in society produced by capitalism.

Some writers argue that teachers are becoming steadily disempowered (Apple, 1986; Whitty 1994). For example, Apple (1986) argues that teachers face the prospect of being deskilled because of the encroachment of technical control procedures into the curriculum in schools. He cites as examples behaviourally based curricula, prespecified competencies for teachers and students, and testing activities.

Southworth (2000) and Poppleton (2000) have both reviewed the major reforms that were introduced by the Thatcher and Major governments and the Blair government in the United Kingdom. They have cited the following:

- the construction and implementation of a National Curriculum;
- introduction of a national system of testing pupils at the ages of 7, 11, 14 and 16 years;
- the publication of schools' test results and the use of league tables to rate schools' apparent success;
- the creation of the Office for Standards in Education (OFSTED), which sets in place week-long inspections of all schools;
- the setting of numerical targets for pupils' attainments in every school;
- the intention to link teacher performance to rewards and pay.

It is evident that both political parties have severely curtailed opportunities for teacher empowerment, brought about a resultant loss of autonomy and increased teachers' resistance to change.

Collaborative Approaches

One approach, when considering teacher collaboration, is to use the principle of 'zone of acceptance' (Hoy and Tarter, 1993). There are some school decisions that teachers are not concerned about or are indifferent about. These might include aspects of financial accounting or head office reporting. Then again there are other decisions about which teachers are most concerned and in which they have a personal stake (relevance), and there are other decisions where teachers have specific expertise and experience and can make a valuable contribution (expertise). According to Hoy and Tarter (1993) it is up to the school principal to ensure that collaborative decision-making occurs with issues relating to teacher relevance and expertise but not for other issues – 'always involving subordinates is as shortsighted as never involving them' (p. 4).

A 'quality system' is an approach developed by Snyder *et al.* (1994). They contend that a school team goes through three stages of growth, namely:

- Awareness: learning about new collaborative approaches; setting goals for improvement; emphasizing team activities.
- Transition: staff begin to appreciate the interdependence of their activities; achieve success with small projects; explore different ways to achieve ends.
- Transformation: a new belief system about work is shared by all staff; emphasis on student and community needs; common agreement about goals, expectations, collaboration and professional development activities.

Snyder *et al.* (1994) contend that the work culture of schools matures over a period of years and that the quality of collaboration and cohesiveness develops in accordance with the stages of growth described above.

Anderson and Cox (1988, pp. 5–6) propose that developing a collaborative climate within schools can be stimulated by a number of actions, which they term 'energizers', namely:

Energizer 1:   Harnessing self-interest: encourage staff to go beyond self-interest and to look at the needs of the organization as a whole.

Energizer 2:   Compacting tasks: use larger purposes to find linkages and overlaps in existing activities – to pack more than one meaning into a task – to work smarter.

Energizer 3:   Acting for cumulative impact: assess one's actions for their contribution to the overall goal – each task should not be seen as an end in itself.

Energizer 4:   Recasting conflict: looking at multiple perspectives rather than only one right way, allows more energy to be concentrated upon the problem and its solution.

Energizer 5:   Enabling communication: to optimize meaning we need to be very careful about the messages we send and how the parts fit the whole.

Energizer 6:   Fostering coherence by focusing on the larger meaning: encourage staff to find the larger connections among things.

Energizer 7:   Transforming reactivity to proactivity: the use of cooperative power rather than coercive power spreads responsibility and control among the players.

Energizer 8:   Building knowledge and skills to undergird change: provide the necessary support and assistance for intended changes.

Energizer 9:   Modelling desired behaviours as the quickest way to produce change: if staff experience collaboration in a positive and useful way they will be likely to consider collaboration in other settings.

Energizer 10:   Creating productive collaboration: this is very time-consuming but is most likely to succeed when:

- there is trust between partners based on interdependence;
- authentic, two-way communication occurs;
- goals are examined from several perspectives;
- power is used with mutual respect.

Mathews and Hudson (1994) have developed a 'collaborative review of teachers planning' model that enables teachers to see themselves and their work in relation to school plans and broader state and national frameworks. The steps involved include:

- teachers themselves identify and describe the various tasks that make up their daily work;
- self-review by teachers is necessary – this may require training so that they can analyse their work objectively;
- classroom observation is undertaken, preferably planned by the group as a whole;
- appraisal discussions occur – focus is on constructive suggestions about work practices;
- plans are made collaboratively with others after thoughtful reflection.

Conditions Necessary for Collaboration

Fullan (1991) and Hargreaves and Fullan (2000) strongly support teacher collaboration and advocate it as an alternative to teacher isolation. They describe learning-enriched schools where staff collaboration is at a high level with shared goals, teacher certainty and teacher commitment (see Figure 15.1).

Fullan and Hargreaves (1991) and others advocate a number of conditions necessary for collaboration to be successful in schools. They include:

- collaboration is linked with norms and with opportunities for continuous improvement;
- interaction sessions are provided whereby teachers develop a greater certainty and sense of efficacy about their teaching (Rosenholtz, 1989);
- opportunities occur for joint work between teachers such as team teaching, planning, observation, peer coaching (Little, 1990);
- informal, pervasive qualities and attitudes exist among staff that are based upon support, trust and openness (Nias *et al.*, 1989);
- there is an open and supportive climate in which to share and discuss failure and uncertainty (Gold and Roth, 1993);
- teachers' purposes are developed and shared with others;
- collaborative cultures respect, celebrate and make allowances for the teacher as a person – the person is not consumed by the group but fulfilled through it (Nias *et al.*, 1989);
- the individual and the group are inherently and simultaneously valued – individuals are valued and so is interdependence;
- the principal plays a major role in enabling and empowering teachers, but not necessarily being the charismatic high-flier (Fullan and Hargreaves, 1991);
- many teachers are leaders;
- there are close working relationships with parents and the wider community.

Figure 15.1: *Learning-enriched schools*

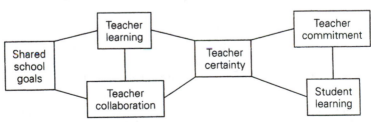

Source: Fullan (1991, p. 133).

There are of course 'disadvantages' in developing collaborative arrangements in some schools if these are superficial and likely to fail. Some forms of collaboration which can lead to undesirable outcomes include:

- Balkanization: where subcultures develop in a school comprised of competing groups with separate loyalties and identities. This can often occur in high schools between subject departments (Fullan and Hargreaves, 1991).
- Superficial collaboration: limited forms of sharing that do not progress beyond advice-giving and material sharing – there are no deeper forms of interaction such as joint planning, observation and experimentation.
- Contrived collaboration: can occur when school principals attempt to control or regulate collaboration – although it may be useful as a preliminary phase in establishing more enduring forms of collaboration, there is the danger that they will be perceived by teachers to be additional formal, bureaucratic procedures.

Hargreaves and Dawe (1990) contend that these collaborative forms of teacher development may in many instances not be empowering teachers towards greater professional independence at all, but incorporating them and their loyalties within processes and structures bureaucratically determined elsewhere. They may be fostering training, not education, instructional closure rather than intellectual openness, dispositional adjustment rather than thoughtful critique (Hargreaves and Dawe, 1990, p. 119).

Campbell and Southworth (1990) provide additional points about collaborative activities, which they perceive to be disadvantages:

- Time: teachers in primary schools and principals of small schools have virtually no non-contact time and so collaborative activities can only occur after school.
- Reduced roles: some teachers and especially some school principals perceive that collaborative activities reduce their autonomy and their power. Campbell and Southworth (1990) consider that a principal's ego-identification with a school can be greatly affected by collaborative activities and could in turn produce feelings of losing control, anxiety and conflict for principals. Teachers may also experience anxiety in moving from closed and isolated settings to more open and communal ones.
- Capacity of teachers to work in groups: it can be argued that not all teachers accept the assumption that teachers should work together. Further, school structures and policies do not facilitate group activities. Some writers may also be over-optimistic about the extent to which agreement can be reached in collaborative activities (Handy, 1981).
- Collaborative activities have been largely recommended by persons outside of schools such as researchers and consultants. There is limited evidence about teachers' views on collaborative activities.

Collaborative Activities and Students

In addition to fostering collaborative activities between teachers there is considerable scope for teachers to embark upon collaborative activities with their respective students. Clark and Moss (1995) highlight some of the contributions that high school students can make in working collaboratively on activities with teachers. Hill and Hill (1990) argue that students should be taught the skills of collaborative learning, group management and organization in primary schools. They contend that there are a number of reasons why collaborative activities are important for students:

- they lead to the development of thinking skills and deeper levels of understanding;
- they enable students to have more enjoyable experiences, especially in cooperative learning groups;
- they provide opportunities for students to develop important leadership and group skills;
- they produce more positive attitudes about school, teachers and other students;
- they promote higher levels of self-esteem in students;
- they promote care and respect for others, especially positive peer relationships;
- they provide a sense of belonging and identity for students.

Collaborative Activities and Principals

School principals are an important factor in supporting collaborative activities among their staff. Fullan and Hargreaves (1991) counsel principals to resist proprietary claims and attitudes 'which suggest an ownership of the school which is personal rather than collective, imposed rather than earned, and hierarchical rather than democratic' (p. 90). If they are not careful, 'collaboration' among staff becomes 'co-optation'.

Sharing leadership and promoting professional development should be a major target for principals. The effective principal is one who searches out and celebrates examples of teacher leadership (Fullan, 2001). Louis and Miles (1990) suggest the following strategies that a principal can use to foster collaboration among staff:

- power sharing;
- rewards for staff;
- openness, inclusiveness;
- expanding leadership roles;
- patience.

Fullan and Hargreaves (1991) also remind principals that it is perilous to assume that collaboration only takes one form – it can take diverse forms. A fixation on specific kinds of collaboration such as mandatory peer coaching or compulsory team teaching could be counterproductive and disempowering: 'Don't force through one particular approach. Develop awareness of, commitment to, and experience in the general collaborative principle. Commit to the principle, but empower teachers to select from the wide range of practices the ones that suit them best' (p. 94).

Empowerment of Teachers and Students

Empowerment can also be considered as teacher and student empowerment, 'jointly developed'. Giroux and McLaren (1986) argue for teachers to democratize schools and to empower students to become critical, active citizens. Boomer (1982) and Green (1988) argue that students must be given opportunities to contribute to, and modify, the curriculum, so that they will have a real investment both in the learning processes and in the outcomes. The negotiation process between a teacher and his or her students empowers both groups as they share commitments and make decisions about class activities. Green (1988) refers to the affective and cognitive tensions in the classrooms as a teacher and his or her students permit and commission various power sanctions. Different learning situations will permit or require certain actions. Actions of power occur with great subtlety and include legal power, informational power, charismatic power, physical power and many other forms exercised by both teachers and students.

Empowerment and School Support

Teachers can also become empowered through increased resources, such as technology. Recently, educators have been proposing that broad-based use of computer technology (for example, word processors, spreadsheets and data bases) can enhance teaching and teachers can match the technology to their own creativity (Valdez, 1986).

With computers, teachers and students can learn together – they can be sharing experiences as they try out new programmes and both groups can become empowered as they master additional uses and ends of computer technology (Palinesar and Herrenkool, 2002). Individuals use computers in different ways and allow the machine to be integrated into their sense of identity – that is the big payoff.

Sizer, in his interview with O'Neil (1995), refers to the satisfactions teachers gain in the coalition of Essential Schools in the USA being able to exhibit/demonstrate meaningful student work.

Increased resources can also be a powerful reward. This may take the form of increased pay incentives or it might be additional teacher-aide assistance or additional resources such as laptop computers (Cornett, 1995). Effective reward systems can be used to increase:

- teacher motivation;
- acceptance of personal accountability;
- continuous professional development;
- acceptance of an enlarged definition of teacher work responsibilities.

Reward systems need to be a mixture of intrinsic satisfactions (for example, exciting work, positive working conditions, interesting co-workers) and extrinsic benefits (for example, promotions, public recognition) (Barth, 2002).

There are also penalties, as indicated in Table 15.1. A new task or opportunity very often requires additional labour-intensive activities, which some teachers at least will perceive to be a 'punishment'. Furthermore, it may be a threat to the teachers' established procedures or may require a teacher to work closely in collaboration with other teachers. As indicated in Table 15.1 these are just some of the perceived 'costs' of getting involved with new tasks.

Ideally teachers can become increasingly empowered by:

- working together on joint projects;
- talking to one another at a level of detail that is rich and meaningful;
- shared planning or evaluation of topics;
- observing their colleagues in peer observation arrangements;
- training together and training one another (for example, teaching others about new ideas and classroom practices);
- having access to appropriate levels of material and human support/ resources.

School administrators have the resources and the opportunities to empower teachers. They can provide leadership opportunities for outstanding staff members. They can increase opportunities during the school day for teachers to interact on teaching problems (Nias, 1990).

Table 15.1: Rewards and costs for teachers in undertaking an innovation

Costs	Rewards
1 Time demands are heavy	1 More stimulating/interesting teaching
2 Need to acquire new skills, acquire new knowledge	2 Improved discipline among pupils
3 Need to prepare new material	3 More time allocated for planning lessons
4 Have to adopt unfamiliar patterns of teaching	4 More resources made available
5 Requires reorganization of administrative structures	5 More status/recognition for 'innovative' teachers
6 Can be a threat to autonomy	6 More active part in decision making
7 Subject expertise can be undermined	7 More money
8 Involves unwanted collaboration with other teachers	8 Promotion
9 Leads to change in power structure among teachers, teacher/pupils	

Clark and Meloy (1990) suggest that problems of schools as organizations can be greatly reduced by developing 'democratic' structures, incorporating the following principles:

- designated teachers (for example, the principal) should be chosen by the teachers;
- the school must be built on shared authority and responsibility, not delegation of authority and responsibility;
- all staff should have terms of work as administrators as well as classroom teachers;
- formal rewards to the staff (for example, forms of promotion) should be under the control of the staff;
- the goals of the school must be formulated by, and agreed to through, group consensus.

Problems and Issues

Some writers consider that teachers are not interested in empowerment because of limiting factors in the culture of teaching. For example, Hargreaves (1989) argues that teachers are present-oriented, conservative and individualistic. They tend to avoid long-term planning and collaboration with their colleagues.

A problem for teacher groups becoming empowered is that teachers are trained to survive in the system as individuals. Teachers have few ways of sharing their experience. As noted by Walker and Kushner (1991, p. 194), 'precious time available for staff meetings tends to be gobbled up by scheduling arrangements and by the need to consider closely each individual child's progress'. There is little opportunity for schools to reflect on their practices. This can be a major deficiency because major problems for teachers are problems of organizations.

For many teachers their career future is featureless, lacking in challenges and just more of the same. Research studies of life histories of teachers (for example, Huberman, 1993; Goodson, 1992; Kelchtermans and Vandenberghe, 1994) indicate that many teachers follow well defined patterns of behaviour – although there is initial excitement and experimentation, this is superseded by boredom and negative attitudes.

Concluding Comments

Collaborative teacher planning is widely cited in the education literature as being highly desirable. Yet, there appears to be only modest acceptance of collaboration by the teaching profession (Riordan, 2001). It might also be argued that teacher empowerment is widely canvassed as desirable by schools but power structures and relationships within many schools and education systems limit the opportunities for it to occur.

Reflections and Issues

1. 'To work collaboratively and effectively as partners takes both time and commitment. Institutional culture is a powerful agent in keeping teachers apart' (Groundwater-Smith, 1992). Explain why it is that teachers typically operate independently. Give examples of activities which facilitate the process of staff work collaboratively.

2. 'Taking small steps, while easier to take in the beginning, are in the long run riskier than bold steps; incremental changes that do not address the fundamental problems, get in the way of powerful student learning and simply put off the day of reckoning' (Sizer, 1989). Explain, using examples from schools with which you have been associated.

3. Although there are many examples of successful collaborative efforts in schools many seem to falter after initial enthusiasm. What are the reasons why some schools cannot maintain their initial momentum? How can these problems be overcome?

4. 'Collaborative cultures are highly sophisticated. They cannot be created overnight. Many forms of collegiality are superficial, partial and even counter-productive. It is not possible to have strong collaborative cultures without strong individual development. We must avoid crushing individuality in the drive to eliminate individualism' (Fullan and Hargreaves, 1991, p. 61). Explain why collaboration and individual development is needed. Describe activities that can be used to foster their development.

5. 'Teachers are thinkers who make many decisions that create the curriculum in classrooms. They have an important function in shaping what students have an opportunity to learn' (McCutcheon, 1988). Are teachers sufficiently empowered to undertake this function?

6. The three major factors that facilitate empowerment include acquisition of support (for example, endorsement by the principal), information (for example, technical data) and resources (for example, human services). Do you agree that these are important factors? Give examples to support your answer.

7. 'Teachers seeking empowerment have to resolve the common tensions between management and curriculum. Decisions are often made in favour of management which emphasizes the need to survive above the urge to learn and to develop' (Walker and Kushner, 1991). Is this the typical pattern in your experience? How can both groups' ends be served more appropriately?

8. 'We are certain of one thing. We will never move within the bureaucratic structure to new schools, to free schools. That structure was invented to assure domination and control. It will never produce freedom and self-actualization. The bureaucratic structure is failing in a manner so critical that adaptations will not forestall its collapse. It is impractical. It does not fit the psychological and personal needs of the workforce' (Clark and Meloy, 1990, p. 21). Discuss this statement and, in particular, point to what some alternatives might be.

16 Decision-makers, Stakeholders and Influences

Introduction

Schooling occurs as a result of decisions made by various individuals and groups, both professionals and lay-persons. To complicate matters, actions occur at different levels, especially national, state and local. It is of considerable value to analyse and understand the contributions of the various players.

Some Basic Terms

A classroom teacher's work is affected by many individuals and groups. Although various myths abound about the freedom of a teacher to do whatever he or she wishes in the privacy of 'behind the classroom door' this is not true in the twenty-first century – if in fact it ever was the case.

'Decision-makers' are those individuals or groups who, because of their professional status or position, are able to make specific decisions about what is to be taught, when, how and to whom. Obvious examples of decision-makers include education systems and their senior officers and school principals and senior teachers. But there are many others, including textbook writers, testing agencies, accreditation and certification agencies.

'Stakeholders' are individuals or groups of persons who have a right to comment on, and have input into, school programmes (Arends, 2000). In many cases they may have the authority to ensure that their inputs/directives are implemented, such as head office education directors or regional directors. Then again, they may have no official powers but rely upon their modes of persuasion, such as parent groups or newspaper editors.

'Influences' are individuals or groups that hold common interests and endeavour to persuade/convince authorities that certain changes should occur. They may be content to push a certain slogan/ideal or they may focus upon specific activities or processes that should occur in schools. Examples of such influences include various local interest/lobby groups representing environmental issues or specific religious beliefs.

There are obviously no clear demarcation lines between some forms of decision-makers, stakeholders and influence groups, as their degree of authority/control depends upon the eye of the beholder. Yet for the purpose of analysis it is useful to produce a tentative list of groups that might be considered under each of these headings.

Classification

So many different groups influence curriculum decision-makers in so many different ways that it is impossible to plot out with precision the various interactions and points of leverage they have at the various levels of educational systems (Fullan, 2001; Scott, 1999). However, it is possible to list some of the most influential groups and to describe in general ways how their influence works. Tables 16.1 and 16.2 list such groups along with some tentative judgements about their levels of involvement and influence. The list includes both professional and non-professional organizations. Some of the groups listed ordinarily have benign motives, such as improving the quality of education in general. Other groups listed usually have narrower interests.

Decision-makers

Table 16.1 lists some individuals and groups ordinarily considered curriculum decision-makers. Their decisions may range from creating highly detailed and individualized plans for specific classrooms to adopting externally created programmes for use throughout a school district or an entire state.

At the school level, teachers and principals are mainly concerned with decisions that are directly related to day-to-day teaching. Teachers tend to focus on the curricula of their own classrooms and the classrooms of other teachers with whom they work most closely. Principals tend to be more concerned with coordination within curricula or across grade levels (Ornstein and Hunkins, 1993; Wildy *et al.*, 2000). At the district level, superintendents are mainly concerned with decisions about general programmes. Usually they work closely with their school boards or school committees (ordinarily not educational professionals but groups of citizens charged by law with making many administrative decisions for their districts).

At the state (or sometimes even the federal) level, commissioners of education or officers of educational agencies make policy decisions about establishing or terminating total programmes, such as programmes for intellectually talented students.

Politicians

Ministers of Education/Secretaries of State at national and state levels have had, and continue to have, an enormous influence on curriculum, especially during the last few decades. In many cases, individual ministers have initiated major curriculum reforms single-handedly, as a result of their position and

Table 16.1: *Decision-makers/stakeholders*

	Title and Focus	Impact on Schools
Politicians	Ministers of Education/Secretary of State; State/National	High
Superintendents	Superintendents, Chief education officers, Directors general region/state	High
State departments	State/LEAs	High
Assessment boards	State/National	High
Teacher unions	State/National	Medium/High
Parents and school councils/boards	School-focused	Medium/High
Principals/Headmasters Teachers	School-focused School-focused	Medium/High
Students	School-focused	Low
Academics	Universities, TAFE, Further education State/National	Medium/High
Employers	State/National	Medium

Table 16.2: *Influences*

	Examples	Impact on Schools
Professional associations	National Association for the Teaching of English (UK)	Medium (at secondary school level)
Textbook writers	Authors of major texts for primary/elementary and secondary students	Medium
National agencies	Office of Education (USA)	Low
Media	Editorials and feature articles in major daily newspapers; daily television news	Medium/High
Educational consultants	Specialists in reading instruction	High in individual schools
Lobby groups	Environmental groups	Low
The courts	Mandating instruction in a school district	High
Research and testing organizations	Literacy tests	Medium
Commercial sponsorship/contracting out	Sponsorship for a computer laboratory	Medium/High

extremely strong personalities – for example John Dawkins in Australia (Marsh, 1994), David Blunkett and his Prime Minister, Tony Blair, in the United Kingdom (Crump, 1998).

For example, Marsh (1994) analysed Dawkins' efforts as Minister for Education in Australia in the 1980s – 'by using "crisis rhetoric" he steered state ministers into collaborative efforts to produce national statements and profiles in eight learning areas. His statements were largely economics-driven, coupled with assertions that education had failed' (p. 44).

Crump (1998) details the New Labour initiatives by the Blair government to drive skills improvement in schools by management and leadership targets, reinforced by national standards testing, the closure of failing schools and the sacking of teachers. Fullan and Earl (2002), as part of a team of consultants from the University of Toronto to monitor the implementation of national literacy and numeracy strategies in the United Kingdom, conclude that the large-scale reform has been successful in raising literacy and numeracy standards but they consider that the strong initiatives from the centre (top-down) now need to be followed by more local capacity-building and local networking.

It might be argued that the education budget is so large in most countries that it is only politicians who can provide direct levels of accountability to the general public to justify the expenditure. It is certainly the case that politicians have excluded the traditional senior educators and made many changes to the secret garden of curriculum (Lawton, 1980).

Superintendents/Chief Education Officers/Directors General

Senior officers in charge of education systems have different titles in the USA, United Kingdom and Australia, but they are typically responsible for a wide range of educational decisions, even though they delegate the authority in various ways and to varying degrees. Their personalities, modes of public relations and establishment of priorities are highly significant for the achievements of the education system.

From time to time a number of these senior officers have shown a major interest in curriculum and have been driving forces in establishing innovatory practices. For example, Bill Honig in California in the 1980s was instrumental in changing the nature of teaching and learning in that state by initiating frameworks and by aligning state-adopted textbooks and state tests to the frameworks (Ball *et al.*, 1994). In the United Kingdom, William Stubbs was an active exponent of local education authority responsibilities during his time as Director of the Inner London Education Authority (Stubbs, 1981).

State Departments/Local Education Authorities

Especially over the last two decades in the USA, state departments have greatly increased their influence over schooling. Standards-based approaches are currently being strongly supported. States have eagerly accepted these new standards because of purported gains in student academic levels, accountability for student outcomes, inclusion of all students in reform initiatives and flexibility to foster instructional change (Goertz, 2001). For example, 49 states have developed content standards and 48 states have state-wide assessments in subjects (Goertz, 2001).

In the United Kingdom, the implementation of the National Curriculum has brought about a diminution of power and responsibilities of the local education authorities (LEAs). The largest LEA, the Inner London Education Authority, was quickly dismantled by the Conservative government. The provision for schools to opt out of their respective LEA and to operate as grant-maintained schools with direct funding from the central government, has further weakened many LEAs (Whitty, 1995).

In Australia, state education systems, protected under the constitution to be solely responsible for the delivery of education, have maintained their responsibilities and influence but economic rationalism has given enhanced emphasis to standards and efficiency. State-led reforms require schools to produce corporate plans and to be accountable for certain budget elements (Caldwell, 2000).

Assessment Boards

Senior Secondary (Year 12) Examination Boards have a long tradition in the United Kingdom and Australia. They are responsible for developing examinations for matriculation entry into universities and, as a consequence, greatly influence the curriculum taught at senior secondary school levels. In Australia, such boards as the Board of Studies in New South Wales control the curriculum for all schooling levels K-12 but have a major impact on teaching in Years 11 and 12. In the United Kingdom, examination boards such as the Cambridge Examination Board produce syllabuses and examinations at GCSE and GCE (A levels).

Examination boards have traditionally been the preserve of university academics, but over recent decades there have been a considerable number of places allocated to senior secondary school teachers and, more recently, to vocational/ further education personnel. As with other major stakeholders, examination boards are now forming alliances with other groups such as universities, research institutes and industry groups, in their endeavours to undertake curriculum development projects, such as those associated with Standard Assessment Tasks (SATs) in the United Kingdom and profile reporting in Australia.

Teacher Unions

In the United Kingdom and Australia, in particular, teacher unions have been a significant influence upon curriculum. Not unexpectedly, in times of rapid expansion of education, or periods of crisis of funding, teacher unions are especially active.

Over recent decades there has been a disempowering of teacher unions, by design or by default.

According to Burrow and Martin (1998) the reason for the decline in union influence in Australia has been the open hostility by 'economic fundamentalist, right wing governments' (p. 98). They argue that the following tactics have been used:

- state governments have rescinded procedures whereby teachers automatically have payroll deductions for union dues and thereby have put strains on union cash flows;
- the removal of teacher unions from representative and consultative committees;
- the winding up of national bodies that had significant union representation (such as the Australian Teaching Council) or influence (such as the Schools Council);
- federal government financial support to other professional associations and especially principal associations;
- attacks on education standards in public schools, especially literacy and teacher standards.

Parents and School Councils/Boards

Parent influence on curriculum issues occurs most frequently through involvement on school boards/councils. In fact, school boards can be an ideal vehicle for parents and teachers to work together on curriculum decision-making. Yet, school councils can never be the sole or even the most important facet of parent participation. They are just one means of trying to provide teacher–parent–student interaction in decision-making. In the everyday life of a school it is important that there are numerous opportunities for this joint decision-making to occur and that it is not restricted to the relatively few, formal meetings of a school council (Pettit, 1984).

Yet, many parent groups are not well represented in decision-making at the school level. This is especially the case for parents of low socio-economic status and for parents of minority ethnic groups. These groups often need special encouragement and support before they are willing to become involved in decision-making (Maclure and Walker, 2000).

School Principals/Heads

The position of school principal is certainly an exacting one to uphold, as so many different groups and individuals have beliefs about what the school principal should do and should achieve (Lambert, 1998). Parents and community members expect a public-minded, highly principled person who is open to outside initiatives and who will communicate information regularly to them. Some of these expectations may conflict with those of the teachers, who expect their school principal to be an instructional leader and a supporter of curriculum initiatives and to be very visible and active around the school buildings. Students might have other expectations, including a sympathetic counsellor and the final arbiter on matters of justice, discipline and penalties, but above all, an inspirational, charismatic figurehead.

State department officials and senior regional officers expect school principals to be thorough, reliable and efficient, to be capable of implementing and monitoring departmental policies, and not to be overly influenced by vocal minority groups. In total, these beliefs about the role of the school principal contain obvious conflicts and ambiguities. Even if it were possible to rationalize some of these conflicting points of view, it is doubtful whether single individuals could embody all the demanding characteristics. It seems that the public is setting unattainable goals and that only 'superstars' can achieve these standards (Copland, 2001).

Schools in the twenty-first century are being engulfed by multiple innovations and policy changes (Fullan, 1996). Overload and fragmentation take their toll even on the superstar principals – their energy sources become so drained that they run on empty (Loader, 1998a).

Principals have the opportunity to make a number of decisions at school level. They are the critical change agents, even though their styles as leaders may vary, encompassing the bureaucratic, visionary, entrepreneurial or pedagogical (Sergiovanni, 1998).

Southworth (2000) contends that, in the United Kingdom, principals are predominantly managerial. Woods (2000) concurs, pointing out that principals increasingly are subject to 'performativity', the expectation that they perform like enterprising, competitive entrepreneurs. Soder (1999) argues that 'school renewal' is now widely seen as secondary to 'school reform', with its emphasis on standards, high-stakes testing and immediate results.

Teachers

Teachers are involved in all the complexities associated with daily teaching and are responsible for a myriad of classroom decisions. They try to create order and stability in potentially chaotic surroundings.

There are various interpretations about the level of decision-making that could be undertaken by classroom teachers and what actually occurs in practice. Guglielmi and Tatrow (1998) note the heightened job pressures on teachers and consequently their reduced interest in decision-making.

Smyth and Shacklock (1998) argue that there is now a widening gulf between manager-principals and teachers. Principals are so engrossed in financial management and meeting targets that teachers have to take on the role of pedagogical leaders, developing collaborative cultures and teamwork.

Fullan (1993) is more cautionary when he notes that teachers have the potential to be major decision-makers but it depends upon the extent to which they have been able to succeed with their *inner* learning (learning to cope with the immediate environment even if it is adverse) and with their *outer* learning (being able to work, learn and network with colleagues).

The emotions of teaching is also an issue taken up by Hargreaves (1998). Leadership by teachers in periods of rapid change is affected greatly by issues of emotion. 'Teaching is a form of emotional labour and teaching and learning involves emotional understanding' (Hargreaves, 1998, p. 319).

Recently, massive intensifications of teachers' workloads have occurred in many Western countries (Easthope and Easthope, 2000). McMahon (2000) identifies the drives to micro-manage schools and to raise standards as counter-productively placing new strains on how teachers use their time.

Beare (1998) suggests that in future teachers will deliver or apply specialist knowledge under contract – they will be one-person businesses. The traditional decision-making structures operating in schools will decline.

Students

Students are an important element in the learning environment and are the ultimate consumers. In some classes teachers may seek out students' views on teaching content and methods, as might be expected in a democratic learning environment.

Of course students affect curriculum policy by mediating it – they come to classrooms with different backgrounds and as a result transform the taught curriculum in various ways (Schubert, 1986). Students can provide vision and be constructive participants in curriculum planning, so long as trusting and supportive environments are developed by teachers and administrators (Holdsworth, 1993).

Although it might be assumed that student decision-making has the potential to occur in secondary schools there are many factors operating that inhibit student participation. Wilson (2002) cites some of these inhibiting factors as teachers' accountability mentality, management priorities for the school, and an unwillingness to provide training for students for decision-making roles.

Academics

It has long been argued that academics are important decision-makers, especially at the secondary school level, as universities dictate the academic curriculum required of senior secondary school students. In many countries senior university academics are active participants on examination boards and do become involved in policy decisions about syllabus content and examinations. However, increasingly they are just one of the players on examination boards, as a result of the emerging roles being shaped by senior Technical and Further Education (TAFE) personnel and industry representatives.

Although key academics were consulted for specific tasks relating to national curriculum initiatives (for example, P. Black on assessment in the United Kingdom and P. Fensham on science education in Australia), academics in general were largely bypassed in the 1980s and 1990s. Their influence occurred via *post-hoc* criticisms, such as Australian academics criticizing the Mathematics National Profile (Guttman, 1993; Ellerton and Clements, 1994) – 'the idea of wresting the control of school curricula from vested interests in universities, has been one of the underlying but relatively silent forces in the national curriculum movement' (p. 314).

In Australia over the last decade, under the chairmanship of Professor Stuart Macintyre, academic members of the Civics Expert Group (Macintyre, 1994) produced a strategic plan for developing citizenship education (Kennedy, 1997). The academics have been less influential since 1996 when new political priorities and government department plans for citizenship education (DEST and the Curriculum Corporation) caused some changes in direction and emphasis (Mellor *et al.*, 2002).

Employers

Employer groups have been a relatively new but increasingly powerful player in the education stakes (Fullan, 2001). In many countries, award restructuring, skills training standards and economic instrumentalism ideology have led many employer groups to agitate for a greater voice in the curriculum of schools. Various vocational programmes, generic and core skills orientations and vocational awards have been implemented as a result of initiatives by these groups.

Economic arguments and rationalities are being used to justify changes to secondary school curriculum (Poole, 1992). In the USA, Apple (1988) notes that schools must be brought more closely into line with policies that will 'reindustrialize' and 'rearm' America so that it will be more economically competitive.

Various writers support the emphasis upon vocation education and the need for schools to prepare students for the working world. Teachers do not have all the knowledge or the skills to prepare students effectively for the world of work (Price, 1991). It is likely that employer groups will continue to have a significant influence on curriculum, especially at the senior secondary school level.

Influences

Professional Associations

Professional associations exercise their influence at national, state and local levels but especially at the national level. Their activities can include lobbying for or against political actions; publishing curriculum guidelines and producing scope and sequence charts; and establishing networks, workshops and conferences (Glatthorn, 1987).

In the USA various professional associations are currently playing a major role in the development of national standards, such as the National Council of Teachers of Mathematics and the National Council for the Social Studies. Professional associations have had mixed fortunes in the United Kingdom and Australia over recent decades. In the 1970s in the United Kingdom, professional associations such as the National Association for the Teaching of English (NATE) were very influential (Stenhouse, 1980), but their influence waned with the implementation of the National Curriculum. In Australia, professional associations were largely ignored in the development of national statements and profiles (Marsh, 1994) but subsequent intensive lobbying has now enabled national associations to play a role in developing teacher development materials for their respective learning area profiles (Ellerton and Clements, 1994).

Textbook Writers

Textbooks are a major learning source for many students. They can provide a core of important learning; up-to-date information; instruction on basic skills; and an introduction or overview of particular topics. Good textbooks are often very popular with teachers because they bring together a massive amount of important material in one volume, thus saving the busy teacher considerable time.

Writers of popular textbooks can be extremely influential about what is taught and how it is taught. If teachers rely very heavily upon a textbook they are likely to accept the content structure and associated pedagogy put forward by a textbook author.

In countries where textbooks are selected by central committees or state committees, a selected few can dominate the market. In several states of the USA, such as Texas and California, state textbook adoptions are a major activity and wield a significant influence on school education. It is interesting to note that alignment policies, especially in California, have required textbook publishers to ensure that their publications are congruent with state curriculum frameworks and state tests.

Some writers, such as Apple (1993) and Pinar *et al.* (1995), are concerned about the influence of textbooks:

They are at once the results of political, economic and cultural activities, battles and compromises. They are conceived, designed and authored by real people with real interests. They are published with the political and economic constraints of markets, resources and power. And what texts mean and how they are used are fought over by communities with distinctly different commitments and by teachers and students as well. (Apple, 1993, p. 46)

The World Wide Web (WWW) is rapidly becoming a de facto textbook for many teachers and students. The WWW has many advantages. It can provide data from a variety of sources all over the world and is available 24 hours a day. Most importantly, it is a cheaper form of accessing data than traditional sources and so is likely to become increasingly attractive for education systems.

National/Federal Agencies

In a number of countries national departments of education can have a major influence upon curriculum but there can be peaks and troughs. For example, in the USA the National Institute of Education/Department of Education oscillated between major and minor involvement in curriculum matters during the 1980s and 1990s due to different political priorities.

The election of the New Labour government in the United Kingdom in 1997 led to increased powers for national agencies with its emphases upon targets, national standards testing, and the Office for Standards in Education (OFSTED) inspections (Macpherson, 1998; Crump, 1998). The increase in national agency control is very evident in the recently released policy paper 'Education and Skills: Investment for Reform' (Department for Education and Skills, 2002). The 'transformation' of secondary education focused upon in this paper will be achieved by the following centralist initiatives:

1. radical reform of school leadership;
2. radical reform of school structures;
3. radical reform of teaching and learning;
4. radical reform of partnerships beyond the classroom.
   (Department for Education and Skills, 2002, p. 2)

The creation of the super-ministry Department of Employment, Education and Training (DEET) in Australia in 1987 produced a major 'implementation arm' for federal ministers. Under the incumbent Minister's direction, DEET established priorities, consonant with political priorities and, in many cases, was able to provide substantial funding to ensure that tangible and visible outcomes were achieved. The current national agency has been renamed the Department for Education, Science and Training.

Media

The media, through newspapers and televisions become increasingly influential over the last decade, due in no small measure to the fact that the topic of education is very newsworthy. Some daily newspapers provide regular education supplements while all newspapers run major feature articles on specific issues from time to time.

The news media rarely deal fully with complex issues involved in education, yet the complexity is precisely what curriculum decision-makers must deal with if their decisions are to be soundly based. Often, therefore, news media create unrealistic expectations in the public about education, while at other times picking up and heightening unrealistic expectations that the public already holds. In either case, the news media indirectly exert influence on curriculum decision-makers because of what they have chosen to report about education and how they have chosen to report it. New sources of news via the Internet also include these biases (Futoran *et al.*, 1995).

Educational Consultants

Educational consultants are specialists who are involved in discussing current or potential problems of a class, department or school. In some cases they may be seconded teachers, located in regional or head offices of systems and available at call to assist classroom teachers. Other consultants may include university lecturers and management personnel, external to the system. Consultants have the potential to be very influential for individual teachers or groups of teachers at particular schools because they can pass on a variety of professional skills relating to such areas as curriculum development, management, pastoral care.

Lobby Groups

Lobby groups are always present in society but become very active and conspicuous when controversy arises over particular topics or policies. The media is always eager to publicize the actions of lobby groups because of their newsworthy nature. Kirst and Walker (1971) contend that there are two kinds of policy-making processes undertaken by lobby groups: normal policy-making and crisis policy-making. The day-to-day activities of lobby groups do not gain media attention but the crisis activities certainly do. Lobby groups can be very influential on school curriculum matters.

The Courts

In a number of countries, but especially in the USA, court cases involving teachers, students and parents are becoming very common (Fischer *et al.*,

1995). In the USA court judges have made decisions about curriculum such as the mandating of specific tasks, methods and materials that schools must use (McNeil, 1985).

Research and Testing Organizations

Large research and testing organizations that are involved in developing and have responsibility for major educational tests have a major influence on curriculum. In the USA testing agencies such as the Educational Testing Service (ETS) have largely produced a 'national' curriculum (McNeil, 1985). Standardized tests for college admission have a major influence on what teachers present to students at the senior secondary school level. National standardized reading and mathematics tests greatly influence the content of the elementary (primary) school curriculum.

In the United Kingdom, the National Foundation for Educational Research (NFER) has played a similar role in the provision of testing and its association with the monitoring of student performance through the Assessment of Performance Unit (APU), set up in 1974. Yet, because standardized testing is far less an educational preoccupation in the United Kingdom, the NFER has had less influence on schools than the ETS.

The Australian Council of Educational Research has developed into a major influence upon curriculum through its research projects on schooling (for example, King, 1998; McGaw *et al.*, 1992); its single-handed validation of national profiles in the eight learning areas (Marsh, 1994); its subsequent development of computer-aided teacher development packages for using the national profiles (Forster, 1994); and its leadership in sponsoring major curriculum seminars and conferences.

In addition, in many countries there are numerous research organizations that undertake public opinion surveys on educational topics (for example Gallup polls in the USA: Drake, 1991) and are successful in tendering for major government-sponsored contracts on specific educational issues (for example, the Institute of Public Affairs: Nahan and Rutherford, 1993).

Commercial Sponsorship/Contracting Out

In a period of privatization and corporate sponsorship, schools are becoming increasingly involved in sponsorship arrangements with private industry. To a certain extent, schools have always been involved in seeking sponsorship support from the local community – for example local firms advertising in the school magazine or paying for the printing of a programme for a school sporting event.

The opportunities and necessity for sponsorship have widened considerably. It is no longer a matter of gaining sponsorship to acquire resources or to supplement ongoing minor expenditure. For some schools it is rapidly becoming their life-blood. It is very evident that sponsors have the potential to greatly influence the curriculum of a school. Long-term sponsorships could be very helpful and produce a positive commitment from the staff and local community, so long as the integrity of the school and its goals are not compromised (Harty, 1990).

Other Categorizations

The above listing of decision-makers, stakeholders and influences is derived from the assumption that spheres of influence are greatest at the school level or state/national level. This is, of course, a highly simplified account of what really happens.

Walker (1990) contends that a better understanding of stakeholders is obtained if consideration is given to the 'needs' and their potential areas of 'control'. For example, school principals need support from teachers and resources; their controls include subject offerings, school timetable, access to parents and community. A Secretary of Education (Federal Minister for Education) needs political support, compliance from states and districts and expertise; controls include federal budget, federal grants, authority of position.

The interactions among the many groups and individuals, arenas and decisions can become quite complex and produce unexpected results. New coalitions of groups keep on occurring. Success factors in one period and in a particular context do not necessarily provide success at other times and in other contexts.

Reflections and Issues

1. Within your situation which agencies/groups appear to have the greatest influence on the school curriculum? Give reasons for your answer.
2. The dominant role of textbooks as a primary factor in the planning of the curriculum is further illustrated by the ways in which citizens and public agencies seek to control the choice of textbooks used. Discuss.
3. To what extent is it legitimate for politicians to make decisions about schooling? Are there other significant stakeholders? How can they coexist? Give examples to support your argument.
4. Consider the impact of national/federal versus state initiatives in curriculum. Which have been the most significant for you in your situation? Explain.
5. Describe a recent alliance by two or more stakeholders associated with an innovatory curriculum or curriculum policy. Why do you think the alliance occurred? How successful has it been? Give reasons.
6. 'School children are for sale to the highest bidder ... Today's corporations are slicker, more sophisticated in their marketing strategies than they were a decade ago. Intrusions into the classroom by business interests continue unabated' (Harty, 1990, p. 77). Are schools been exploited by these initiatives? Give exam-

ples that have occurred in your community. What checks and balances would you advocate?

7. How might greater harmony be developed between competing stakeholders on matters of curriculum? Choose two or more stakeholders and give examples to illustrate your argument.

8. 'Much of the information the media offers about education comes from single troubled schools in large cities' (Drake, 1991). Do the media provide a balanced picture of schooling? If not, what steps might be taken to provide a more balanced coverage?

17 Action Research/Teachers as Researchers

Introduction

According to Calhoun (2002) action research is about seeking to understand and acting on the best we know. As professionals, teachers want to grow – to develop new insights, skills and practices (Elliott and Chan, 2002). Yet, action research can also be regarded as a very demanding professional activity because it requires introspection which can challenge an individual's personal practice and beliefs (Hannay and MacFarlane, 1998).

Some Basic Terms

Stenhouse (1975) referred to action research as a self-reflexive process that is systematic and public.

Kemmis and McTaggart (1984, p. 6) describe action research 'as a method for practitioners to live with the complexity of real experience, while at the same time, striving for concrete improvement'.

Calhoun (2002) has a wider definition indicative of her interest in school-wide and district-wide action research: '[action research] asks educators to study their practice and its content, explore the research base for ideas, compare what they find to their current practice, participate in training to support needed changes, and study the effects on themselves and their students and colleagues' (p. 18).

According to Wallace (1987), action research originated in the USA and its name was coined by Collier in 1945. It can be traced to Lewin's (1948) studies of the impact of change on community workers, originally referred to as action-training-research. Subsequently, other educators such as Corey (1953) used action research with groups of teachers to improve their schools through democratic means. Although action research was largely forgotten by educators in the 1960s, it was revived in the 1970s as a result of the efforts of Stenhouse (1973) and Elliott (1975) in the United Kingdom and Clark (1976) and Tikunoff et al. (1978) in the USA.

This revival continued in the 1980s and 1990s and is still ongoing in the twenty-first century in the United Kingdom (Elliott, 1999; McKernan, 1993), USA (Feldman et al., 1999; Noffke, 1997; Calhoun, 2002), Canada (Clandinin, 1986; Hannay and Seller, 1998) and Australia (Grundy, 1982; Carr and Kemmis, 1986; Brooker et al., 2000).

Action research can be conducted entirely by individual teachers, by small groups of teachers, or by school-wide or district-wide groups.

Frequently, 'external facilitators' are invited to enhance the processes. There is some evidence that without ongoing support from facilitators, teachers find it difficult to sustain their action research. Calhoun (2002) argues that district-wide action research projects can benefit from multiple sources of data as an information source to guide practice. Adequate organizational support (for example, externally run workshops, external technical assistance) and external knowledge bases can greatly assist action research teams.

Action research involves groups of teachers in systematically analysing educational problems of concern to them, planning programmes, enacting them, evaluating what they have done, and then repeating the cycle if necessary. As such, action research is very much central to the approaches to curriculum planning and development taken by progressive educators throughout the twentieth century and currently. First, they identify a field of action. (The implementation of an innovative curriculum might fall within this field.) Next, they develop and then enact a specific plan. Throughout the steps of development and enactment the teachers continuously monitor what they are thinking and doing: observing, reflecting, discussing, learning, and replanning. Eventually they evaluate what they have enacted in some kind of formal sense, using what they have discovered as the basis for revising plans and actions as they repeat the spiral (see Figure 17.1).

Making a Start with Action Research

Kemmis and McTaggart (1984, pp. 18–19) suggest that participants in action research should commence by 'addressing questions' such as:

- What is happening now?
- In what sense is this problematic?
- What can I do about it?

And then go on to consider:

- How important is the issue to me?
- How important is it to my students?
- What opportunities are there to explore the area?
- What are the constraints of my situation?

To do action research, according to Kemmis and MacTaggart (1988), a person or group must undertake four fundamental processes or 'moments':

(a) Develop a 'plan' of action to improve what is already happening:
- it must be forward looking;
- it must be strategic in that risks have to be taken.
(b) 'Act' to implement the plan:
- it is deliberate and controlled;

Figure 17.1: *The action research spiral*

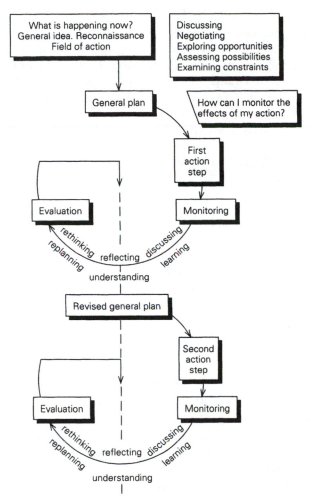

Source: Kemmis (1982).

- it takes place in real time and encounters real constraints;
- it may involve some negotiations and compromises.

(c) 'Observe' the effects of action in the context in which it occurs:
- it is planned;
- it provides the basis for critical self-reflection;
- it must be open-minded.

(d) 'Reflect' on these effects as a basis for further planning and a succession of cycles:
- it recalls action;

- it comprehends the issues and circumstances
- it judges whether the effects were desirable.

Although these fundamental processes are useful in describing likely phases of action, McKernan (1991) argues that teachers need additional assistance in selecting techniques for collecting data (see Table 17.1). For example, teachers can decide from a range of observational techniques (for example, unstructured observation in a classroom by a teacher-colleague) or non-observational techniques (for example, getting students in a class to complete a questionnaire). Alternatively, a group of teachers might decide to get technical assistance from an external consultant in collecting appropriate data, especially product-centred data. A practical/collaborative approach might focus more upon process-oriented data.

Modes of Action Research

Action research cannot simply be characterized as following the basic steps of a spiral. There are additional points to consider. Feldman *et al.* (1999) contend that action research is located in a three-dimensional space, the three dimensions being *purpose*, *theoretical orientation* and *types of reflection*.

Purposes Dimension

There can be a variety of purposes for action research including:

- professional purposes including staff development;
- promoting school reform (Hursh, 1995);
- reforming teacher education and increasing the problem-solving skills of pre-service teachers (Price and Vallie, 2000);
- changing teaching practice (Burnaford *et al.*, 1996);
- personal purposes to better understand self and others (Noffke, 1997);
- political purposes – to critique the nature of teachers' work and workplaces (Noffke, 1997);
- to create social change (Carr and Kemmis, 1986).

Theoretical Orientation Dimension

Technical

- directed by a person or persons with special expertise;
- the aim is to obtain more efficient practices as perceived by the directors;
- the activities are product-centred;
- operates within existing values and constraints.

Table 17.1: Techniques available to teachers

Observational
- unstructured observation in a classroom by a teacher-colleague
- participant observation
- structured observation using checklists or rating scales by the teacher or a teacher-colleague
- anecdotal records completed by the teacher or a teacher-colleague
- short case study accounts of a project or an event
- keeping a diary or journal
- photographs, video tape-recording, audio recording

Non-observational
- attitude scales completed by students
- questionnaires completed by students
- interviews of selected students
- document analysis

Technical action/research
- directed by a person or persons with special expertise
- the aim is to obtain more efficient practices as perceived by the directors
- the activities are product-centred
- operates within existing values and constraints

Practical/collaborative action research
- directed by the group
- the aim is to develop new practices
- the activities are process-oriented
- personal wisdom is used to guide action

This orientation is towards control.

Practical/Collaborative

- directed by the group;
- the aim is to develop new practices;
- the activities are process-oriented;
- personal wisdom is used to guide action.

This orientation is based upon consensus.

Emancipatory

- directed by the group;
- the aim is to develop new practices and/or change the constraints;
- involves a shared radical consciousness.

This orientation arises from a critical perspective.

Tripp (1987) suggests that emancipatory action research is very rare because it can only occur in circumstances where a critical mass of radical participants can work together over a considerable period of time.

Type of Reflection Dimension

- individual, autobiographical reflection to examine the literal meaning of his or her stories;
- collaborative reflection – sharing personal theories;
- collaborative reflection with groups in a larger context/wider communities.

Limiting Factors

According to Hannay and MacFarlane (1998) 'Action research is perhaps the most demanding professional learning activity for a practitioner as it requires introspection which can challenge the individual's personal practice and beliefs. Participants engaged in action research need to have the personal confidence and system support to challenge their teaching and learning practice' (p. 36).

Carr and Kemmis (1986) identify problems of lack of autonomy and lack of emancipation as major limiting factors. McKernan (1993) lists the major limiting factors as:

- lack of time to do action research;
- lack of resources;
- school organization (for example, problems of timetable);
- lack of research skills and knowledge.

Impact of Action Research upon Schools

A number of authors such as Zeichner (1993), Cochran-Smith (1994) and Calhoun (2002) use terms such as 'overwhelming evidence', 'real power' and 'transformational qualities' of action research. The many claimed advantages of action research can be summarized as follows:

Positive

- increased self-confidence for teachers;
- feelings of empowerment;
- greater school–staff collegiality;
- greater willingness to experiment;
- involved teaching practice and performance;
- increased understanding of research processes;
- increased practical knowledge;
- increased understanding and reflection;
- increased teacher autonomy (Cochran-Smith and Lytle, 1993; Burnaford *et al.*, 1994).

Yet, there can be a variety of negative impacts due to barriers and impediments. These include the following:

Negative

- limited impact on school staff not directly involved;
- limited impact because teachers are not allocated time or resources to engage in action research;
- teachers are not free to make changes that they might feel are educationally worthwhile;
- teachers are not skilled in examining and reflecting upon what is actually happening in classrooms – it takes considerable time to develop these skills;
- difficulties can arise about areas of confidentiality such as who has control of materials gathered and who has access to them (Beattie, 1989; G.H. Bell, 1988; Day *et al.*, 1990).

Concluding Comments

Although action research is complex and involves a number of tensions, there is considerable evidence from many countries that it is a successful vehicle for educational change.

Reflections and Issues

1. To what extent do you consider that school-based curriculum development (SBCD) has encouraged action research initiatives? If you have been involved recently in SBCD describe your experiences in this regard.

2. 'Action research provides a way of working which links theory and practice into the one whole: ideas-in-action' (Kemmis and McTaggart, 1984, p. 5). From your experience does this happen? Give details.

3. Action research involves values and norms of behaviour. What are the rights and responsibilities of participants in action research? Can this cause unrealistic demands or expectations on the part of participants/administrators?

4. 'Emancipatory action research is essentially a political act – to change the consciousness of and constraints for those other than the immediate participants' (Tripp, 1987, p. 11). To what extent can action research transform practices, understandings and situations?

5. 'One of the characteristics of action research is that it is research which people get on with and do quickly ... Academics are watchers of the world: teachers are actors in it. Teachers make decisions and search for "right" decisions' (Bassey, 1990, p. 161). Comment upon how action research differs from traditional academic research. What are its strengths and limitations compared with academic research?

6. 'Action research stands or falls by its demonstrable relevance to the practical ethic of education, as well as whether it is reliable, valid and refutable as a methodology' (Adelman, 1989, p. 177). Have published studies demonstrated the relevance of action research? Is it difficult to prove the quality (reliability, validity) of action research? What solutions can you offer to this dilemma?

7. 'Action research provides the necessary link between self-evaluation and professional development' (Winter, 1989, p.10). Explain why reflection and self-evaluation are so important to action research. Should action research lead to actual changes in practice? If so, does this provide professional development for teachers?

8. 'To place the teachers' classroom practice at the centre of the action for action researchers is to put the most exposed and problematic aspect of the teachers' world at the centre of scrutiny and negotiation' (Goodson, 1991, p. 141). Do you agree that it could be undesirable to start a collaborative mode of research from a study of classroom practice? Are teachers sensitive to these studies? Are there advantages which outweigh the possibility of exposing teacher vulnerability?

18 Parent–Teacher Participation

Introduction

There is widespread support among educators and the community for the notion that parents have a major role to play in education and in schooling in particular (Cavarretta, 1998). What is more difficult to get agreement upon is how to nurture a collaborative relationship between parents and teachers to enhance students' learning. There are various interpretations about activities that are perceived to be effective or ineffective. In this chapter some of the historical and political contexts are examined, along with existing practices in various states and territories.

Some Basic Terms

The ways that parents work with schools can vary enormously. For many parents their role is of limited involvement via attendance at:

- parent–teacher nights;
- school sports days;
- fetes;
- tuck shops;
- working bees;
- parents and citizens/parents and friends meetings;
- school council meetings.

McGilp and Michael (1994) sum up types of parent involvement in terms of: 'as audience, spectators, fund raisers, aides, organizers, instructors, learners, policy makers, decision makers and advocates of school happenings' (p. 2).

As noted by Vick (1994) parents are usually on the sidelines when it comes to their children's education. 'Involvement' means very limited opportunities whereby parents undertake activities that have been designed and initiated by the school principal and staff. 'Participation' is to do with sharing or influencing decisions on policy matters and includes an active decision-making role in such areas as school policy, staffing and professional development of staff, budget, grounds and buildings, management of resources and the school curriculum. Participation can involve students too, especially at the secondary school.

Claims and Counterclaims about Parent Participation

A major reason for parent participation in schools is a powerful pedagogical one: 'the closer the parent is to the education of the child, the greater the impact on child development and education achievement' (Fullan, 1991, p. 227).

Of course this is a gross generalization and, although many educators support it, can it be verified? There are likely to be all kinds of variations related to the age and gender of students and cultural, ethnic and class differences.

There are a number of *claims* in favour of parent participation (Table 18.1).

- Parents are also teachers and can and should support the teaching that goes on in classrooms. Parents have their own curriculum and teaching styles that are used in out-of-school learning situations (and in increasing numbers they are choosing home schooling: Finn, 1998). Hence there is a need for close collaboration between parents and teachers if children are to gain the full potential from their in-school and out-of-school learning experiences.
- Parents possess a variety of skills, talents and interests that can enrich the curriculum in so many ways beyond the capabilities of any one classroom teacher, no matter how talented he or she happens to be (Stevenson, 1998). Having a number of parents as active participants in a school will create a multiplier effect because of the energies, enthusiasm and motivation generated by these additional adults (West, 1993).
- If parents become involved in schools they begin to understand the complexities of the teaching roles and structures. Too often parents are swayed by media accounts that frequently present derogatory accounts about schools, teachers and students (Dodd, 1998). If parents can experience at first hand the complicated issues that can arise in the school environment they are less likely to be influenced by superficial media accounts (see Table 18.1). As a specific example, research studies have demonstrated that when parents are employed as paid teacher-aides in a school, they have more positive attitudes about schooling and their children attending the same school develop better attitudes towards their work (Melaragno *et al.*, 1981).
- Parents have a democratic right and responsibility to further their children's education in whatever ways they can (Allen, 1990). Other writers argue that democratic decision-making rarely operates in other institutions and agencies so why should it apply to schools (Lareau, 1986)?
- Parent participation on school councils and in the general governance of a school contributes to student learning at that school. However, research evidence undertaken in the USA (Bowles, 1980) and the United Kingdom (Mortimer *et al.*, 1988) did not find any empirical

Table 18.1: Claims in favour of parent participation

- Parent participation will generally lead to improved student learning, intellectually, socially and emotionally
- Parent participation increases richness and variety of the school learning environment because of a wide range of skills that can be provided by parents
- It increases the sense of identity for the local school community
- it enables parents to understand education processes more fully and to support the goals of schooling
- By increasing the number of interest groups involved in education there is greater likelihood that the interests of all students will be taken into account
- Parents and other citizens have the right in democratic countries to participate in school decision-making

support for this contention. Fantini (1980) noted that the participating adults on councils benefited from their experiences but there was no evidence to confirm or reject any impact on student learning. Hatch (1998) argues that increases in student learning do occur when parents, teachers and students participate in intensive projects (see Table 18.1).

There are also a number of *counterclaims* about why parents should not participate actively in school decision-making (see Table 18.2):

- Schools are dominated by middle-class norms. In schools where there is active participation by parents, these tend to be articulate, well-educated parents. Parents who cannot speak English, who have difficulty communicating well in groups, or who are poorly educated, are usually not represented (Cohn-Varas and Grose, 1998). That is, a significant number of parents are poorly equipped to be active participants in school decision-making (Power and Clark, 2000).
- It places additional burdens of time on the teachers. There is more likelihood that parents will be contacting teachers during out-of-school hours – teachers could be constantly on call to various demands, both trivial and important, and teacher exhaustion and 'burn-out' is a very real problem. It is small wonder that research studies indicate that only a minority of teachers in schools have goals and programmes for parent participation. For example, Rosenholtz's (1989) study showed that the

Table 18.2: Claims against parent participation

- Many parents do not have the necessary problem-solving and communication skills to be effective participants
- Many parents make conscious decisions not to participate and as a result a small number of articulate parents can monopolize the decision-making
- School staff are sometimes reluctant or opposed to parent participation activities
- Governments have not devolved professional authority to parents and community – the rhetoric is stronger than the reality
- Parents are being encouraged to be individual consumer-citizens and to see schooling as another product in the market place

majority of teachers were in 'stuck' schools rather than 'moving' schools. Teachers from 'stuck' schools held no goals for parent participation while teachers in 'moving' schools 'focussed their efforts on involving parents with academic content, thereby bridging the learning chasm between home and school' (p. 152). In another study Becker (1981) surveyed 3700 primary school teachers and 600 principals and concluded that 'very few appear to devote any systematic effort to making sure that parental involvement at home accomplishes particular learning goals in a particular way' (p. 22).

- Parents and community members should not be active participants because it leads to a reduction in professional responsibilities of teachers:

No teacher's school or work should be in any way controlled by the decisions of any non-professional or unpaid body or person, except with the teacher's concurrence. (NSW Teachers Federation, 1976, as reported in Hunt, 1981, p. 4)

An Australian Council of Educational Research (ACER) survey of over 7000 school stakeholders which culminated in the report 'Making Schools more Effective' (McGaw *et al.*, 1992), revealed some opposition by school respondents to parent participation, namely: 'The principal concern was that inappropriate roles for lay people were being envisaged and pressed on schools and that this development undervalued the professional role and contribution of teachers' (p. 94).

- Parents are being increasingly perceived by governments to be 'consumer-citizens' (Woods, 1988). That is, parents operate largely as individual consumers in making decisions about schooling and schooling practices for their children. They rarely share school-related interests with other parents or lack the opportunity to do so:

They do not constitute a monolithic group. Individualism and difference (in priorities, preference, philosophy) characterizes the consumer-citizens. (Woods, 1988, p. 328)

A Continuum of Parent Participation

Various accounts in the educational literature refer to 'tapping parent power' and 'effective parent participation in schooling'. A number have been written by individual enthusiasts or vested interest groups and so their laudatory comments are not surprising (for example, Morris, 1992; Gamage, 1992; Meadows, 1993; Scherer, 1998). To provide a balanced picture it is useful to distinguish between the different activities/roles that might be undertaken by parents and depict them on a continuum (see Figure 18.1). The activities range from 'one-

Figure 18.1: Continuum of parent participation

One-way information giving	Reporting progress	Special events	Sharing of ideas	Parent assistance at school in non-instruction	Parent assistance at school in instruction	Governance	Interaction partnerships
• Notices sent home • Posters	• Home–school notebooks • Call-in times • Newsletters • Telephone calls	• Picnics • Art shows • Concerts • Open days • Tuckshops • Working bees	• Seminars • Classroom observation days • Informal discussions	• Playground • Assistance on excursions • Liaison with local business • Organizing sports days • Preparing art material	• Guest speakers • Leaders on school camps • Teaching various skills	• Chairing subcommittees • Members of school council	• Specific parent–teacher working groups

way information giving' to 'interactive partnerships' and there are a myriad of possible positions in between these two extremes of passive and active.

The examples listed in the second column of the continuum in Figure 18.1 are simply 'reporting progress' to parents. Variations of this category can include parent–teacher conferences. These face-to-face meetings can be most satisfying to the parent and to the teacher, but few parents tend to take advantage of this opportunity because of their busy daily schedule or their reticence about appearing personally at the school (MacLure and Walker, 2000). Teachers will often complain that the parents they really need to meet to discuss urgent school problems do not come to parent–teacher conferences.

Home–school notebooks are another interesting variation whereby a parent and a teacher correspond with each other in a notebook that is sent regularly between the two participants. It requires, of course, a substantial commitment of time by both parties and a willingness to maintain a regular schedule. Yet it does have the potential for keeping contact between the teacher and parents and is a reasonably effective and time-saving alternative to face-to-face meetings.

In addition, teachers are likely to request parents to be involved in a number of learning activities with their children at home (e.g. giving reading assistance and listening to reading, home tutoring in other subjects). Research studies have demonstrated that teacher requests to parents for assistance are likely to be far more effective if individualized instructions and/or training are provided and if there are mechanisms for monitoring parents' and children's progress in the home instruction (Fullan, 1991; Finn, 1998).

Special events for parents are depicted in the third column of Figure 18.1. These can take various forms including parent evenings, open days, concerts and plays. Such events enable teachers to demonstrate certain special student skills (for example: dance routines, art work), but they also provide an opportunity for teachers and parents to interact socially. Special occasions like these can enable a positive rapport to be developed between individual parents and a teacher.

Fund-raising activities have also been included under 'special events' although some parents might prefer to describe them as 'special chores'! Resources are always scarce in any school – funds are always needed to purchase additional library books or sporting equipment or microcomputers. Parents are usually very willing to be involved in fund-raising activities such as school fetes, jumble sales, cake stalls and managing a school canteen if they can see that the funds generated will provide additional resources that will benefit their children. However, it is very limited if this is the only contact that parents have with their school. Fortunately, the availability of federal funds in the form of direct grants to schools rather than subsidy schemes has to some extent reduced the need for parent organizations to devote most of their energies to fund-raising.

Sharing of ideas, as indicated in the fourth column in Figure 18.1, typically takes the form of informal discussions, special seminars and workshops

(Gorman and Balter, 1997). The seminars in particular, if held on the weekends or in the evenings, can be valuable occasions for parents and school staff to share ideas about school goals, values analysis, sex education/AIDS, mathematics skills, etc.

Parents can be involved in assisting school staff with a number of non-instructional activities. At the primary school level in particular, parents are in considerable demand to assist as additional supervisors for excursions and visits. If handled sensitively by the school principals, developing a group of volunteer parents for these activities can establish strong links between them and their school. More and more, parents are being sought after to assist school staff with a number of instructional activities (see Figure 18.1). To a certain extent, changes in employment patterns and resultant early retirement and redundancy packages have enabled parents to become available and willing to take on some of these tasks (Halstead, 1994).

In the junior primary school, parents are often sought after to assist with reading and miming stories to small groups of children and also to assist with various art and craft activities. Parents possess a wide range of specialist skills that can be a welcome and varied addition to the school curriculum. For example, Love (1986, p.4) lists the activities provided by eighteen parents who carry our specialist teaching at his secondary school for periods of half a day per week: maths; art; library; knitting and crochet; job interviews; tennis; social studies; choir; and fitting and turning (metalwork).

Governance activities by parents is in the penultimate column in Figure 18.1. Many school councils/boards make major decisions about staffing, school building, resources and curriculum for their school.

No outstandingly successful prototype for school councils has yet been found. Various combinations of membership, functions and legal status have been initiated, but these initial versions are often found to be unsuitable and different versions have replaced them.

Intended Practices and Actual Outcomes

To date there have been few accounts in the literature about how parents operate within school communities. It is therefore not known what percentage of parent communities operate at the different points on the continuum depicted in Figure 18.1. For example, there have been some accounts of successful governance by school councils (Gamage, 1993; Knight, 1995) but they are relatively few in number. Some parents maintain social networks among other parents, which can lead to very active participation at a local school (Sheldon, 2002).

It may be that only small numbers of parents are involved in the other categories listed in Figure 18.1. Although governments establish structures by legislation for parent participation in schools there are enormous difficulties in bringing about a relocation of power and in many instances 'toothless tigers' have been established (Pettit, 1987).

The problem is multifaceted, and the blame does not lie solely with any one group. It is true that there are difficulties for parents, many of whom venture into the school environment with various anxieties, are considerably overwhelmed and are often poorly informed about typical school activities.

According to Power and Clark (2000) the problems that parents experience are not imaginary: 'Their sense of frustration, and often humiliation, of consultations with teachers is genuinely felt' (p. 44).

An area of major concern in Australia is Aboriginal parents and the extent to which their views and concerns are acted upon by school administrators. McInerney's (1989) study noted that Aboriginal parents (despite negative media portrayals) hold positive attitudes towards education. A typical Aboriginal response was 'Without proper schooling our children have no future' (p. 47). Yet, these parents were also concerned about negative consequences of attending school, such as:

- my child receives no praise or support from school;
- my child is ridiculed by others;
- even if my child does well at school he still can't get work.

McTaggart (1984, p. 12) notes that: 'Parents' knowledge of what goes on in schools tends to be restricted to the treatment of educational problems given by the media ... The images are both incomplete and confrontationist' .

For parents of lower socio-economic backgrounds, the problem is especially severe (Zady *et al.*, 1998; Mutimer, 1999). They often perceive the school council to be an appendage of the principal, espousing traditional middle-class values. They often consider that the problems of their immediate neighbourhood are not translated into programmes at the school. These parents need special encouragement and support before they will become regular participants in the school community. Andrews (1985, p. 30) maintains that the typical response from such parents tends to be 'Every other time I've complained or spoken out too much, my kid has been picked on' or 'It doesn't affect my kid, she or he is doing OK'.

Teachers' language to the lay person can be almost incomprehensible. Not surprisingly, teachers receive new training in the academic disciplines and theory building of various kinds and as a result of interaction with their peers establish their educational jargon. This is particularly evident when teachers are asked to explain to parents why a child is not coping with a subject. In many cases, teachers use technical terms that lay persons simply cannot understand. MacLure and Walker (2000) contend that the discourse between teachers and parents is rather like the discourse between doctors and patients. The teacher is in control, chooses the topics of discussion and dominates the interaction.

Perhaps all stakeholder groups are to blame for building up their unique set of language modes, norms and expectations. Parents can certainly build up their barriers around their family life, interests and ambitions (Kenway *et al.*, 1987). These barriers take a considerable amount of time and goodwill to break down. Boomer (1986) refers to this as a kind of: 'Educational apartheid . . . they develop their own special forms of protection; an array of the equivalent of moats, barricades, deflection and passwords' (Boomer, 1986, p.1).

In the final analysis, it is likely that all stakeholders need skills training if they are to communicate effectively with each other. This is especially the case for parents and teachers.

Training Needs

Parents

Although some parents, as a result of their schooling and professional activities, are highly articulate, enthusiastic and very capable of participating in school decision-making, there are many who are not (McGilp and Michael, 1994; Sheldon, 2002). The majority of parents do need assistance in such matters as knowledge of the educational system and interpersonal and communication skills (Zady *et al.*, 1998).

Many parents do not have a clear idea of the education system in which their local school operates (Hughes and Greenhough, 1998). They need information about the various levels of the hierarchy and the respective powers and functions of head office, regions and individual school principals. In particular, parents need to know the kinds of activities that a principal and his or her staff can initiate and maintain at a local school level, and an awareness of the constraints and monitoring procedures used by head office officials.

Training needs for many parents are most evident in the areas of interpersonal and communication skills (MacLure and Walker, 2000). Experienced parent participants need to be able to break down the apathy of other parents and seek out their support by informal home visits, telephone calls and parent meetings. They have to be able to develop and demonstrate empathy for the needs of the apathetic or uninvolved parent and be able to devise ways of gradually wearing down that person's resistance.

Parent 'drop-in centres' are becoming more widespread in schools as principals realize that the provision of a meeting place for parents is a valuable strategy for getting them more involved in school activities. A drop-in centre can enable parents to interact socially and discuss various matters relating to their school community. In so doing, it may enable parents to increase their level of confidence and skills in communicating with other adults.

Special provisions need to be made to assist parents with language difficulties. Staff with second-language expertise can be used on home visits to encourage those parents to support school affairs. Community liaison officers can also be used with good effect to maintain regular home visits to parents. Migrant adviser services are sometimes available to offer assistance.

Information booklets about the school, printed in several languages, can also be a useful measure to attract the interest of parents of migrant families.

The building up of positive attitudes about school participation among parents is a time-consuming process and requires the concentrated efforts of many participants, including teachers, liaison officers from various departments, and experienced, supportive parents/friends (Griffith, 1997; Brandt, 1998).

Teachers

Training for many teachers revolves around learning about and demonstrating competence in planning and executing student lessons. Few pre-service courses focus upon the role of parents in the school community, especially in terms of techniques for communicating effectively with parents. As a result, some teachers tend to make minimal use of parent assistance or, in some instances, actively resist communicating with parents (Fullan, 1991).

According to Rich (1998) if parents were given the opportunity to rate their child's teacher, the rating might be very low indeed. She argues that many teachers would score low marks about the extent to which they know and care about the children and their willingness to communicate with parents.

Bauch and Goldring (2000) contend that a school that has a caring atmosphere has the greatest influence on positive relationships between teachers and parents.

Hiatt-Michael (2000) argues that beginning teachers need pre-service training modules in parent involvement.

Lasky (2000) asserts that emotionality is a major factor in teacher–parent relationships. She argues that emotions are not solely internal, personal, phenomena but are also social in nature. Consequently, any training of teachers must focus upon the deep-seated emotions that can cause limited interactions between a teacher and parents.

School Councils

School councils/boards are an important element of schooling. Although the composition and powers of school councils vary, the membership typically consists of the principal and representatives of the staff, parents, the community and students (in the case of secondary schools).

'Alternative schools' have a major commitment to a participative democratic process, and most of them operate some kind of school council. These alternative schools have typically very small enrolments and so it is feasible for all parents, teachers and students to meet regularly and make decisions jointly about all major school issues including the curriculum, deployment of staff and the use of resources. For a number of years, many small parish schools operating within Catholic education systems have also maintained their own local boards of management, and these have had independent control over staff appointments, school buildings and finances (including the setting of school fees).

School councils have been established in many of the large government schools and there is some evidence that progress is being made. Gamage (1993) refers to successful examples in New South Wales. Knight (1995, p. 273) describes some successes in Victoria, despite problems occurring due to a current government priority to promote 'self-managed entrepreneurial schools' versus 'democratic control of school decision-making'.

In some cases school councils can be radically powerful and can bring about rapid change (Fullan, 1991). Gamage's (1993, p. 102) studies revealed that 'councils have become effective and efficient organizations, and the principals are highly satisfied and totally committed to the collaborative form of governance adopted in terms of the school council system'.

La Rocque and Coleman's (1989) study of school councils in British Columbia and Hatch's (1998) study of Alliance Schools in the USA, conclude that school councils can make a difference. School council members can develop a clear sense of what they want to accomplish and engage in activities to bring about these ends (Johnson, 2003).

Harold (1997) describes the Boards of Trustees in New Zealand and notes that they have had a pivotal role in developing partnerships between teachers and parents. Each board consists of five elected parent representatives; an elected student representative (for schools with secondary students); the principal; and an elected staff representative. Clearly, this structure allows much wider powers of decision to be given directly to parents. Harold (1997) concludes that Boards of Trustees are operating successfully in the majority of schools.

However, as noted by Fullan (1991), how to increase or improve the effectiveness of school councils is an unstudied problem. There are still many unanswered issues and problems, and some of these are listed in Table 18.3.

Lutz (1980) questions whether school councils really practise democratic decision-making. He argues that school council participation of parents from a local school community is very limited and sporadic; that few council members are closely involved in decision-making; and that few issues are ever made public and widely debated. It is certainly evident that for large schools it is extremely difficult for school board members to represent more than a few of the community interests. Many of the disadvantaged community groups are never represented. Yet it might be argued that democracy means the freedom to participate or not to participate and that if individuals and groups feel strongly enough about an issue then they will participate vigorously.

Questions might also be raised whether school councils actually reduce conflicts between various interest groups or heighten the conflicts still more (Table 18.2). For example Knight (1995) highlights some of the conflicts between teacher and parent members. It is possible that parent priorities (for example, school discipline, and literacy and numeracy) are likely to be different

Table 18.3: Problems and issues for school councils

1 Do councils have real power if their control over finances is limited?
2 Are school councils really able to practise democratic decision-making?
3 Is an adequate supply of dedicated and well-informed parents and community members available to fill school council positions?
4 Does the size of a school influence the effectiveness of school councils?
5 How can school council members understand and represent all sections of a local community if they tend to be better educated and more affluent than the majority of local citizens?
6 Will school councils ever be able to represent effectively such disadvantaged groups as migrants, the unskilled, the unemployed and low income earners?
7 Do school councils really provide a structure for school principal, teachers and parents to coexist harmoniously?
8 Do school councils in the Australian context ever get complete control over decision-making?

from the priorities expressed by teachers (for example, providing a caring atmosphere and building student self-esteem).

Finally, questions might also be raised about whether school councils operating an education system can ever anticipate becoming fully independent from head office policies and requirements. Recent accountability measures introduced into a number of education systems would seem to indicate that centralist requirements are increasing rather than decreasing.

Reflections and Issues

1. Fullan (1991) argues that parent participation at the school and classroom level is a fundamental mission of an effective school. Present arguments for and against this statement.
2. Some school council members complain that they suffer from a lack of direction, the feeling of being a rubber stamp, and parent and staff apathy. How might some of these problems be resolved?
3. 'Many parents and teachers are overloaded with their own work-related and personal concerns. They also may feel discomfort in each other's presence due to lack of mutual familiarity and to the absence of a mechanism for solving the problems that arise' (Fullan, 1991, pp. 249–50). Discuss this statement. What are some practical solutions to the problem?
4. Stevenson (1998) contends that parents want to:
   • feel confident that their children will be happy;
   • trust teachers; and
   • share their insights about their children with the teacher.
   Have you experienced parents who share these goals? What steps can you take to bring about a more productive partnership with parents?
5. Are parents or teachers mainly responsible for creating students' interest in learning? Explain, giving reasons.

6.   MacLure and Walker (2000) contend that many of the meetings between parents and teachers are ceremonial, where both parties enact ritual performances of interest and concern. In your experience, is this a realistic assessment? How can these meetings be used more successfully for both parties?

7.   To what extent do you consider that computer technology (especially e-mail) enables teachers and parents to connect more successfully with each other?

8.   Hughes and Greenhough (1998) argue that the knowledge bases of parents and teachers is one of 'difference and diversity' rather than 'superiority and deficit'. If this is the case, how might this affect communications between teachers and parents?

9.   'It is important that parent governors should be the choice of parents, people that parents feel they can approach with trust and confidence'. (Edwards and Redfern, 1988, p. 109). Are there difficulties in getting representative governors? What are some possible solutions?

Part VI

Curriculum Ideology

19 Curriculum Theorizing

Introduction

Over the years, curriculum theorizing has not advanced steadily. Over the last decades of the twentieth century, scholars grappled with vexing questions such as: 'What is curriculum theory?', 'How might we obtain one?', 'What is one good for?' (McCutcheon, 1982), 'Can an example be found?' (Kliebard, 1977). The answers to these questions have been many and varied, and they have revealed differences in basic assumptions about what counts as valid curriculum purposes and content. On one hand, Westbury (1999) contends that these are not relevant questions at all, since the day-to-day reality of schools revolves around much less lofty and idealistic questions, such as: 'What might we want to do in this here-and-now world?' and 'How can or might we begin to do it?' (p. 357). On the other hand, curriculum specialists such as Giroux (1991) and Ornstein and Hunkins (1993) contend that we have to construct new vocabulary and new terms or metaphors if we are to make any advances.

Certainly, new approaches, with new terms and metaphors, began to be developed during the 1970s. Whether they offer increasingly promising insights and directions is problematic. John Dewey's remark in the 1920s that in curriculum matters we are still 'groping' may be equally pertinent today. Jackson (1992) has observed that the curriculum field remains 'confusing'. Wright (2000) contends that at the beginning of the twenty-first century curriculum theorizing is still highly contested and in a state of flux.

Approaches

The frustration for curriculum writers is that, although the conceptualizing of curriculum theories still eludes us, the potential use of curriculum theories is very clear. Appropriate curriculum theories (if we had them) could guide the work of teachers, policy-makers, administrators, and anyone else involved in curriculum planning and development. They would help researchers analyse data and provide a much-needed impetus and direction for curriculum research with the benefits flowing on to classroom teachers.

One approach is to attempt to establish the key questions that need to be answered by a curriculum theory. For example, Kliebard (1977) suggested that the fundamental question for any curriculum theory is: 'What should we teach?' This question then leads us to consider other questions, such as:

Why should we teach this rather than that?
Who should have access to what knowledge?
What rules should govern the teaching of what has been selected?
How should various parts of the curriculum be interrelated in order to create a coherent whole?

Beyer and Apple (1998), Posner (1998) and Ross (2000) extend this list to include broader, more politically sensitive questions:

What should count as knowledge? As knowing? What does not count as legitimate knowledge?
Who defines what counts as legitimate knowledge?
Who shall control the selection and distribution of knowledge?

Curriculum Models

Another possible approach to curriculum theory is to abandon ambitious plans for producing all-embracing curriculum theories and to concentrate on models of curriculum. Vallance (1982) and Posner (1998) advocate the development of models of curriculum and suggest that models, although they may lack statements of rules and principles that theories include, can identify the basic considerations that must be accounted for in curriculum decisions and can show their interrelationships.

Curriculum Theorizing

Yet another solution, and one that has been proposed by many recent curriculum writers, is 'to shift focus from the end product (the curriculum theory) to the process by which a theory is sought (the process of theorizing)' (Vallance, 1982, p. 8). Although theorizers are apparently involved in activities; the outcome of which is the completion of a theory, their real involvement is actually with the processes of arriving at such an outcome. Theorizing is thus a general process involving individuals in three distinct activities:

* being sensitive to emerging patterns in phenomena;
* attempting to identify common patterns and issues;
* relating patterns to one's own teaching context.

If theorizing is defined in this way, then it can-and should be undertaken by all persons with an interest in curriculum, including teachers, academics and members of the community (Brady, 1984). Teachers in their daily work attempt to become increasingly sensitive to what is significant in their own classrooms and to establish some appropriate framework or orientation to guide what they do (Schubert, 1992). Academics, even though their primary motive may be to theorize in general rather than to guide teaching specifically, still interpret their experience with specific examples or episodes of teaching and attempt to identify patterns that may prove useful in orienting actions. In this way, the traditional dichotomy of theory–practice disappears since all now become practitioners who theorize about their teaching–learning experiences.

Categories

To understand what has been achieved in curriculum theorizing over the decades it is necessary to categorize the contributions. Three broad categories are used here to demonstrate different emphases, namely:

1. *Prescriptive theorizers.* This group attempts to create models or frameworks for curriculum development that improve school practices. Many members of this group have, in fact, held the belief that finding the best way of designing curricula will lead to the best possible curricula for schools. Ralph Tyler and Hilda Taba are members of this group.
2. *Descriptive theorizers.* This group attempts to identify how curriculum development actually takes place, especially in school settings. The idea is to understand the various steps and procedures in curriculum development and the relationships among them. Decker Walker and Joseph Schwab are members of this group.
3. *Critical-exploratory theorizers.* This group attempts to understand deficiencies in past practices of curriculum development and to replace them with more adequate practices, particularly by considering curriculum in the broadest possible intellectual and social contexts. This group looks at curriculum in terms of its diversities and continuities, emphasizing what curriculum has been, is, and might be. Elliot Eisner and William Pinar are members of this group.

Prescriptive Theorizers: Creating the Best Curricula Possible

Up until the 1960s nearly all theorizing about curriculum development focused on ways to improve practices in schools. The major problem with most of these prescriptive approaches was that they assumed the characteristics of traditional, bureaucratized schools to be givens. Therefore, they rarely questioned – and thus frequently served to support existing educational, social, and political systems.

Some specialists worked closely with laboratory schools located on university campuses. Others were involved in major studies of schools or with major curriculum development projects. As a consequence, they wrote directly out of their experiences with specific schools. Hlebowitsh (1999) describes the common concern of these specialists for the improvement of school systems as 'dedicated to offering curriculum development frameworks centred on using the school for the maintenance and improvement of the public interest'. Yet, other commentators have seen these endeavours much less positively, describing them as 'control mechanisms' (Perkinson, 1993), 'traditionalist' (Pinar, 1978) and 'quasi-scientific' (Apple, 1979).

Tyler is often quoted as a major figure of the prescriptive theorizers. In the 1940s, Tyler worked at the University of Chicago and produced an approach to curriculum planning that was subsequently published in 1949 as *Basic Principles of Curriculum and Instruction* (Tyler, 1949). The book has been widely used over the decades in many countries and is a fine example of common sense and clarity.

Tyler describes in his book a number of principles that have come to be known as the 'Tyler rationale'. Tyler argues that his book is not a prescriptive approach – it is not a manual for curriculum construction since it does not describe and outline in detail the steps to be taken by a given school or college that seeks to build a curriculum (p. 1). He goes on to state that it is merely 'one way of viewing an instructional program', and 'the student is encouraged to examine other rationales and to develop his own conception of the elements and relationships involved in an effective curriculum' (p. 1). Yet it is also fair to say that Tyler's book does describe various steps in some detail and it does have an air of prescription about it. Many educators have used and continue to use it as a manual for curriculum planning (Hlebowitsh, 1992).

Tyler's model states *how* to build a curriculum. He argues that there are really four principles or 'big questions' that curriculum makers have to ask (see Figure 19.1). These questions are concerned with selecting objectives, selecting learning experiences, organizing learning experiences and evaluating. For Tyler, these questions can be answered systematically, but only if they are posed in this order, for answers to all later questions logically presuppose answers to all prior questions.

Evaluation of Tyler's Approach

Despite certain ambiguities about how to select objectives and how to use some sources of data, the Tyler rationale encompasses most of our basic concerns about curriculum (Walker, 1990; Hlebowitsh, 1992, 1999). Many other approaches have been based on Tyler. The excesses of some of these have been criticized, but there has also been a tendency to criticize – perhaps fairly, perhaps unfairly – the Tyler rationale itself.

In reflecting on curriculum in 1975, nearly 30 years after the publication of his rationale, Tyler summed up what he thought his approach was about:

> [Curriculum planning is] a practical enterprise not a theoretical study. It endeavours to design a system to achieve an educational end and is not primarily attempting to explain an existential phenomenon. The system must be designed to operate effectively in a society where a number of constraints are present and with human beings who all have purposes, preferences, and dynamic mechanisms in operation. (Tyler, 1975, p. 18)

Figure 19.1:   *Tyler's framework for answering the four basic curriculum questions*

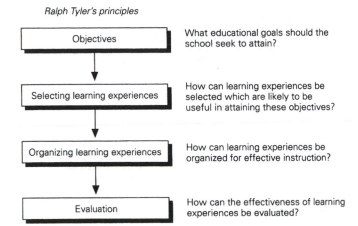

Ralph Tyler's principles

This quotation captures the basic reasons why the Tyler rationale has proved so persuasive to curriculum workers over such a long period of time and also why it has left teachers to deal with the gaps that arise among the planned, the enacted and the experienced curricula. As Tyler suggests, his rationale is primarily a way of simplifying complex situations sufficiently so that plans and procedures can be carried out rationally – that is, in ways that people engaged in the process can understand and, at least potentially, reach agreement about. For the purposes of communication and consensus building, it has had immense practical utility. It is not a way, however, of dealing with the underlying existential complexity that creates the lived character of the experienced curriculum or even with many of the characteristics of individual classrooms that teachers need to take into account in making their decisions about how to flexibly enact curricula that have been planned with precision.

In 1949, Tyler's rational-linear approach broke new ground in curriculum (see Figure 19.2). It had a relatively liberating effect at that time (Helsby and Saunders, 1993). Curriculum workers had for the first time an approach that appeared both comprehensive and workable. They were advised to concentrate on student behaviours in devising objectives for a unit and to emphasize appropriate learning experiences rather than simply identifying content to be covered. The guidelines for evaluating a curriculum were very different and far more comprehensive than were the summative tests used during the 1940s.

Descriptive Theorizers: Mapping the Procedures of Curriculum Development

Descriptive theorizers are not concerned – at least not directly – with providing specific answers to questions concerning what a curriculum should be. Rather,

Figure 19.2:   *Advances made by Tyler's 1949 rationale*

	Before Tyler	Tyler
Purposes of Instruction	General statements about what the teacher should do.	Specific statements about students' behaviours to be used to bring about certain ends.
Topics Selected	Statements about content to by taught.	Statements about learning experiences needed to achieve objectives.
Organization of Teaching	Support in general for teacher-directed, didactic methods.	Support for teacher-directed methods but emphasis on concept development, vertical and horizontal integration of concepts, student awareness of the purpose of learning activities.
Methods of Assessment/Evaluation	Use of content-based tests and standardized tests at the completion of a teaching unit.	Tests to be based upon course objectives; informal and formal methods of evaluation to be used; evaluation to occur throughout the teaching of a unit.

they are concerned with how such answers can be arrived at. To use an ana-
logy, they are concerned with creating a map of the terrain on which curriculum decision-making takes place, not with moving specific plots of earth
involved in school construction projects. An accurate map may be essential
to a good construction project, but where specific roads and structures are built
depends on the beliefs and values of the designers of the project, on budgets
and the availability of building materials, and on numerous other practical
matters that vary from project to project.

Descriptive theorizers are similar to the prescriptive theorizers of our first
category, however, to the extent that both groups view curriculum decision-
making as taking place primarily in schools or in large curriculum development
projects that see schools as givens, thus supporting existing educational, social
and political systems. Nonetheless, descriptive theorizers do tend to have a
broader vision, primarily because they perceive curriculum problems as being
largely indeterminate and open-ended. They understand there are no curriculum development procedures that ensure practical success. They argue that it is
futile to search for a single best curriculum because of the diversity of curriculum problems and possible solutions. Therefore, most descriptive theorizers
actually hold a wide vision about the organization of schools and the interaction of diverse individuals and groups. Technical, operational procedures are
seen to be of less importance than deliberate processes (Reid, 1999a).

Because they view curriculum decision-making broadly, as taking place in
the same multiple and complex ways in which people make practical decisions
within their own lives, they stress that the procedures of curriculum development also take place through what Schwab (1969, 1970), in working out
Dewey's line of reasoning, has termed 'practical inquiry'. Schubert (1986)

notes that the practical inquiry approach to curriculum theorizing can be characterized as follows:

- It involves everyday problem-solving.
- It assumes that every teaching situation is unique.
- It focuses more on questions to be asked than on finding answers.
- It proceeds through the process of deliberation.
- It does not provide general solutions to problems, for each specific situation must be considered separately.

Walker's naturalistic approach to the processes of curriculum deliberation is one example of mapping how practical inquiry takes place.

Walker's Naturalistic Approach

Walker (1971) was especially interested in how curriculum planners 'actually' went about their task, rather than following Tyler's advice about how they 'should' go about the task. He had an excellent opportunity to find out when he was appointed as participant observer and evaluator for the Kettering Art Project during the late 1960s in California. For a period of 3 years he meticulously recorded the actions, arguments and decisions of the project team. By analysing transcripts of their meetings and other data, Walker was able to isolate important components in the curriculum development process. During the 1960s and 1970s a number of major, national curriculum projects were in operation and so he was able to compare his findings from the Kettering Art Project with several other projects. He developed his concepts into a process framework, which he termed a 'naturalistic model'.

Walker used the term 'naturalistic' because he wanted to portray how curriculum planning actually occurs in practice, compared with other approaches which prescribe how curriculum planning should occur. His three-step sequence of 'platform-deliberation-design' has since been used at various levels of curriculum development including small-scale projects with pre-service teachers (Holt, 1990; Kennedy, 1988; Ross, 1993), as well as in large-scale programmes (Ben-Peretz, 1990; Orpwood, 1985). This model is illustrated in Figure 19.3.

Platform

Walker (building on the ideas of Schwab, 1969) suggests that any individuals who come together as a group to undertake curriculum development activities approach the task with certain beliefs and values. They will have certain perceptions of the task, ideas about what the chief problems are, assertions about what should be prescribed and certain commitments which they are prepared to pursue and argue about. The preliminary step is therefore to get everyone to join in, to talk, discuss and even argue about what the platform is or should be. Walker used the term 'platform' because it provides a benchmark or basis for the future discussions.

Figure 19.3: Walker's naturalistic model

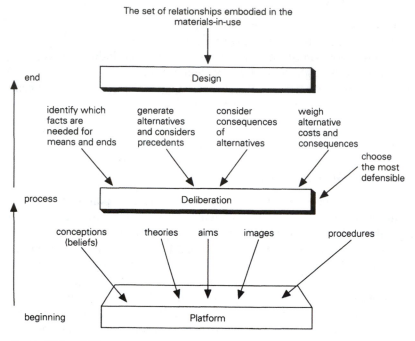

Source: Walker, 1971

Deliberation

Whether a group achieves much or little consensus about their platform, planning eventually moves into the second phase: 'deliberation'. There is not necessarily a clear separation between these phases, for the process of deliberation is also concerned with consensus, but in deliberation attention turns away from beliefs themselves and towards how they are used is assessing actual states of affairs and possible courses of action – towards what Schwab refers to as 'the practical'. In general, planners should identify as far as possible what is problematic about the situation in which their curriculum is to implemented and how the curriculum they develop can mitigate problems.

Design

Deliberation finally leads to some decisions for action: planning enters the 'design' phase when a group has achieved sufficient consensus about beliefs, problematic circumstances and potential solutions so that particular courses of action can be taken more or less automatically, without further consideration of alternatives. That is, what the travails of the previous phases have made explicit for the group now forms the implicit basis for the group's actual curriculum design. Walker argues that the design phase of a curriculum development project typically contains both implicit and explicit considerations. Even though a project may have passed through the platform and deliberation phases, decisions may still be influenced as much by personal preferences as by rational discussion. The culminating activity for the design phase is the creation of the planned curriculum, which may include whatever specific subjects, instructions, teaching materials or activities that the group believes advisable.

Walker's deliberative approach attempts to accurately portray what actually happens during curriculum planning. Because Walker based his approach on studies of planning that had occurred during actual curriculum projects, he claims that it can be supported on empirical grounds. It can be argued that Walker's approach is normative as well as descriptive. Donmoyer (1982) suggests that although the specifics within it are empirically based, it 'resembles in a general way, if not in all important details, Schwab's normative model of how curriculums *ought* to be made' (p. 3).

Certainly, Walker's approach is of considerable value to teachers and other curriculum planners. Knowing what typically happens during planning – the assertions of personal beliefs in the struggle toward consensus, the use of deliberation in identifying problematic situations and weighing alternative solutions, and the interplay of the implicit and the explicit in designing a curriculum – can at least help identify potential pitfalls and frustration in curriculum development and perhaps even guide planners around them. Walker's descriptions of what typically *does* happen during planning certainly present a highly useful alternative to Tyler's prescriptions of what *should* happen. Tyler does not describe what happens when consensus cannot be reached in practice; Walker describes how curriculum planning proceeds even when consensus is not reached.

Critical-Exploratory Theorizers: Understanding Curriculum in Terms of What Has Been, Is, and Might Be

Theorizers in the critical-exploratory category are particularly diverse. Nonetheless, there are just two general approaches to how they treat problems of schooling and curriculum. One general approach emphasizes the connections between schooling and the existing social order. This approach provides critical analysis of prevalent social structures and mainstream curriculum practices. These critiques are concerned with such issues as domination, exploitation, resistance, and what constitutes legitimate knowledge. Collectively, this approach tends to use similar technical terms, such as 'cultural capital' (the ability of certain groups in society to transform culture into a commodity and to accumulate it) and 'cultural reproduction' (the idea that the school's role is to pass on to succeeding generations the present culture without changing it). Many of these theorizers maintain – and with some justification – that a new technical language is needed to provide new insights and interpretations about existing social structures.

The second general approach within this group is an emphasis on the personal nature of learning and on people, rather than ideas, as the basis for action. In other words, these theorizers' primary concern is with individual experience itself and with how systematic education can contribute to high-quality experiencing. They locate the value of curriculum planning and development in the experienced curriculum, not in the planned curriculum. Although most recognize the importance of the preconscious realm of experience and emphasize that often knowledge is personally constructed by each individual, they believe that teachers, in planning and in enacting what is planned, play a key role in influencing the quality of their students' experiences.

Of course, despite the diversity of the critical-exploratory category, many of its theorizers find ways of linking their analyses of the external social context of curriculum and schooling with the personal experience of individual students and teachers.

We need to consider the term *reconceptualist*, which has been used as an umbrella term since the 1970s and early 1980s to describe new forms of theorizing that were then emerging. It is still frequently used today, especially to capture the sense of exploration, but its use has created some avoidable confusion.

Initially, the term proved useful, for it seemed to suggest that whatever reconceptualists stood for was new – and probably better – than what had gone before, and reconceptualists certainly were united in their opposition to the rationalistic and scientific.

However, as theorizers interested in reconceptualizing the field grew in number and in influence, it became increasingly important to clarify what they did – and did not – have in common. For instance, some theorizers used philosophical analysis and methods drawn from mainstream social science, while others used case studies, biography, psychoanalytical techniques and literacy theory. Perhaps the most successful effort to map the common characteristics of reconceptualists was undertaken by Klohr (1980), who identified nine foci of their efforts:

1. A holistic, organic view is taken of people and their relation to nature.
2. The individual becomes the chief agent in the construction of knowledge; that is, he or she is a culture creator as well as a culture bearer.
3. The curriculum theorists draw heavily on their own experiential base as method.
4. Curriculum theorizing recognizes as major resources the preconscious realms of experience.
5. The foundational roots of this theorizing lie in existential philosophy, phenomenology and radical psychoanalysis; they (reconceptualists) also draw from humanistic reconceptualizations of such cognate fields as sociology, anthropology and political science.

6. Personal liberty and the attainment of higher levels of consciousness become central values in the curriculum process.
7. Diversity and pluralism are characteristics both of the social ends and of the means proposed to attain these ends.
8. A reconceptualization of supporting political–social operations is basic.
9. New language forms are generated to translate fresh meanings, for example, metaphors. (Klohr, 1980, p.3)

However, a close examination of Klohr's foci reveals that some are clearly not appropriate to all reconceptualists. For example, a focus on the 'preconscious realms of experience' applies to theorists such as Pinar and Grumet, who use psychoanalytical techniques in their theorizing, but it does not apply to Apple. Conversely, a focus on a 'reconceptualization of supporting political-social operations' applies to Apple but far less to Pinar or Huebner.

Despite these difficulties with the term reconceptualist, readers should be aware of its history in carrying forward new forms of curriculum theorizing that emerged in the 1970s (see, for example, Pinar *et al.*, 1995).

Whether the endeavours over the decades since the 1970s represent a shift in basic thinking about curriculum sufficiently profound to be considered a paradigm shift in Kuhnian terms (Kuhn, 1962) is debatable. Pinar *et al.* (1995) suggest that there has been such a shift and, along with Rogan and Luckowski (1990), that the work of reconceptualists represents a paradigmatic advancement over the Tyler rationale. Brown (1988) concludes that a first approximation to a paradigm shift has been under way and that the new generation of curriculum scholars, as they gain a firm foothold in universities, will begin to challenge the received wisdom of traditional points of view.

There is certainly nothing finished or final about reconceptualism, for ideas and methods are constantly evolving. Rather, a 'proliferation of schools' (Brown, 1988, p. 28) has developed with considerable differences among them.

Although these theorizers often write from a neo-Marxist perspective, their critiques have attacked the problems of society and schooling in a variety of ways. Giroux (1982) described traditional educational theorizing as 'dancing on the surfaces of reality ... ignoring not only the latent principles that shape the deep grammar of the existing social order, but also those principles underlying the genesis and nature of its own logic' (p. 1). Apple suggests a number of political questions that should be asked about the legitimacy of the knowledge included in a curriculum. For example:

> Why and how are particular aspects of a collective culture represented in schools as objective factual knowledge?
>
> How, concretely, may official knowledge represent the ideological configurations of the dominant interests in a society?
>
> How do schools legitimate these limited and partial standards of knowing as unquestioned truths? (Apple, 1979, p. 7)

There is no doubt that these curriculum theorizers have had a considerable impact on curriculum writings. They have alerted curriculum planners and developers to a number of ingrained problems in the usual – and usually unexamined – relationship between schools and the society in which they are embedded. Their approach has exposed classroom practices that have remained hidden when approached by prescriptive theorizers (Taylor, 1979).

Literacy Artist

Under this subcategory are scholars whose approach to curriculum theorizing can be exemplified by Eisner's approach to curriculum planning. In some ways this approach is similar to the deliberate approach of the descriptive theorizers already discussed. The main difference is that the deliberations of curriculum development committees usually lead towards public meanings and group decisions, whereas literacy artists are concerned with personal experience as well (Barone, 1982; Eisner, 1979; Eisner and Vallance, 1974). Indeed, all theorizers in this subcategory emphasize to one degree or another that learning is highly personal.

Essentially, members of this group see themselves, curriculum developers, teachers, students, and virtually every other person as involved in an ongoing process of making meaning in their own lives and conveying meaning to others. This process centers on personal perception and choice. In it, the curriculum is considered a medium through which individuals learn how to deepen.

Existential and Psychoanalytical

Writers who do existential and psychoanalytical theorizing begin with individual experience but point to the importance of how schooling influences experience. Schools represent nature (things that exist prior to human intervention, such as physical sites and space) and culture (things that are human creations, such as beliefs and objects), but the culture of schools tends to be taken for granted. Whenever people take culture for granted, they tend to become less aware – hence, less free. Therefore, we need to attend especially to those parts of culture that are not compelled directly by nature and about which we can make decisions. In particular, the task is to transform schooling that constrains human freedom (Grumet, 1981; Miller, 1992; Pinar, 1980).

Autobiographical/Biographical

The autobiographical/biographical approach to theorizing focuses on the centrality of personal experience in the curriculum. In 1972, Pinar first wrote about his interest in the autobiographical method. Subsequently, he formulated the term *currere* to explain his emphasis. Currere refers to an existential experience of institutional structures. The method of currere is a strategy for self-reflection that enables the individual to encounter an experience more fully and more clearly, as if creating a highly personal autobiography (Pinar and Grumet, 1976).

Gender Analysis and Feminist Pedagogy

Pinar *et al.* (1995) describe a growing interest in theorizing about curriculum as 'gender text'. Doing so involves analysing the unequal ways in which people are treated because of their gender and sexuality, and how knowledge and values develop under society's prevailing assumptions about gender. Many different terms may be used in examining how gender and curricula are related. For example, Kenway and Modra (1992) use the phrase *feminist pedagogy* to describe the social theory and politics of feminists, explaining several variations of feminism, including liberal feminism (working toward equality with males in access to education), socialist feminism (criticizing educational practices exploitative of females) and radical feminism (seeking a distinctively women's educational culture). Analysis of schooling in terms of gender points out how it has been organized around different socially perceived roles and status for men and women (see Chapter 20).

Gender Analysis and Male Identity

Feminist curriculum theorizers have not been the only scholars exploring the frontier of gender studies. Increasingly, a number of scholars have theorized about male identity. In particular, they have been challenging 'heteronormativity'.

Sears (1992a, b, 1999) has been a major figure in highlighting homosexual issues and supporting the struggle for social justice for gays and lesbians. He uses the term 'queer' to signify 'those who have been defined or have chosen to define themselves as sexual outsiders' (1999, p. 4). He defines teaching queerly as 'creating classrooms that challenge categorical thinking, promote interpersonal intelligence, and foster critical consciousness' (1999, p. 5), contending that such teaching requires a re-examination of taken-for-granted assumptions about diversity, identities, childhood and prejudice (see Chapter 20).

Racial

Race is a 'complex, dynamic, and changing construct' (Pinar *et al.*, 1995, p. 316). Race has a powerful influence on schooling in general and the curriculum in particular, yet McCarthy (1988) contends that theorizing about race and racial inequality did not come into its own in curriculum until recent decades. Past neglect has been supplanted, however, by recent theorizers such as Watkins (1993), McCarthy (1988), Villenas and Deyhle (1999) and Pinar (2000). Race can be a powerful, autonomous focal point for theorizers, yet it also intersects with other foci such as gender and postmodernism.

Postmodern

Since the early 1980s the term 'postmodern' has been applied to various pursuits or occupations, as in 'postmodern art' and 'postmodern architecture'. Presumably, what is postmodern replaces what is modern as a defining characteristic. Postmodern curriculum theorizing – at least when it is sufficiently farsighted – should be, therefore, on the leading edge of future changes in education.

Not only are there numerous interpretations of postmodern, but there are also distinctions that can be made between postmodernism and postmodernity and related terms such as poststructuralism, deconstruction, postcolonialism and postindustrialism (see Chapter 21).

Concluding Comments

The examples of theorizing included here should be analysed in the light of history. They illustrate the divergent approaches that have been taken and continue to be developed by curriculum specialists. Some approaches have been more dominant at some times than others. In the last decade, approaches based on the analysis of social structures or personal experience became increasingly common. New classifications of theorizing continue to appear in the literature. These conceptions of curriculum add insights about diversity and directions in theorizing, but further studies of the effects of theorizing at the school level are needed.

What is needed more urgently, however, is increasing and continuing dialogue between theorizers at all levels, from teachers to academics, so that we can learn from our history and our diverse perspectives. Walker (1980) claimed that a 'rich confusion is the right state for curriculum writing' (p. 81). We believe this is so, but writing is only one of many ways to contribute to the dialogue about the richness of curriculum theorizing in which this chapter has invited readers to participate.

Reflections and Issues

1. 'Schools persist in using curriculum models grounded in technical rationality (for example, Tyler's approach) because it fits well with the bureaucratic organization of schools' (Olson, 1989). Is this the major reason? Consider other reasons why schools might support or reject the Tyler approach.
2. 'The real world of teaching is messy, indeterminate and problematic situations arise because of conflicting values' (Carr and Kemmis, 1986, p. 9). To what extent is the Tyler approach or the Walker approach able to accommodate these situations?
3. To what extent is the Tyler model value-free? Do you see this as an advantage or a disadvantage? Give reasons for your answers.
4. The use of technical/rational administrative solutions to complex social issues of equity and access in schools is wrong-headed, superficial and fundamentally flawed, according to Smyth and Shacklock (1998). Critically analyse this statement.

5. 'It is significant that Tyler's first question gets more than twice the attention of any of the other three because Tyler's scheme depends on the careful predetermination of the objectives of the curriculum' (Kliebard, 1992, p. 81). Present points for and against the issue of predetermining objectives.
6. The naturalistic model explodes the myth that curriculum planning must commence with objectives. Do you support this statement? Are there additional caveats to consider?
7. Until we know a particular value we hold, it holds us – we are not in possession of it; it affects our work and thinking although we are unaware of it. Reflect upon the major explicit and implicit values that have guided your teaching. How do they relate to the values implicit in the theorizing described in this chapter? Try to describe your current value orientation and its influence on how you now theorize about curriculum.
8. 'Curriculum theorizing has been overtly politicized, it has been variously institutionalized ... queered, raced, gendered, aestheticized, psychoanalysed, moralized, modernized and postmodernized ... [so] that it presently demands a high degree of flexibility and tolerance from all involved' (Wright, 2000, p. 10). Consider the implications of this point of view for the future of curriculum theorizing and school practice.

20 Gender Inequalities and the Curriculum

Introduction

As regards curriculum there are various terms used to describe the nature and impact of inequalities between the sexes at all levels of education. Robertson (1992) emphasizes the problems of androcentric or male-centred teaching, which involves seeing and valuing the world from a male point of view, and assuming that this is the universal experience. Schools try to achieve better sex equity by establishing teaching programmes that are purported to be gender-neutral.

Pinar *et al.* (1995) argue that there is a growing interest in 'curriculum as gender text'. This involves analysing the unequal ways people are regarded due to their gender and sexuality and the ways they develop knowledge and values under the prevailing system of gender.

Gender Analysis and Feminist Pedagogy

Kenway and Modra (1992) use the term 'feminist pedagogy' to describe not only the social theory and social movement aspects of feminists but its 'personal political practice', in its many forms. They cite a number of variations of feminism including:

- liberal feminists: aspire to access and success and equality with males;
- socialist feminists: concerned about exploitative practices and their effects upon 'women as gendered and classed social beings';
- radical feminists: argue for a 'distinctively women's educational culture'.

The term 'pedagogy' refers to the processes of teaching and involves interactions between the teacher, learners, knowledge and milieu. Lusted (1986) considers that pedagogy includes what is taught, how it is taught and how it us learned and wider issues of knowledge and learning. It is these wider social issues of pedagogy – the problematics in many of the accepted assumptions about pedagogy, that are of major concern to feminist academics and teachers.

Historical Background

Schooling over the decades has been organized in terms of perceived roles and statuses of men and women in society. The dominant and enduring trend until the 1960s and 1970s has been for education structures to be male-oriented.

The accounts of schooling in the nineteenth century in Western countries are strikingly similar about their male domination. Labaree's (1988) account of Central High School in Philadelphia, founded in 1838, indicates that its major purpose was to provide an academic curriculum for the children (mainly sons) of shopkeepers and master craftsmen in the district. It gave these proprietors' sons the 'cultural property' to ease into a middle-class existence.

Sydney Girls' High School was an early school for girls, established in 1893 in Australia. According to Norman (1983): 'one has a sense of girls, hundreds of them, held back like a dam by a wall of superficiality and lack of education. With the opening of Sydney High the dam broke, and the first enrolment spilled out, followed by a flood of others' (Norman, 1983, p. 21). The subjects available over a period of 3 years which culminated in matriculation standard included:

- Latin;
- elementary mathematics;
- modern languages – French, German;
- English language and literature, elocution;
- history;
- physical science;
- drawing – freehand and perspective;
- music;
- cookery;
- needlework (Goodson and Marsh, 1996).

In keeping with earlier priorities that a girl's education should be fitting her for decorative wifehood, Norman (1983) asserts that 'cooking, music and drawing were on the curriculum partly as a sop to those who feared that higher education would make a girl unfeminine and unfit for her basic role of wife and mother' (p. 16).

In most Western countries by the beginning of the twentieth century coeducational and single-sex schools were operating. The teacher workforce was comprised mainly of female teachers who worked for lower wages than male teachers. Administrators of schools were almost entirely male. The curriculum was overwhelmingly male-centred – 'it represented the values and interests of white, Anglo-Saxon, Protestant, middle class males' (Tyack and Hansot, 1990).

Pinar *et al.* (1995) refer to the various ways that gender differences were reinforced and that the male domination continued over the decades. For example, organized sports arose in schools due partly to a fear that boys were becoming feminized due to the few male role models at school (teachers).

Organized sports glorified 'competition', and 'violence'. Girls were 'unable to find the same sense of glory and prestige in sports and were sidelined to the roles of spectators and cheerleaders' (p. 363).

Differentiation also occurred in terms of subject choices. Boys were directed into manual arts (woodwork, metalwork, technical drawing) while girls were required to attend home economics classes. Peer pressure and parental pressures also caused many girls to opt for subjects in a commercial programme while boys did the 'hard' sciences and mathematics. However, it was not until the 1960s and 1970s that the feminist movement of liberation commenced. It appeared to occur at two levels:

- analyses and critiques of sexism and gender: stereotyping in schools;
- analyses and critiques of gender differences in society: including theoretical accounts of how they were produced and maintained.

These analyses have continued as various aspects of education have come under scrutiny by feminist critics; for some 'women's studies' is *the* solution while other feminist groups have been concerned with reconceptualizing curriculum theory, ecological dimensions of feminist theory and knowledge, identity and popular culture, gender and postmodernism.

Feminist Critiques of Schooling

Early critiques of schooling in the 1960s and 1970s examined sex stereotyping and gender bias in content.

The list of activities in Table 20.1 indicates some early endeavours to critique sex stereotyping. Other endeavours have focused upon ways of reforming the curriculum, especially in terms of reworking school knowledge and improving teaching practice.

In some countries national action plans have been established, such as the National Policy and Action Plan for the Education of Girls in Australia, which states that:

Curriculum reform requires a fundamental reworking of what knowledge is valued in the curriculum, how that knowledge is made available (for example, its placement on timetabling lines and competition with other subjects) and how it is taught.

Such curriculum reform should:

- consider where, how and why women's and girls' experiences, achievements and contributions have been excluded from the knowledge that is valued in society;
- provide both females and males with access to a wider range of knowledge, skills and ways of being. It should contain those areas of knowledge and living that are of particular significance to women and girls, to

Table 20.1:   Some teaching activities to reduce sex stereotyping

1   Ask the students to describe their image of the 'typical' male and the 'typical' female. The students should then share their views with the rest of the class, the aim of the exercise being to make the students aware of sex-role stereotyping as an assumption, underpinning the socialization of males and females.

2   Students should be asked to complete the following activities:
What do you feel it means to be male or female? Check off everything on the list in the box below that you feel applies to you.

Boys only	Girls only
Because I am a boy, I would not:	Because I am a girl, I would not:
• cook	• dress like a man in a play
• knit	• climb a tree
• wash dishes	• wear a tie
• help my mother around the house	• play football
• wear a dress in a play	• beat a boy at a sport or game
• cry	• try to join a boys' club or team
• hit a girl	• kiss my mother
• wear jewellery	• get in a fist fight
• babysit	• mow the lawn
• back out of a fight	

3   Encourage the students to think carefully about their own actions and the extent to which they may be perpetuating gender-role stereotyping. For example, ask them to complete the following and to analyse their responses:
• Book

Item	Girl	Boy	Girl or Boy

• Lego
• Computer
• Ball
• Ice skates
• Train set
• Clothing

Source: SEMP, (1977).

the same extent as it includes those areas that are of significance to men and boys;
•   acknowledge the multiple perspectives that women have because of ethnicity, culture and class;
•   students will be as knowledgeable about female as male contributions to society;
•   there will be no difference by gender in the classroom interaction of students and teachers or in expectations for student success;

- there will be no sex bias in the content of courses taught or instructional materials used;
- there will be no sex stereotyping in the hidden curriculum of the school;
- unravel the ways through which social and institutional structures act to maintain the dominant position of men in society;
- explore system and personal models that fulfil expectations of social justice, and that are based on broad rather than narrow views of what it means to be female or male. (Department for Employment, Education and Training (DEET), 1987)

These action plans and related policies have been designed to reduce sexism and gender bias in schooling, yet it appears after nearly two decades that differential outcomes from schooling still exist for girls in comparison with boys (Smith, 2004; Kenway and Willis, 1997).

Students

Stephens (1997) and Jobe (2003) both contend that the gendered life experience that students bring to the classroom will affect students' frame of reference.

Shore (2001) puts the problem very succinctly: 'a girl in the process of her schooling, learns to layer the messages of a logo/androcentric culture over the insights born of her lived experience, muffling and silencing the still, small voice within' (p. 132).

Lundeberg (1997) argues that gender bias is often present in classrooms, even though it may be subtle and not immediately noticeable. Crowley *et al.*'s (1998) study concluded that not only in the classroom but in the home, parents are more likely to explain scientific matters to boys than to girls.

Sex-based harassment can be a disruptive factor in schools and can be promoted by particular subgroups and individuals and even by teacher expectations about typical and least typical boys and girls. For example, Abraham (1995) describes harassment that occurred in a secondary school between girls 'who mixed too much with the boys', the 'conscientious quiet' ones and the 'lads' and the 'gothic punks'.

Research studies have demonstrated that some forms of assessment seem to advantage males, for example multiple-choice tests (Allen, 1990). By contrast, females often achieve higher scores than males on essay tests. In pragmatic terms, therefore, multiple-choice tests are more commonly used by teachers because they are more convenient to set and mark and so female students overall are at a disadvantage to their male counterparts. However, the assessment issue is complex because sex difference is just one of the factors – others include achievement variability across cultures and age levels and subject areas (Feingold, 1992). Then again there are wider issues relating to assessment that may discriminate against girls, such as the test-taking behaviours of males versus females (O'Connor and Robotham, 1991).

Teachers

As noted by Smith (2004) 'not only do schools provide a gendered experience for students, they also provide a gendered experience for teachers' (p. 354).

Milligan (1994) observes that gender is a powerful factor in the daily lives of teachers. She also concludes, using Australian Bureau of Statistics data, that women remain heavily under-represented in school leadership and promotions positions.

Put simplistically, teachers have to either make decisions about continuing the status quo (and maintaining the inequalities and discrimination) or to get involved in reforms. In practice, it is not so easy.

As an example of the complexities involved, Kenway *et al.* (1996) suggest that a number of female teachers try to bring about improved learning situations by assuming the needs of the 'normal girl' and making the erroneous assumption that 'all girls have similar needs, interests, pleasures and anxieties, that what oppresses one, oppresses all, and that what "empowers one" "empowers" all'.

The same authors (Kenway *et al.*, 1996) point to the 'authoritarian' and 'therapeutic' approaches used by teachers to improve teaching practice and suggest that both approaches ignore the emotional dimensions of teaching and learning. Authoritarian attempts, to the point of dogmatism by female teachers, often alienated many students. However, therapeutic approaches where the focus is upon female students enjoying themselves and feeling good about feminism underplays the need for girls to 'become critical, informed and skilled advocates for a better world' (p. 7).

Hubbard and Datnow (2000) studied women teachers' involvement in school reforms. They concluded that reforms that were compatible with women teachers' beliefs about nurturing and caring were well supported and advocated by women teachers, which in turn facilitated the success of the reforms. It was also found that an over-representation of women teachers in a reform effort had the potential of causing negative political reactions.

Robertson (1992) argues that staff development activities to improve teaching practice, such as those developed by Joyce and Showers (1988) and used widely in the USA and Canada, largely ignore gender issues and that workshop discussions benefit males. Sadker and Sadker (1986) conclude that 'men are more likely to influence group discussions and that women's comments are more likely than those of men to be ignored'. This gender gap in communications, they contend, puts women teachers and administrators at a disadvantage as regards having their ideas heard and implemented.

Gender Differences in Society

In addition to critiques of schooling, radical feminists over recent decades have criticized the academic disciplines – the reality interpreted by males in higher education and compartmentalized into disciplines with claimed objectivity. Studies undertaken by feminist critics have noticed that:

- research methodology of these academic disciplines excluded/prevented certain kinds of information;
- areas of enquiry related to women were minimal;
- generalizations made about males and females were based on the study of males only;
- research studies often claimed objectivity but were highly value-laden;
- extant knowledge and modes of inquiry prevented the introduction of new ideas;
- women were devalued in all the disciplines;
- much of the research was based upon highly rational, technological assumptions (Pinar *et al.*, 1995).

A result of these critiques, especially at the higher education level, has been for feminists to introduce 'feminist critiques and theories within their various disciplines and departments as well as starting separate women's studies programs' (Middleton, 1992, p. 18).

'Women's studies' programmes have attempted to redefine and reconstruct the academic disciplines. It might be argued that some programmes have been very optimistic, as revealed by the Charter document of the National Women's Studies Association in the USA:

> Women's Studies, diverse as its components are, has at its best shared a vision of a world free not only from sexism but also from racism, class-bias, ageism, heterosexual bias – from all the ideologies and institutions that have consciously or unconsciously oppressed and exploited some for the advantage of others ... The uniqueness of Women's Studies has been its refusal to accept sterile divisions between academy and community, between intellect and passion, between the individual and society. Women's Studies ... is equipping women ... to transform [society]. (National Women's Studies Association, 1977)

Klein (1986) considers that 'women's studies' curricula can be summarized as being:

- re-action and re-vision, as women confront the androcentric world view;
- action and vision as women assess women's experience from within a gynocentric perspective;
- a combination of these approaches that fuses critique and new vision.

However, it is debatable whether fusion has occurred, rather a myriad of advocacy movements. Pagano (1992) considers that 'the educational challenge in the foreseeable future will be to teach people to acknowledge and understand their own passions, their own advocacy positions, without being reduced to them' (p. 150).

Some of these advocacy movements have included:

- *Essentialism*: male/female differences are innate. The unique feminine characteristics that emerge from women's biology enable them to appropriate many societal functions previously done by males and to do them better (Belensky *et al.*, 1988).
- *Social constructionists*: gender is socially constructed by economic, cultural and political forces in society (Chodorow, 1978; Kenway and Longmead, 1998).
- *Ecological feminist theory*: the humankind–nature relationship (De Mocker, 1986).
- *Political feminist theory*: relationships between gender politics and democratic education (Arnot and Dillabough, 1999; Blackmore, 1998; Yates, 1998).
- *Post-structuralist*: an exploration of the contradictions and injustices in society – to promote feminist self-understanding and self-determination (Lather, 1998; Grumet and Stone, 2000).

Gender Analysis and Male Identity

Feminist curriculum theorists have not been the only scholars who have advanced the frontier of gender studies. Increasingly, a number of scholars are theorizing about male identity. In particular, they have been challenging heteronormativity.

Sears (1992a, b, 1999) has been a major figure in highlighting homosexual issues and supporting the struggle for social justice for gays and lesbians. He uses the term 'queer' to signify 'those who have been defined or have chosen to define themselves as sexual outsiders' (p. 4). He defines teaching queerly as 'creating classrooms that challenge categorical thinking, promote interpersonal intelligence, and foster critical consciousness' (Sears, 1999, p. 5).

Sears (1999) contends that teaching queerly requires a re-examination of taken-for-granted assumptions about diversity, identities, childhood and prejudice. He elaborates upon this by offering five basic propositions, namely:

- Diversity is a human hallmark – despite the evidence, many educators, in terms of sexuality and gender, 'mold children into curriculum cookie-cutter identities' (p. 5) such as male/female; heterosexual/homosexual. 'This is a make-believe world of self and other' (p. 5).
- (Homo)Sexualities and constructed essences – sexual identity is constructed within a cultural context but the predisposition for sexual behaviour is biologically based.
- Homophobia and heterosexism are acquired – 'The belief in the superiority of heterosexuality ... and the deep-seated hatred or fear of those who love the same gender (homophobia) are acquired early in life and serve a variety of functions' (p. 7).

- Childhood innocence is a fictive absolute – 'This is a veneer that we as adults impress onto children, enabling us to deny desire comfortably and to silence sexuality' (p. 9).
- Families are first – 'The concepts of family and parenthood have become "unhinged" in this era of postmodernity' (Stacey, 1999).

Other theorizers within this group who also challenge heteronormativity include Leck (1999), Sumara and Davis (1999), Aitken (1999) and Pinar (1983, 2000). Leck (1999) contends that 'many of the consequences we see in the lives of racialized, gendered and sexualized minorities are the results of the dogmas that have disallowed teachers, parents and schools from participating in an open dialogue about children, sexuality and diversity' (p. 257). Sumara and Davis (1999) take an even stronger line in asserting that curriculum theorizers must interrupt heteronormative thinking. Their propositions for a queer curriculum theory include (p. 203):

- The need to work toward a deeper understanding of the forms that curriculum can take so that sexuality is understood as a necessary companion to all knowing.
- The need to call into question the very existence of heterosexuality as a stable category and to examine the unruly heterosexual closet.
- The need to understand and interpret differences among persons rather than noting differences among categories of persons.
- The need to interrupt common beliefs of what constitutes experiences of desire, of pleasure and of sexuality.

Aitken's (1999) editorial to *Curriculum Inquiry* 29:2 captures the purposes of 'queer' curriculum theorists by his title 'Leaping Boundaries of Difference'. And they are doing it successfully. Aitken concentrates especially upon flawed premises of society such as a patriarchal notion of civil society and culturally sanctioned expressions of heterosexuality.

Pinar (1983, 1994, 1997, 2000) has also written extensively about homosexual issues within autobiographic frameworks. He warns that theorists must be aware of politically enforced heterosexuality, stating 'as a feminist man it is clear to me I must confront my own manhood, understood of course not essentialistically, but historically, socially, racially, in terms of class and culture' (Pinar, 2000, p. 2).

Concluding Comments

The perspectives provided in this chapter highlight issues of power, oppression and inequalities. The severity of gender disadvantage can apply to both girls and boys (Gilbert and Gilbert, 1998).

Disadvantage and discrimination often occurs due to different sexual preferences. As noted by Letts and Sears (1999) 'much of the research on lesbian, gay, bisexual, transgender and queer youth has been testimonial to the fallout from oppression by heterosexualized silences ... and that not enough has been done to speak of the risks and costs of extinction of unique and diverse individuals, and of certain cultural characteristics within our human symbioses' (p. 260).

Reflections and Issues

1. 'Feminist pedagogy consists of a diversity of voices and practices and it exists in a wide variety of educational settings and modes' (Kenway and Modra, 1992). Discuss.
2. In theorizing about feminist pedagogy we need to consider 'such concepts as pleasure, nurturance, pain, blame, shame, risk, investment, fantasy and positionality' (Kenway *et al.*, 1996). To what extent are feminist educators failing to attend to the subtleties of what girls think, feel, say and do in schools?
3. 'If feminism cannot criticize itself, it cannot facilitate a multitude of emancipatory possibilities' (Miller, 1990). To what extent has feminist theorizing been uncritical and oversimplified? Give examples of recent initiatives by feminists to overcome a failure to critically reflect upon their theory-building.
4. 'A teacher's general ideology about sex roles is a major factor in determining their willingness to use non-sexist or anti-sexist curriculum materials' (Abraham, 1995, p. 133). Discuss.
5. 'The time to make children aware of the ways they are limited, and the ways they limit themselves through gendered identities, is in the early childhood years' (Alloway, 1995, p. 26). What are some of the restrictions that can occur? Are there asymmetries in power relations at this level of schooling? How can teachers encourage children to contest inequitable gender relations?
6. 'Feminist theorizing is clearly both the condition for a recognition of our unity across national boundaries but also the condition for recognizing our diversity, between nations and within nations' (Arnot, 1993, p. 2). Are there commonalities of women's experiences of schooling across different societies? Give examples to illustrate the commonalities and diversities.
7. 'Homophobia and the vilification and violence it generates need to be seen as part of the construction of dominant masculinity' (Gilbert and Gilbert, 1998, p. 164). Discuss.
8. Is the major problem that modern societies have cemented our ideas of child development around behaviours that are assumed to be 'normal'? What understandings and actions regarding this problem can be taken by teachers?
9. As we study constructions of power, we can see the often defensive, reactionary and diverse responses of those who are in positions of power. Explain with reference to the treatment of boys with different sexual preferences.

21 Postmodernism and the Curriculum

Introduction

The term 'postmodern' is used frequently in accounts of society and descriptions of various occupations – and so we have, for example, 'postmodern society', 'postmodern art', 'postmodern architecture'. The term has been interpreted in many ways but before it is analysed here it is necessary to examine what is being replaced – what is the 'modern' which is to be relegated to a previous era or replaced?

Some Major Terms

According to Hargreaves (1995) 'modernity' is a social condition which was dominant in many countries up to the 1960s. Its characteristics included:

- a major emphasis upon rational, scientific methods and the use of technology to control nature;
- the division of production methods involving separation of family and work;
- the development of specialized, hierarchical bureaucracies to control decision-making;
- achievement of social progress by systematic development and rational applications;
- economic and social organizations focused upon capitalist production.

Modernity has had the potential to bring about progress. To a certain extent it has been successful – as witnessed by efficiency, productivity, prosperity in some quarters, creation of the welfare state, mass education. Yet there are also signs that modernity as a social condition has become exhausted and no longer relevant, in terms of:

- economic markets have become saturated, profitability is declining; many Western economies are in fiscal crisis;
- bureaucracies are being blamed for inefficiencies and inflexible decision-making.

Of course, it may be the case that we are entering a new phase of 'modernity'. Giddens (1990) uses the term 'high modernity' to describe a social condition where decisions and actions are more diffuse, radicalized and universalized than before. He argues that it is not sufficient to invent a new term such as 'postmodernism', rather we should be examining the nature of modernity to understand the extension and intensification of conditions.

Habermas (1970) argues that modernity offers considerable promise of integrating science, morality and art back into society through the use of reason. Yet many others argue that modernism is on the wane and must be replaced (Jencks, 1992; Griffin *et al.*, 1993; Slattery, 1995).

Doll (1993a) contends that postmodernism, as characterized by open systems, indeterminacy, the discrediting of metanarratives and a focus on process, will bring about megaparadigmatic changes. McLaren and Farahmandpur (2000) argue that postmodernism has made impressive advances in helping educators map the hidden trajectories of power and to peel away layers of ideological mystification.

Not only are there numerous interpretations of the term 'postmodern', but there are also distinctions which can be made between 'postmodernism' and 'postmodernity' and related terms such as 'poststructuralism', 'deconstruction', 'postcolonialism' and 'post-industrialism'.

Hargreaves (1995) uses the term 'postmodernity' to refer to a social condition – patterns of social, economic, political and cultural relations – whereas he perceives 'postmodernism' as a set of styles and practices such as intellectual discourse or cultural forms. Others, such as Slattery (1995), use the term 'postmodern' to refer to both social conditions and practices.

This also appears to be the stance of other writers describing 'postmodern':

- as a diffuse sentiment rather than any set of common doctrines (Griffin *et al.*, 1993, p. vii);
- it is in continual growth and movement and thus no firm definitions are possible (Jencks, 1986, p. 9).

Atkinson (2000) cites some characteristic features of postmodernism, which she sums up as a 'release from certainties' (p. 6). Her list includes:

- resistance towards certainty and resolution;
- rejection of fixed notions of reality, knowledge or method;
- acceptance of complexity, of lack of clarity and of multiplicity;
- refusal to accept boundaries or hierarchies in ways of thinking (p. 7).

Poststructuralism

Poststructuralism is a variation of postmodernism that criticizes modernity by challenging a structuralist view of the world. For example, structuralists believe in invariant forms of knowledge and of society that give meaning to the world, whereas Foucault (1972) argues that attempts to establish such a system of homogeneous relationships – a network of causality – fail to take into account the underlying but changing social and political assumptions such systems are ultimately built on. Structuralists identify systems to create meaning, whereas poststructuralists endeavour to dismantle systems to expose their variable and contingent nature (Slattery, 1995).

Deconstructionism

Deconstructionism is another variation involved in exposing the contradictions and fallacies embedded within modernity. The idea of deconstruction does not imply a tearing down; rather, it is simply being alert to contradictions and fallacies in Western thought and rationality, 'alert to the implications, to the historical sedimentation of the language we use' (Derrida, 1972).

Lather (1991a) in *Getting Smart: Feminist Research and Pedagogy with/in the Postmodern* takes a deconstructivist stance. She argues that the modernist system of power, language and meaning has imploded and collapsed (p. 88) and that what is needed is knowledge constructed from self-understanding. Lather contends, using feminist research, that an emancipatory concept of language and power will emerge in education – self-understanding and self-determination is required.

Postcolonialism

Postcolonialism is a third and more specific variation of the postmodern that, according to Giroux (1992), challenges the ideological and material legacies of imperialism and colonialism.

Giroux's (1992) *Border Crossings: Cultural Workers and the Politics of Education* provides an account of the shifting borders that affect the different configurations of culture, power and knowledge. He uses the term 'border pedagogy' to signal a recognition of those margins (epistemological, political, cultural, social) that structure the language of history, power and difference. The term also signals the need for teachers to create learning situations so that students become border crossers – allowing them to write, speak and listen in a language in which meaning becomes multiaccentual and dispersed and resists permanent closure. Giroux states that:

> border pedagogy necessitates combining the modernist emphasis on the capacity of individuals to use critical reason to address the issue of public life with a postmodernist concern with how we might experience agency in a world constituted in differences unsupported by transcendent phenomena or metaphysical guarantees. In that way, border pedagogy can reconstitute itself in terms that are both transformative and emancipatory. (Giroux, 1992, p. 29)

Postcolonial adherents challenge imperial centres of power and contest the dominant Eurocentric writing of politics, theory and history. Spivak (1985) argues that it is necessary to unlearn one's own privilege; the legacy of colonialism must be examined to make visible the various exclusions and repressions that permit specific forms of privilege to remain (for example, privilege that benefits males, whiteness, heterosexuality, and property holders).

The 'post-industrial' society is another term used to connote worldwide changes in social, economic, political and technological relations. In 1980, Toffler (1980) was making predictions about a 'third wave'. Naisbitt and Aberdene (1990) as reported in Swanson (1993) refer to 'megatrends' whereby the changes in the present age are of a magnitude similar to the shift from feudalism to capitalism or from an agriculturally based economy to industrialization.

Postmodernism and Schooling

While different postmodernists may disagree on specific details of their critiques of the hidden political, social and cultural assumptions of the present, they (and related groups) collectively agree that schooling is far more complex and ambiguous than traditional curriculum writers describe it and, therefore, that modernist standardized curriculum packages are likely to be grossly inappropriate in the present, if they ever were appropriate. Thus, teachers need to enter into dialogue about the uncertainties, the concerns, the doubts and the questions that pervade teaching, including those that surround selecting and enacting curricula. The challenge is to transcend traditional, positivist approaches to curriculum development. Teachers need to create methods to develop and incorporate various postmodern discourses into their daily teaching. Examples of how this challenge can be met include the following:

- Teachers and students need to become engaged in telling their life stories, and especially to reflect upon ideas that appear to have been hidden or forgotten (Graham, 1991).
- Curriculum experience in schools must be open to reflection, because from a postmodern standpoint everything requires recursive interpretation. Thus the official syllabuses and curriculum documents cannot be used in any passive way – as a teacher-proof curriculum (Mitchell, 1996).
- Through dialogue and debate, teachers and students must deconstruct norms and values about race and gender, especially those that perpetuate religious bigotry, political repression and cultural elitism (Parker, 1997).
- Teachers need to encourage students to undertake aesthetic reflections whereby they can gain some intrinsic coherence about the body, the spirit and the cosmos.
- Teachers need to promote holistic inquiry with their students in terms of the classroom environment, the natural environment and the inner environment of students and teachers (Atends, 2000).

- 'Teachers and student will be encouraged to become ironic in reconciling the foundationless status of their beliefs and commitments – and the commitments of others – with the desire to create, develop and defend them' (Parker, 1997, p. 142).
- Teachers should encourage students to accomplish their learning in diverse ways using written, numerical, oral, visual, technological or dramatic media. Hierarchical distinctions of worth among different forms of representation are eliminated. In a postmodern approach, the student's voice in the process of assessment is fundamental (Hargreaves *et al.*, 2001).

Just as the term 'reconceptualist', has many perspectives, so too does the term 'postmodern'. Postmodern theorizing is eclectic and takes many stances and directions.

Slattery (1995) focuses upon eight different perspectives: it is worth remembering that postmodernism promotes eclecticism – there are no unified conceptions. His listing of perspectives includes:

- historical: ongoing reinterpretation; the primacy of subjective experience of history, interrelating events unified with time and space;
- aesthetic, qualitative: to prioritize the dramatic, artistic, non-rational, intuitive dimensions of the human person;
- social criticism: exposing contradictions and deconstructing notions of truth, language, knowledge and power in economic and political systems;
- cultural analysis: critiquing the negative impact of modern technology on the human psyche and the environment;
- a radical eclecticism: a discourse that accepts and criticizes, that constructs and deconstructs;
- cosmological dialogue: a search for personal and universal harmony;
- globally interdependent ecological perspective: the interrelated destruction of the ecosphere and the human psyche and how it can be halted;
- reconceptualizing and transcending the interlocking categories of race, gender and class: 'excavating the unconscious assumptions' (Miller, 1987).

Postmodernism and the Curriculum

Curriculum is a central aspect of schooling. If it is accepted that schooling is currently in crisis (Schon, 1991; Duke, 1984), then it is crucial for teachers to reflect deeply about the curriculum that is planned and implemented. Some possible examples are included below:

Methods

Autobiographical Reflection

Postmodern educators can no longer teach a subject in terms of facts, or a series of events to be memorized. What is needed is:

- for the teacher to continually tell his or her life story in terms of the subject: subjective reflections on what it has meant/what it could mean;
- for students to become engaged in telling their life stories about the subject;
- to encourage students to keep a journal during a particular course and to record their personal perspectives;
- to arrange classroom chairs in a circle to enable informal sharing by students of their personal perspectives;
- to reflect upon ideas that appear to have been hidden or forgotten: 'redeeming a lost sense of historical consciousness' (Graham, 1991, p. 13);
- to question linear descriptions and artificially contrived categories and to reflect upon events of the present and how they provide access to the future.

Collaborative Interpretation

Postmodern educators need to engage in collaborative interpretation with their colleagues. The curriculum experience in schools must be open to reflection, because from a postmodern standpoint everything requires recursive interpretation. Thus, the official syllabuses and curriculum documents cannot be used in any passive way – as a teacher-proof curriculum. It requires:

- teachers to share ideas collaboratively with other teachers, and in so doing, to create a community of interpreters;
- collaborative interpretation to be viewed as a creative activity rather than a technical function;
- teachers to respect the interplay of individuals and to expect infuriating and inciting experiences as well as rewarding ones. Once teachers enter this hermeneutic circle they become involved in frank and candid interpretations, clarifications, deconstructions and challenges to all fields of study.

Multicultural Debates

Postmodern teachers must depart from the notion of curriculum as being 'radically, gender and culturally neutral' (Slattery, 1995, p. 133). Through dialogue and debate between a teacher and students it is necessary to:

- shatter myths about race and gender, especially those that perpetuate religious bigotry, political repression and cultural elitism;

- encourage investigation of confrontational ideas outside a student's prior knowledge and experience in order to develop wide insights about self and society;
- use race and gender studies as vehicles to expose 'the impotence of traditional curriculum development in the face of the tragedies of contemporary global society' (Slattery, 1995, p. 136);
- deconstruct norms and values about race and gender through discussion and debate and through autobiographical accounts.

Aesthetic, Integrated Inquiry

Postmodern teachers need to encourage aesthetic reflections that help students to gain some intrinsic coherence about the body, the spirit and the cosmos. Activities toward this end include:

- encouraging teachers and students to use multisensory phenomena and perceptions;
- encouraging a multiplicity of voices in making judgements;
- giving a higher priority to music, fine arts, drama, dance, poetry, speech, band, painting and to use these sources to encourage interdisciplinary integrated inquiry.

Ecological Sustainability and Holistic Inquiry

Postmodern educators realize the crisis of surviving due to ongoing destruction of both the ecosphere and forms of violence to the human psyche (Slattery, 1995).

According to Sloan (1993, p. 1), 'the world is collapsing under the impact of the homogenizing influences of the modern mindset and its attendant institutions [where] educational systems ... force children at an ever-earlier age into an adult culture already shot through with futility, greed and banality.'

What is needed is:

- a holistic perspective to enable students and teachers to explore the dangers of environmental pollution and destruction and to search for alternatives;
- to give a higher priority to teaching activities that span the classroom and the outside community and to include field trips, guest speakers, nature studies and visits to museums;
- to focus upon holistically, the classroom environment, the natural environment and the inner environment of teachers and students.

Critics of Postmodernism

Postmodern theorizing is not without its critics. Barrow (1999) concludes 'that the label "postmodern" is simply too confused to be useful' (p. 419).

Proponents of postmodernism postulate a theory that seeks to deny the coherence of theory – this is a central contradiction.

Green (1994) contends that postmodernism 'has so far contributed little that is distinctive or theoretically fruitful and it seems unlikely that it will' (p. 73). 'Postmodernism taken to extremes, can only lead to moral nihilism, political apathy and the abandonment of the intellect to the chaos of the contingent' (p. 74).

Behar-Horenstein (2000) contends that the postmodern interpretation is shortsighted, 'represents a gross distortion of reality and a reductionist critique of the field' (p. 20).

Within the ranks of postmodern theorists there are some who take a more moderate stance compared with stances taken by theorists such as Lather (1991a), Giroux (1992) and Doll (1993a).

For example, Kincheloe (1993) is concerned about mapping the postmodern terrain historically and politically. He also constructs a philosophical and aesthetic theory of post-formal thinking. He perceives post-formal thinking as seeing relationships between ostensibly different things – making connections between logic and emotion – transcending simplistic notions of cause and effect. He attempts to create a middle ground by accepting progressive and democratic features of modernism but then moves to post-formal thinking 'as a new zone of cognition' (Slattery, 1995, p. 27).

Griffin *et al.*'s (1993) *Founders of Constructive Postmodern Philosophy* also takes a more moderate stance, some might consider it to be high modernist, by advocating an integration of the desirable features of premodern rural agrarian societies (for example, family/tribal community values) and the desirable features of the modern societies (for example, advances in health care) to construct a more balanced and ecologically sustainable global community. A new unity of scientific, ethical, aesthetic and religious perspectives is proposed to contribute to the construction of a worldview.

Hargreaves' (1995) and Hargreaves *et al.* (2001) provide an analysis of the postmodern social condition and the challenges they posit for teachers. Hargreaves (1995) argues that 'while society moves into a post-industrial postmodern age, our schools and teachers continue to cling to crumbling edifices of bureaucracy and modernity' (p. x). He contends that it is the struggle between and within modernity and postmodernity that is the major challenge for teachers.

Although Hargreaves shares similar concerns about modernist priorities he is not so optimistic about postmodern developments when he states that:

Modernity has survived for centuries; its more recent forms for decades. It is not yet clear whether our generation will be witness to its complete demise, to the end of an epoch. Many facets of modernity clearly are in retreat or under review – standardization, centralization, mass production and mass consumption among them. Deeper continuing structures of power and control in society may not be eliminated so easily. They may, however, be changing their form: renovated and refurbished with postmodern facades of accessibility and diversity. (Hargreaves, 1995, p. 32)

Hargreaves *et al.* (2001) are concerned about change in postmodern society and that 'the worthy pursuit of continuous improvement can turn into an exhausting process of ceaseless change ... If people are forever in a state of becoming, they never have the chance to be' (p. 123).

Concluding Comments

Postmodernism provides opportunities for dialogue about the hidden political, social and cultural assumptions of present-day curriculum planning and schooling. Whilst not necessarily providing solutions to modernity issues, postmodern proponents provide mechanisms for challenging traditional, positivist approaches to curriculum development.

Reflections and Issues

1. 'The postmodern world is fast, compressed, complex and uncertain. Already it is presenting immense problems and challenges for our modernistic school systems and the teachers who work within them' (Hargreaves, 1995, p. 9). Discuss.
2. Teaching is more than well-formatted lesson plans with carefully crafted objectives and outcomes – this is a simplistic modernist/positive view of the world. Critique this statement from a postmodern stance.
3. 'The postmodern curriculum, in all its kaleidoscopic perspectives, offers an opportunity for education to move beyond moribund modes of analysis to a new understanding of curriculum development' (Slattery, 1995, p. 257). Discuss.
4. To what extent have modern economies been beset by such massive changes in economic, political and organizational life that postmodern alternatives are inevitable? Examine some of these changes that have occurred and several postmodern alternatives.
5. Doll (1993b) suggests a new set of criteria for determining a quality postmodern curriculum. These criteria include 'richness' (multiple layers of interpretation to challenge the learner); 'recursion' (to revisit ideas, reflection); 'relations' (the more interconnections the better – non-linear explorations); 'rigour' (the process of moulding problems and perturbations into a coherent and dynamic unity). Comment on the potential of using these four 'R's in teaching. Do they constitute a new educational mindset and curriculum frame?
6. 'Poststructuralism encourages ambiguity and multiplicity, opens up traditional boundaries and breaks out of frames' (Rhedding-Jones, 1995). What are the implications for classroom teachers? How might a diversity of meanings be addressed by the teacher? How does one acquire heightened awareness of wider discourses?
7. 'In a postmodern curriculum there must be a sense of indecision and indeterminacy to curriculum planning. The ends perceived are not so much ends as beginnings' (Doll, 1993a, p. 19). Explain how this transformation might occur. Would

this bring about changes in the locus of power? Give examples to illustrate your stance.

8. 'The free-form processive dance of postmodernism is indeed preferable to the lock-step progressive control of modernity' (Slattery, 1995, p. 28). Explain and take a position that supports or refutes this statement.

9. According to Slattery (1995) we must move from 'curriculum development in the disciplines to the postmodern paradigm of understanding curriculum in various contexts – in this sense curriculum development becomes kaleidoscopic – it is always shifting perspectives and constantly reflecting new and liberating visions of learning and living' (p. 257). Discuss.

References

ABBOTT-CHAPMAN, J., HUGHES, P. and WILLIAMSON, J. (2001) 'Teachers' perceptions of classroom competencies over a decade of change', *Asia-Pacific Journal of Teacher Education*, **29**, 2, pp. 171–185.

ABRAHAM, J. (1995) *Divide and School*, London, Falmer Press.

ADELMAN, C. (1989) 'The practical ethic takes priority over methodology', in CARR, W. (Ed) *Quality in Teaching*, London, Falmer Press.

AINLEY, J., FLEMING, M. and ROWE, K. (2002) 'Evaluating systemic school reform: Literacy advance in the early years', Paper presented at the Annual Conference of the American Educational Research Association, New Orleans.

AITKEN, J.A. (1999) 'Leaping boundaries of difference', *Curriculum Inquiry*, **29**, 2, pp. 149–157.

ALLEN, J.R. (2002) *The Effect of the Writing Task: A First Analysis*, Brisbane, BSSSS.

ALLEN, S. (1990) 'The parent–teacher partnership in schooling', *Education Australia*, **8**, pp. 5–6.

ALLOWAY, N. (1995) 'Eight's too late: Early childhood education and gender reform', *Unicorn*, **21**, 4, pp. 19–27.

ANDERSON, B.L. and COX, P.L. (1988) 'Configuring the education system for a shared future: collaborative vision, action, reflection', Regional Laboratory for Educational Improvement of the North-East and Islands, Andover, MA.

ANDERSON, G.L. and DIXON, A. (1994) 'Paradigm shifts and site-based management in the United States: Toward a paradigm of social empowerment', in SMYTH, G. (Ed) *A Socially Critical View of the Self-managing School*, London, Falmer Press.

ANDERSON, K.L. (2001) 'Voicing concern about noisy classrooms', *Educational Leadership*, **58**, 7, pp. 77–87.

ANDERSON, L.W. and SOSNIAK, L.A. (1994) (Eds) *Bloom's Taxonomy: A Forty-Year Retrospective, Ninety-Third Yearbook of the National Society for the Study of Education*, Chicago, University of Chicago Press.

ANDERSON-INMAN, L.A. and HORNEY, M. (1993) 'Profiles of hypertext readers: Results from the Electro Text Project', Paper presented at the Annual Conference of the American Educational Research Association, Atlanta.

ANDREWS, G. (1985) *The Parent Action Manual*, Schools Community, Melbourne, Interaction Trust.

ANGUS, L. (1994) 'Quality schooling: Responding to the issues', in CHAPMAN, J., ANGUS, L. and BURKE, G. (Eds) *Improving the Quality of Australian Schools*, Melbourne, ACER.

ANGUS, M. (1995) 'Devolution of school governance in an Australian state school system: Third time lucky–', in CARTER, D.S.G. and O'NEILL, M.H. (Eds) *Case Studies in Educational Change: An International Perspective*, London, Falmer Press.

ANGUS, M. (1998) *The Rules of School Reform*, London, Falmer Press.

APPLE, M.W. (1979) *Ideology and Curriculum*, London, Routledge and Kegan Paul.

APPLE, M.W. (1986) *Teachers and Texts*, New York, Routledge and Kegan Paul.

APPLE, M.W. (1988) 'What reform talk does: Creating inequalities in education', *Educational Administration Quarterly*, **24**, 3, pp. 272–281.

APPLE, M.W.(1993) *Official Knowledge*, New York, Routledge.

APPLE, M. W. (2000) 'Can critical pedagogies interrupt rights policies?', *Educational Theory*, **50**, 2, pp. 229–258.

ARENDS, R.I. (2000) *Learning to Teach*, 5th edn, McGraw-Hill, Boston.

ARNOT, M. (1993) 'Introduction', in ARNOT, M. and WEILER, K. (Eds) *Feminism and Social Justice in Education: International Perspectives*, London, Falmer Press.

ARNOT, M. and DILLABOUGH, J. (1999) 'Feminist politics and democratic values in education', *Curriculum Inquiry*, **29**, 2, pp. 174–190.

ASP, E. (2000) 'Assessment in education: Where have we been? Where are we headed?', in BRANDT, R.S. (Ed) *Education in a New Era*, Alexandria, VA, ASCD.

ATKINSON, E. (2000) 'What can postmodern thinking do for educational research?', Paper presented at the Annual Meeting of the American Educational Research Association, New Orleans.

AUSTRALIAN COLLEGE OF EDUCATORS (2002) *Teacher Standards, Quality and Professionalism, Towards a Common Approach*, Australian College of Educators, Canberra.

AYERS, W. (1993) *To Teach: The Journey of a Teacher*, New York, Teachers College Press.

AZZARA, J. (2000) 'The heart of school leadership', *Educational Leadership*, **58**, 4, pp. 62–68.

BAILEY, D.B. and PALSHA, S.A. (1992) 'Qualities of the stages of concern questionnaire and implications for educational innovations', *Journal of Educational Research*, **85**, 4, pp. 226–232.

BALL, D.L., COHEN, D.K., PETERSEN, P.L. and WILSON, S.M. (1994) 'Understanding state efforts to reform teaching and learning: Learning from teachers about learning to teach', Paper presented at the Annual Conference of the American Educational Research Association, New Orleans.

BALL, S.J. (1994) *Education Reform*, Buckingham, Open University Press.

BARONE, T. (1982) 'Insinuated theory from curriculum-in-use', *Theory and Practice*, **21**, 1, pp. 38–43.

BARROW, R. (1999) 'The need for philosophical analysis in a postmodern era', *Interchange*, **30**, 4, pp. 415–432.

BARRY, K., KING, L., PITTS-HILL, K. and ZEHNDER, S. (1998) 'An investigation into student use of a heuristic in a series of cooperative learning problem solving lessons', Paper presented at the Annual Conference of the American Education Research Association, San Diego.

BARTH, R.S. (2002) 'The culture builder', *Educational Leadership*, **59**, 8, pp. 6–11.

BASS, B.M. and AVOLIO, B.J. (1994) *Improving Organisational Effectiveness Through Transformational Leadership*, Sage, Thousand Oaks.

BASSEY, M. (1990) 'Action research in action', in DADDS, M. and LOFTHOUSE, B. (Eds) *The Study of Primary Education, A Source Book*, Vol. 4, *Classroom and Teaching Studies*, London, Falmer Press.

BAUCH, P.A. and GOLDRING, E.B. (2000) 'Teacher work context and parent involvement in urban high schools of choice', *Educational Research and Evaluation*, **6**, 1, pp. 1–23.

BEAGLEY, D. (1997) 'Enabling effective parent participation', Paper presented at the Biennial Conference of the Australian Curriculum Studies Association, Sydney.

BEANE, J.A., TOEPFER, C.F. and ALESSI, S.J. (1986) *Curriculum Planning and Development*, Boston, Allyn and Bacon.

BEARE, H. (1995) 'New pattern for managing schools and school systems', in EVERS, C. and CHAPMAN, J. (Eds) *Educational Administrations*, Sydney, Allen and Unwin.

BEARE, H. (1999) 'How will it be in ten years' time?', *EQ Australia*, 1, Autumn, pp. 47–48.

BEARE, H. (1998) 'Who are the teachers of the future?', *IARTV Seminar Series*, August, No. 76, Melbourne, IARTV.

BEATTIE, C. (1989) 'Action research: A practice in need of theory?', in MILBURN, G., GOODSON, I.F. and CLARK, R.J. (Eds) *Re-Interpreting Curriculum Research: Images and Arguments*, London, Falmer Press.

BEAUCHAMP, G.A. (1981) *Curriculum Theory*, 4th edn, Itasca, IL, Peacock.

BECKER, H. (1981) 'Teacher practices of parent involvement at home: A statewide survey', Paper presented at the Annual Meeting of the American Educational Research Association, Chicago.

BECKER, H.J. (1998) 'Running to catch a moving train: schools and information technologies', *Theory into Practice*, 37, 1, pp. 20–30.

BEHAR-HORENSTEIN, L. (2000) 'Can the modern view of curriculum be refined by postmodern criticism?', in GLANZ, J. and BEHAR-HORENSTEIN, L. (Eds) *Paradigm Debates in Curriculum and Supervision*, Westport, CT, Bergin and Garvey.

BELENSKY, M., CLINCHY, B., GOLDBERG, N. and TARULE, J. (1988) *Women's Ways of Knowing: The Development of Self, Voice and Mind*, New York, Basic Books.

BELL, G.H. (1988) 'Action inquiry', in NIAS, J. and GROUNDWATER-SMITH, S. (Eds) *The Enquiring Teacher: Supporting and Sustaining Teacher Research*, London, Falmer Press.

BELL, L. (1988) *Appraising Teachers in Schools*, London, Routledge.

BELL, P.A., FISHER, J.D. and LOOMIS, R.J. (1976) *Environmental Psychology*, Philadelphia, W.B. Saunders.

BENNETT, H. (1992) *Teacher Appraisal: Survival and Beyond*, London, Longman.

BENNETT, R.E. (2002) 'Inexorable and inevitable: The continuing story of technology and assessment', *Journal of Technology, Learning and Assessment*, 1, 1, pp. 2–23.

BENNETT, S.N. (1981) 'Time and space: Curriculum allocation and pupil involvement in British open-space schools', *The Elementary School Journal*, 82, 1, pp. 18–26.

BENNIS, W.G., BENNE, J. and CHIN, K. (1976) *The Planning of Change*, New York, Holt, Rinehart and Winston.

BEN-PERETZ, M. (1990) *The Teacher–Curriculum Encounter*, Albany, State University of New York Press.

BETTS, F. (1997) 'Scoreboards for schools', *Educational Leadership*, 55, 3, pp. 70–71.

BEYER, L.E. and APPLE, M.W. (Eds) (1998) *The Curriculum: Problems, Politics and Possibilities*, 2nd edn, Albany, State University of New York Press.

BIDDLE, B.J. and BERLINER, D.C. (2002) 'Small class size and its effects', *Educational Leadership*, 59, 5, pp. 12–23.

BIGUM, C. (1997) 'Teachers and computers: in control or being controlled?', *Australian Journal of Education*, 41, 3, pp. 247–262.

BILLING, D. (1994) 'The development of appraisal in Tasmania', in INGVARSON, L. and CHADBOURNE, R. (Eds) *Valuing Teachers' Work: New Directions in Teacher Appraisal*, Melbourne, ACER.

BINNEY, G. and WILLIAMS, C. (1995) *Leaning into the Future: Changing the Way People Change Organizations*, London, Brearley.

BLACK, P. (2001) 'Dreams, strategies and systems: Portraits of assessment, past, present and future', *Assessment in Education*, **8**, 1, pp. 80–93.

BLACK, P. and WILLIAMS, D. (1998) 'Inside the Black Box: Raising standards through classroom assessment', London, King's College School of Education.

BLACKMORE, J. (1988) *Assessment and Accountability*, Geelong, Deakin University Press.

BLACKMORE, J. (1998) 'Gender, restructuring the emotional economy of higher education', Unpublished paper, Deakin University.

BLANK, R.K. (1993) 'Developing a system of education indicators: Selecting, implementing and reporting indicators', *Educational Evaluation and Policy Analysis*, **15**, 1, pp. 65–80.

BLOOM, B.S., ENGELHART, M.D., FROST, E.J., HILL, W.H. and KRATHWOHL, D.R. (1956) *Taxonomy of Educational Objectives, Handbook 1: Cognitive Domain*, New York, David McKay.

BLYTH, A. (2002) 'Outcomes, standards and benchmarks', *Curriculum Perspectives*, **22**, 3, pp. 13–22.

BOOMER, G. (Ed) (1982) *Negotiating the Curriculum*, Sydney, Ashton Scholastic.

BOOMER, G. (1986) 'Long division: A consideration of participation, equality and brain-power in Australian education', Paper presented at the ACSSO Annual Conference, Launceston.

BOSTON, K. (1994) 'A perspective on the so-called "National Curriculum"', *Curriculum Perspectives*, **14**, 1, pp. 43–44.

BOURKE, S. (1994) 'Some responses to changes in Australian education', *Australian Educational Researcher*, **21**, 1, pp. 1–18.

BOWLES, D. (1980) 'School community relations, community support, and student achievement: A summary of findings', Madison, University of Wisconsin.

BOYD, W.L. (1990) 'Balancing competing values in school reform: International efforts in restructuring education systems', in CHAPMAN, J.D. and DUNSTAN, J.F. (Eds) *Democracy and Bureaucracy*, London, Falmer Press.

BOYD, W.L. (1994) 'National "systemic" school reform: Lessons from the British experience', Paper presented at the Politics of Education Association Conference, Temple University, Philadelphia.

BOYLE, M. (2000) 'The "new style" principal: Roles, reflections and reality in the self-managed school', *The Practising Administrator*, **22**, 4, pp. 40–42.

BRADY, L. (1996) 'Outcome-based education: A critique?', *The Curriculum Journal*, 7, 1, pp. 5–16.

BRADY, L. and KENNEDY, K. (2003) *Curriculum Construction*, 2nd edn, Sydney, Pearson.

BRADY, P. (1984) 'Chasing ghosts out of the machine: A deconstruction of some curriculum theory'. *Curriculum Perspectives*, **4**, 2, pp. 64–66.

BRANDT, R. (1998) 'Listen first', *Educational Leadership*, **55**, 8, pp. 25–30.

BRENNAN, M. (1994) 'For schools to ignore realities', in SMYTH, J. (Ed) *A Socially Critical View of the Self-managing School*, London, Falmer Press.

BRENNAN, R.T., KIM, J., WENZ-GROSS, M. and SIPERSTEIN, G.N. (2001) 'The relative equitability of high-stakes testing versus teacher-assigned grades: An analysis of the Massachusetts Comprehensive Assessment System (MCAS)' *Harvard Educational Review*, **71**, 2, pp. 173–12.

BROADFOOT, P. (1979) *Assessment, Schools and Society*, London, Methuen.

BROOKER, R., MACPHERSON, I. and ASPLAND, T. (2000) 'Taking action research from the local to the global via an hermeneutic spiral', Paper presented at the Annual Conference of the American Educational Research Association, New Orleans.

BROPHY, J. (1981) 'Teacher praise: A functional analysis', *Review of Educational Research*, **51**, 1, pp. 5–32.

BROWN, D.J. (1990) *Decentralization and School-based Management*, London, Falmer Press.

BROWN, M., RALPH, S. and BREMBER, I. (2002) 'Change-linked work-related stress in British teachers', *Research in Education*, **67**, pp. 1–12.

BROWN, T.M. (1988) 'How fields change: A critique of the "Kuhnian" view', in PINAR, W.F. (Ed), *Contemporary Curriculum Discourses*, Scottsdale, AZ, Gorsuch Scarisbrick.

BUDIN, H. (1999) 'The computer enters the classroom', *Teachers College Record*, **100**, 3, pp. 656–670.

BURNAFORD, G., BRODHAGEN, B. and BEANE, J. (1994) 'Teacher action research at the middle level: Inside an integrative curriculum', Paper presented at the Annual Conference of the American Educational Research Association, New Orleans.

BURNAFORD, G., FISCHER, J. and HOBSON, D. (1996) *Teachers Doing Research: Practical Possibilities*, Mahwah, NZ, Lawrence Erlbaum.

BURNETT, P.C. and MEACHAM, D. (2002) 'Measuring the quality of teaching in elementary school classrooms', *Asia-Pacific Journal of Teacher Education*, **30**, 2, pp. 141–154.

BURROW, S. (1994) 'McDonalds in the classroom', in Deakin Centre for Education and Change, *Schooling What Future?* Geelong, Deakin University.

BURROW, S. and MARTIN, R. (1998) 'Speaking up for public education workers — the Australian Education Union in hard times', in REID, A. (Ed), *Going Public: Education Policy and Public Education in Australia,* Canberra, ACSA.

CAIRNS, L. (1992) 'Competency-based education: Nostradamus's Nostrum', *Journal of Teaching Practice*, **12**, 1, pp. 1–31.

CALDWELL, R. (1993) 'Paradox and uncertainty in the governance of education', in BEARE, H. and BOYD, W.L. (Eds) *Restructuring Schools*, London, Falmer Press.

CALDWELL, B.J. (1994a) 'School-based management' in HUSEN, T. and POSTLETHWAITE, T.N. (Eds) *International Encyclopaedia of Education*, 2nd edn, Oxford, Pergamon Press.

CALDWELL, B.J. (1994b) 'The principal's role in radical decentralisation in Victoria's schools of the future', Paper presented at the Annual Meeting of the American Educational Research Association, New Orleans.

CALDWELL, B.J. (1995) 'The impact of self-management and self-government on professional cultures of teaching: A strategic analysis for the 21st century', Roehampton Institute Conference, London.

CALDWELL, B. (2000) 'Scenarios for leadership and abandonment in the transformation of schools', *School Effectiveness and School Improvement*, **11**, 4, pp. 475–499.

CALDWELL, B. (2002a) Policy priorities for the transformation of Australia's Schools, Paper No. 2, Occasional Paper Series, Australian College of Education, Canberra.

CALDWELL, B. (2002b) 'Autonomy and self-management: Concepts and evidence', in BUSH, T. and BELL, L. (Eds) *The Principles and Practice of Educational Management*, London, Paul Chapman.

CALDWELL, B.J. and SPINKS, J.M. (1993) *Leading the Self-managing School*, London, Falmer Press.

CALDWELL, B.J. and SPINKS, J.M. (1998) *Beyond the Self-managing School*, London, Falmer Press.

CALFEE, R. and PERFUMO, P. (1996) (Eds) *Writing Portfolios in the Classroom*, Mahwah, NJ, Lawrence Erlbaum.

CALHOUN, E.F. (2002) 'Action research for school improvement', *Educational Leadership*, **59**, 6, pp. 12–17.

CAMPBELL, P. and SOUTHWORTH, G. (1990) 'Rethinking collegiality: Teachers' views', Paper presented at the Annual Meeting of the American Educational Research Association, Boston.

CAMPBELL, R.J. (1993) (Ed) *Breadth and Balance in the Primary Curriculum*, London, Falmer Press.

CARLESS, D. (2004) 'Continuity and teacher-centred reform: Potential paradoxes in educational change', *Curriculum Perspectives*, **24**,1, pp. 13–21.

CARR, M. (2001) *Assessment in Early Childhood Settings: Learning Stories*, London, Paul Chapman.

CARR, W. and KEMMIS, S. (1986) *Becoming Critical: Education, Knowledge and Action Research*, London, Falmer Press.

CASAS, F.R. and MEAGHAN, D.E. (2001) 'Renewing the debate over the use of standardised testing in the evaluation of learning and teaching', *Interchange*, **32**, 2, pp. 147–181.

CAVANAGH, R. and MACNEIL, N. (2002) 'School visioning: Developing a culture for shared creativity', *The Practising Administrator*, **3**, 1, pp.15–18.

CAVARRETTA, J. (1998) 'Parents are a school's best friend, *Educational Leadership*, **55**, 8, pp. 12–15.

CHAPIN, J.R. and MESSICK, R.G. (1999) *Elementary School Studies*, 2nd edn, New York, Longman.

CHASE, C.I. (1999) *Contemporary Assessment for Educators*, New York, Longman.

CHATTERJI, M. (2002) 'Models and methods for examining standards-based reforms and accountability initiatives: Have the tools of inquiry answered pressing questions on improving schools?', *Review of Educational Research*, **72**, 3, pp. 345–387.

CHODOROW, N. (1978) *The Reproduction of Mothering*, Berkeley, University of California Press.

CHURCHILL, R. and WILLIAMSON, J. (1999) 'Traditional attitudes and contemporary experiences: Teachers and educational change', *Asia-Pacific Journal of Teacher Education and Development*, **2**, 2, pp. 43–51.

CIBULKA, J. (1990) 'American educational reform and government power', *Educational Review*, **42**, 2, pp. 13–29.

CLANDININ, J. (1986) *Classroom Practice: Teachers Images in Action*, London, Falmer Press.

CLARK, A.F. (Ed) (1976) *Experimenting with Organisational Life: The Action Research Approach*, New York, Plenum Press.

CLARK, C.T. and MOSS, P.A. (1995) 'Researching with ethical and epistemological implications of doing collaborative, change-oriented research with teachers and students', Paper presented at the Annual Meeting of the American Educational Research Association.

CLARK, D.L. and GUBA, E.G. (1965) 'Potential change roles in education', Paper presented at the Symposium of Innovation and Planning School Curricula, Airlie House, VA.

CLARK, D.L. and MELOY, J.M. (1990) 'Recanting bureaucracy: A democratic structure for leadership in schools', in LIEBERMAN, A. (Ed) *Schools as Collaborative Cultures: Creating the Future Now*, London, Falmer Press.

CLARKE, S. (1998) *Targeting Assessment in the Primary Classroom*, London, Hodder and Stoughton.

CLARKE, S. (2001) *Unlocking Formative Assessment*, London, Hodder and Stoughton.

CLOUGH, E., ASPINWALL, K. and GIBBS, B. (Eds) (1989) *Learning to Change: An LEA School-focussed Initiative*, London, Falmer Press.

COCHRAN-SMITH, M. (1994) 'The power of teacher research in teacher education', in HOLLINGSWORTH, S. and SOCKETT, H. (Eds) *Teacher Research and Educational Reform*, Ninety-Third Yearbook of the National Society for the Study of Education, Chicago, University of Chicago Press.

COCHRAN-SMITH, M. (2001a) 'The outcomes question in teacher education', *Teaching and Teacher Education*, **17**, 1, pp. 527–546.

COCHRAN-SMITH, M. (2001b) 'Higher standards for prospective teachers: What's missing from the discourse?', *Journal of Teacher Education*, **52**, 3, pp. 179–181.

COCHRAN-SMITH, M. and LYTLE, S.L. (1993) *Inside Outside: Teacher Research and Knowledge*, New York, Teachers College Press.

COHEN, L., MANION, L. and MORRISON, K. (1998) *A Guide to Teaching Practice*, 4th edn, London, Routledge.

COHN-VARAS, B. and GROSE, K. (1998) 'A partnership for literacy', *Educational Leadership*, **55**, 8, pp. 45–48.

COLLINS, C. (1994a) 'Is the national curriculum profiles brief valid?', *Curriculum Perspectives*, **14**, 1, pp. 45–48.

COLLINS, C. (1994b) *Curriculum and Pseudo-Science. Is the Australian National Curriculum Project Built on Credible Foundations?*, Canberra, ACSA.

CONSERVATIVE PARTY (1987) *General Election Manifesto*, London, Conservative Central Office.

CONWAY, J.A. and CALZI, F. (1996) 'The dark side of shared decision making', *Educational Leadership*, **53**, 4, pp. 45–49.

COOMBS, P. (1985) *The World Crisis in Education: The View from the Eighties*, Oxford, Oxford University Press.

COOPER, B.S. (1990) 'Local school reform in Great Britain and the United States: Points of comparison—points of departure'. *Educational Review*, **42**, 2, pp. 68–79.

COOPER, I. (1982) 'The maintenance of order and use of space in primary school buildings', *British Journal of Sociology of Education*, **3**, 3, pp. 45–63.

COPLAND, M. (2001) 'The myth of the superprincipal, *Phi Delta Kappan*, **82**, 7, pp. 528–533.

CORBETT, H.D. and ROSSMAN, J.B. (1989) 'Three paths to implementing change: A research note, *Curriculum Inquiry*, **19**, 2, pp. 163–190.

COREY, S. (1953) *Action Research to Improve School Practices*, New York, Teachers College Press.

CORNBLETH, C. (1990) *Curriculum in Context*, London, Falmer Press.

CORNETT, L.M. (1995) 'Lessons from 10 years of teacher improvement reforms', *Educational Leadership*, **52**, 5, pp. 26–31.

COULBY, D. (2000) *Beyond the National Curriculum*, London, Routledge/Falmer Press.

COUNCIL of CHIEF STATE SCHOOL OFFICERS (1996) Interstate School Leaders Licensure Consortium: Standards for school leaders, Council of Chief State School Officers, Washington, DC.

CRANDALL, D.P. (1988) 'Implementation aspects of dissemination: Reflections towards an immodest proposal', Paper presented at the Annual Meeting of the American Educational Research Association, New Orleans.

CROWLEY, K., CALLANAN, M., TENEBAUM, H. and ALLEN, E. (1998) 'Evidence of early gender bias in informal science activity: A study of everyday parent–child explanation', Unpublished paper, University of Pittsburgh.

CROWTHER, F., HANN, L., McMASTER, J. and FERGUSON, M. (2000) 'Leadership for successful school revitalisation: Lessons from recent Australian research', Paper presented at the Annual Conference of the American Educational Research Association, New Orleans.

CRUICKSHANK, D., JENKINS. D. and METCALF, K. (2003) *The Act of Teaching*, 3rd edn, Boston, McGraw-Hill.

CRUMP, S. (1998) 'New Labour, new conservatism?', Paper presented at the Annual Conference of the American Educational Research Association, San Diego.

CUBAN, L. (1988) 'Reforming again, again and again', *Educational Researcher*, **19**, 1, pp. 3–13.

CUBAN, L. (1992) 'Curriculum stability and change', in JACKSON, P.W. (Ed) *Handbook of Research on Curriculum*, New York, Macmillan.

CUNNINGHAM, G.K. (1998) *Assessment in the Classroom*, London, Falmer Press.

DANIELSON, C. (2001) 'New trends in teacher evaluation', *Educational Leadership*, **58**, 5, pp. 12–15.

DARLING-HAMMOND, L. (1994) 'Performance-based assessment and educational equity', *Harvard Educational Review*, **64**, 1, pp. 5–30.

DARLING-HAMMOND, L. (1997) *The Right to Learn: A Blueprint for Creating Schools that Work*, San Francisco, Jossey-Bass.

DARLING-HAMMOND, L. (1998) 'Teacher learning that supports student learning', *Educational Leadership*, **55**, 5, pp. 6–11.

DARLING-HAMMOND, L. and FALK, B. (1997) 'Using standards and assessments to support student learning', *Phi Delta Kappan*, **79**, 3, pp. 190–199.

DARLING-HAMMOND, L., ANCESS, J. and FALK, B. (1995) *Authentic Assessment in Action*, New York, Teachers College Press.

DAVID, J.L. (1996) 'The who, what and why of site-based management', *Educational Leadership*, **53**, 4, pp. 4–9.

DAVIES, R. and ELLISON, T. (2000) 'Site-based management: myths and realities', Paper presented at the Annual Conference of the American Educational Research Association, New Orleans.

DAY, C. and ROBERTS-HOLMES, T. (1998) 'Beyond transformational leadership', *Educational Leadership*, **57**, 7, pp. 56–59.

DAY, C., JOHNSTON, D. and WHITAKER, P. (1985) *Managing Primary School*, London, Harper and Row.

DAY, C., POPE, M. and DENICOLO, P. (Eds) (1990) *Insight into Teachers' Thinking and Practice*, London, Falmer Press.

DE CASTELL, S. (2000) 'Literacies, technologies and the future of the library in the "information age"', *Journal of Curriculum Studies*, **32**, 3, pp. 359–376.

DELANDSHERE, G. and ARENS, S.A. (2001) 'Representations of teaching and standards-based reform: Are we closing the debate about teacher education?' *Teaching and Teacher Education*, **17**, 1, pp. 547–566.

DE MOCKER, S. (1986) *A Trail of Desire: Aspects of Relationship with Nature*, Unpublished doctoral dissertation, University of Rochester.

DEPARTMENT FOR EDUCATION AND SKILLS (1997) White Paper, 'Excellence in Schools', London, HMSO.

DEPARTMENT FOR EDUCATION AND SKILLS (2001) *Education and Skills: Investment for Reform*, London, HMSO.

DEPARTMENT FOR EDUCATION AND SKILLS (2002) *Education and Skills: Investment for Reform*, London, HMSO.

DEPARTMENT OF EDUCATION, WESTERN AUSTRALIA (2002a) *The School Accountability Framework*, Perth, Government Printer.

DEPARTMENT OF EDUCATION, WESTERN AUSTRALIA (2002b) *Forming Judgments about School Performance: A Resource for Successful Self-Assessment*, Perth, Department of Education

DEPARTMENT FOR EMPLOYMENT, EDUCATION AND TRAINING (DEET) (1987) *National Policy for the Education of Girls*, Canberra, Australian Government Printing Service.

DERRIDA, J. (1972) 'Discussion: Structure, sign and play in the discourse of the human sciences', in MACKSEY, R. and DONATO, E. (Eds) *The Structuralist Controversy*, Baltimore, Johns Hopkins University Press.

DESIMONE, L. (2002) 'How can comprehensive school reform models be successfully implemented?', *Review of Educational Research*, **72**, 3, pp. 433–480.

DE VANEY, A. (1998) 'Educational technology', *Theory into Practice*, **37**, 1, pp. 2–3.

DEWEY, J. (1916) Democracy and Education, Macmillan, New York.

DIMMOCK, C. (1993) (Ed) *School-based Management and School Effectiveness*, London, Routledge.

DINKELMAN, T. (2001) 'Service learning in student teaching: "What's social studies for?"', *Theory and Research in Social Education*, **29**, 4, pp. 617–639.

DODD, A.W. (1998) 'What can educators learn from parents who oppose curricular and classroom practices?', *Journal of Curriculum Studies*, **30**, 4, pp. 461–478.

DOLL, R.C. (1996) *Curriculum Improvement: Decision Making and Process*, 9th edn, Boston, Allyn & Bacon.

DOLL, W.E. JR (1993a) *A Post-modern Perspective on Curriculum*, New York, Teachers College Press.

DOLL, W.E. JR (1993b) 'Curriculum possibilities in a "post" future', *Journal of Curriculum and Supervision*, **8**, 4, pp. 277–292.

DONMOYER, R. (1982) 'Curriculum and the common good', Paper presented at the Annual Conference of the American Educational Research Association, New York.

DONMOYER, R. (1998) 'Educational standards: moving beyond the rhetoric', *Educational Researcher*, **27**, 4, p. 203.

DONNELLY, K. (2002) 'A review of New Zealand's school curriculum, *Education Forum*, October, pp. 1–69.

DOWN, B., CHADBOURNE, R. and HOGAN, C. (2000) 'How are teachers managing performance management?', *Asia-Pacific Journal of Teacher Education*, **28**, 3, pp. 213–222.

DRAKE, N.M. (1991) 'What is needed most: School reform or media reform?', *Phi Delta Kappan*, **73**, 1, p. 57.

DRYFOOS, J. (2000) 'The mind–body building equation', *Educational Leadership*, **57**, 6, pp. 14–17.

DU FOUR, R. (2002) 'The learning-centred principal', *Educational Leadership*, **59**, 8, pp. 12–15.

DUKE, (1984) *Teaching: The Imperilled Profession*, Albany, New York, SUNY.

DUNN, R., BEAUDRY, J.S. and KLAVAS, A. (1989) 'Survey of research on learning styles', *Educational Leadership*, **46**, 6, pp. 50–58.

DYER, K.M. (2001) 'The power of 360-degree feedback', *Educational Leadership*, **58**, 5, pp. 35–39.

EASTHOPE, C. and EASTHOPE, G. (2000) 'Intensification, extension and complexity of teachers' workload', *British Journal of Sociology of Education*, **21**, 1, pp. 43–56.

EDUCATION COMMISSION OF THE STATES (1998) Comprehensive school reform: Allocating federal funds, Denver, Education Commission of the States.

EDWARDS, V. and REDFERN, A. (1988) *At Home and School: Parent Participation in Primary Education*, London, Routledge.

EGAN, K. (2003) 'Testing what for what?', *Educational Leadership*, **61**, 3, pp. 27–30.

EISNER, E.W. (1979) *The Educational Imagination*, New York, Macmillan.

EISNER, E.W. (1992) 'Educational reform and the ecology of schooling', *Teachers College Record*, **93**, 4, pp. 610–627.

EISNER, E.W. (1993) 'Reshaping assessment in education: Some criteria in search of practice', *Journal of Curriculum Studies*, **25**, 3, pp. 219–233.

EISNER, E.W. (1997) 'The promise and perils of alternative forms of data representation', *Educational Researcher*, **26**, 6, pp. 4–9.

EISNER, E. and VALLANCE, E. (1974) (Eds) *Conflicting Conceptions of Curriculum*, Berkeley, CA, McCutchan.

ELLERTON, N.F. and CLEMENTS, M.A. (1994) *The National Curriculum Debacle*, Perth, Meridian Press.

ELLIOTT, J. (1975) 'Initiation into classroom discussion', in ELLIOTT, J. and MACDONALD, B. (Eds) *People in Classrooms*, Norwich, Centre for Applied Research in Education, University of East Anglia.

ELLIOTT, J. (1991) 'Changing contexts for educational evaluation: The challenge for methodology', *Studies in Educational Evaluation*, **17**, pp. 215–238.

ELLIOTT, J. (1999) *The Curriculum Experiment*, Milton Keynes, Open University Press.

ELLIOTT, J. (2002) 'Action research as the basis of a new professionalism for teachers in an age of globalisation', Paper presented at the Centenary Year Conference, Beijing, Beijing Normal University.

ELLIOTT, J., CHAN, K.K. (2002) 'Curriculum Reform East & West: Global Trends and Local Contexts', Unpublished Paper, University of East Anglia,

ELLIS, A.K. and FOUTS, J.T. (1993) *Research on Educational Innovations, Eye on Education*, New Jersey, Princeton Junction.

ELMORE, R.F. (1988) 'Modes of restructured schools', Unpublished paper, Michigan State University.

EMMER, E.T., EVERTSON, C. and WORSHAM, M. (2000) *Classroom Management for Secondary Teachers*, 5th edn, Boston, Allyn and Bacon

EMMER, E.T. and GERWELL, M.C. (1998) 'Teachers' views and uses of cooperative learning, Paper presented at the Annual Conference of the American Educational Research Association, San Diego.

ERAUT, M., GOAD, L. and SMOOTH, G. (1975) *The Analysis of Curriculum Materials*, Brighton, University of Sussex.

ERIKSEN, A. and WINTERMUTE, M. (1983) *Students, Structure, Spaces: Activities in the Built Environment*, Washington, DC, ERIC Research in Education, ED233796.

EVANS, K. (1990) 'Messages conveyed by physical forms', in LOFTHOUSE, B. (Ed) *The Study of Primary Education: A Source Book*, Vol. 2, *The Curriculum*. London, Falmer Press.

FANTINI, M. (1980) 'Community participation: Alternative patterns and their consequence on educational achievement', Paper presented at the Annual Meeting of the American Educational Research Association, San Francisco.

FEINGOLD, A. (1992) 'Sex differences in variability in intellectual abilities: A new look at an old controversy', *Review of Educational Research*, **62**, 1, pp. 74–81.

FELDMAN, A., REARICK, M. and WEISS, T. (1999) 'Teacher development and action research: Findings from five years of action research in schools', Paper presented at the Annual Conference of the American Educational Research Association, Montreal.

FERNANDEZ, C., CHOKSKI, S., CANNON, J. and YOSHIDA, M. (2003) 'Learning about lesson study in the United States', *New and Old Voices on Japanese Education*, Armonk, NY, M.E. Sharpe.

FIELD, T. (1980) 'Imaginative alternative use of learning spaces', in POOLE, M. (Ed) *Creativity Across the Curriculum*, Sydney, George Allen and Unwin.

FINN, J.D. (1998) 'Parental engagement that makes a difference', *Educational Leadership*, **55**, 8, pp. 20–24.

FINN, J.D. and ACHILLES, C.M. (1999) 'Tennessee's class size study: Findings, implications, misconceptions', *Educational Evaluation and Policy Analysis*, **21**, 2, pp. 97–110.

FINN, J.D., GERBER, S.B., ACHILLES, C.M. and BOYD-ZAHARIAS, J. (2001) 'The enduring effects of small classes', *Teachers College Record*, **103**, 1, pp. 145–183.

FISCHER, L., SCHIMMEL, D. and KELLY, C. (1995) *Teachers and the Law*, 4th edn, New York, Longman.

FISHER, D.L. and FRASER, B.J. (1981) 'Validity and use of the "My class inventory"', *Science Education*, **65**, pp. 3–11.

FORD, N. and CHEN, S.Y. (2001) 'Matching/mismatching revisited: An empirical study of learning and teaching styles', *British Journal of Educational Technology*, **32**, 1, pp. 5–22.

FORSTER, M. (1994) 'DART: Assisting teachers to use the English profile in assessing and reporting, in WARHUST, J. (Ed), *Teaching and Learning, Implementing the Profiles,* Canberra, ACSA.

FOSTER, W. (1989) 'Toward a critical practice of leadership', in SMYTH, J. (Ed) *Critical Perspectives of Educational Leadership*, London, Falmer Press.

FOUCAULT, M. (1972) *The Archaeology of Knowledge and the Discourse on Language*, New York, Pantheon.

FRANCIS, D. (2001) 'The challenge of involving students in the Evaluation Process', *Asia-Pacific Journal of Teacher Education*, **29**, 2, pp. 13–37.

FRANKLIN, J. (2002) 'Assessing assessment: Are alternative methods making the grade?', *ASCD Curriculum Update*, Spring, 1–8.

FRASER, B.J. (1981) 'Australian research on classroom environment: State of the art', *Australian Journal of Education*, **25**, pp. 31–42.

FRASER, B.J. (1986) *Classroom Environment*, London, Croom Helm.

FRASER, B.J. and WALBERG, H.J. (1991) (Eds) *Educational Environments*, London, Pergamon Press.

FRASER, B.J., McROBBIE, C.J. and FISHER, D.L. (1996) 'Development, validation and use of the personal and class forms of a new classroom environment instrument', Paper presented at the Annual Conference of the American Educational Research Association, New York.

FROESE-GERMAIN, B. (2001) 'Broadening the discourse on student assessment: Response to Casas and Meaghan', *Interchange*, **32**, 2, pp. 183–190.

FULLAN, M.G. (1982) *The Meaning of Educational Change*, New York, Teachers College Press.

FULLAN, M. (1986) *School Improvement Efforts in Canada*, Toronto, Council of Ministers of Education.

FULLAN, M.G. (1988) *What's Worth Fighting for in the Principalship?*, Toronto, Ontario Teachers Federation.

FULLAN, M. (1989) *Implementing Educational Change: What We Know*, Ottawa, Education and Employment Division, Population and Human Resources Department, World Bank.

FULLAN, M.G. (1991) *The New Meaning of Educational Change*, London, Cassell.

FULLAN, M. (1993) *Change Forces*, London, Falmer Press.

FULLAN, M.G. (1996) 'Turning systemic thinking on its head', *Phi Delta Kappan*, **78**, 2, pp. 87–95.

FULLAN, M.G. (1999) *Change Forces: The Sequel*. London, Falmer Press.

FULLAN, M. (2001) *Leading in a Culture of Change*, San Francisco, Jossey-Bass.

FULLAN, M. (2002) 'The change leader', *Educational Leadership*, **59**, 8, pp. 16–21.

FULLAN, M. and EARL, L. (2002) 'United Kingdom National literacy and numeracy strategies', *Journal of Educational Change*, **3**, pp. 1–5.

FULLAN, M. and HARGREAVES, A. (1991) *Working Together for Your School*. Melbourne, Australian Council for Educational Administration.

FULLAN, M.G. and POMFRET, A. (1977) 'Research on curriculum and instruction implementation', *Review of Educational Research*, **47**, 2, pp. 335–397.

FULLAN, M. and WATSON, N. (2000) 'School-based management: Reconceptualizing to improve learning outcomes', *School Effectiveness and School Improvement*, **11**, 4, pp. 453–473.

FURLONG, J. (2002) 'Ideology and reform in teacher education in England: Some reflections on Cochran-Smith & Fries', *Educational Researcher*, **31**, 6, pp. 23–25.

FUTORAN, G.C., SCHOFIELD, J.W. and EURICH-FULMER, R. (1995) 'The Internet as a K-12 educational resource: Emerging issues of information access and freedom', *Computers in Education*, **24**, 3, pp. 229–236.

GALBRAITH, J. (1997) 'The Internet, past, present and future', *Educational Technology*, **37**, 6, pp. 39–45.

GALTON, M., GRAY, J. and RUDDUCK, J. (2003) *Impact of Transitions and Transfers on Pupil Progress*, London, Department for Education and Skills.

GAMAGE, D.T. (1992) 'School-centred educational reforms of the 1990s: An Australian case study', *Educational Management and Administration*, **20**, 1, pp. 5–14.

GAMAGE, D.T. (1993) 'A review of community participation in school governance: An emerging culture in Australian Education', *British Journal of Educational Studies*, **41**, 2, pp. 134–163.

GARDNER, P. (1997) Managing Technology in the Middle School, Hawker Brownlow, Melbourne.

GAY, K. (1986) *Ergonomics*, Hillsdale, NJ, Enslow Publishers

GEORGE, C.J. and McKINLEY, D. (1974) *Urban Ecology*, New York, McGraw-Hill.

GEORGE, P., LAWRENCE, G. and BUSHNELL, D. (1998) *Handbook for Middle School Teaching*, 2nd edn, New York, Longman.

GIBBS, D. and KRAUSE, K.L. (2000) (Eds) *Cyberlines*, Melbourne, James Nicholas.

GIDDENS, A. (1990) *The Consequences of Modernity*, Cambridge, Cambridge University Press.

GILBERT, R. and GILBERT, P. (1998) *Masculinity Goes to School*, Sydney, Allen and Unwin.

GIPPS, C.V. (1994) *Beyond Testing*, London, Falmer Press.

GIPPS, C. and MURPHY, P. (1994) *A Fair Test?: Assessment, Achievement and Equity*, Buckingham, Open University Press.

GIPPS, C., McCALLUM, B. and HARGREAVES, E. (2000) 'Classroom assessment and feedback strategies of "expert" elementary teachers', Paper presented at the Annual Conference of the American Educational Research Association, New Orleans.

GIROUX, H.A. (1982) 'Power and resistance in the new sociology of education: Beyond theories of social and cultural reproduction', *Curriculum Perspectives*, **2**, 3, pp. 1–14.

GIROUX, H.A. (1991) *Postmodernism, Feminism and Cultural Politics*. Albany, State University of New York Press.

GIROUX, H.A. (1992) *Border Crossings: Cultural Workers and the Politics of Education*, New York, Routledge.

GIROUX, H.A. and McLAREN, P. (1986) 'Teacher education and the politics of engagement: The case for democratic schooling', *Harvard Educational Review*, **56**, 3, pp. 213–238.

GLATTHORN, A.A. (1987) *Curriculum Leadership*, Glenview, Scott, Foresman and Company.

GLATTHORN, A.A. and FONTANA, J. (2002) *Standards and Accountability: How Teachers See Them*, Washington, DC, National Education Association.

GLATTHORN, A.A. and JAILALL, J. (2000) 'Curriculum for the new millennium', in BRANDT, R.S. (Ed) *Education in a New Era*, Alexandria, VA, ASCD.

GLICKMAN, C.D. (2003) 'Symbols and celebrations that sustain education', *Educational Leadership*, **60**, 6, pp. 34–39.

GOERTZ, M.E. (2001) 'Redefining government roles in an era of standard-based reform, *Phi Delta Kappan*, **83**, 1, pp. 62–66.

GOLD, Y. and ROTH, R.A. (1993) *Teachers Managing Stress and Preventing Burnout*, London, Falmer Press.

GOLDRING, E.B. (1993) 'Principals, parents and administrative superiors', *Educational Administration Quarterly*, **29**, 1, pp. 93–117.

GOLDSMITH, L.T. and MARK, J. (1999) 'What is a standards-based mathematics curriculum?', *Educational Leadership*, **57**, 3, pp. 40–45.

GOOD, T. and BRADEN, J. (2000) 'Charter schools: Another reform failure or a worthwhile investment?', *Phi Delta Kappan*, **81**, 10, pp. 745–750.

GOODLAD, J. (1979) *Curriculum Inquiry: The Study of Curriculum Practice*, New York, McGraw-Hill.

GOODLAD, J. and SU, Z. (1992) 'Organisation of the curriculum', in JACKSON, P. (Ed) *Handbook of Research on Curriculum*, New York, Macmillan.

GOODSON, I.F. (1981) 'Becoming an academic subject', *British Journal of Sociology of Education*, **2**, 2, pp. 56–83.

GOODSON, I.F. (1985) (Ed) *Social Histories of the Secondary Curriculum*, London, Falmer Press.

GOODSON, I.F. (1988) *The Making of Curriculum*, London, Falmer Press.

GOODSON, I. F. (1991) 'Teachers' lives and educational research', in GOODSON, I.F. and WALKER, R. (Eds) *Biography, Identity and Schooling: Episodes in Educational Research*, London, Falmer Press.

GOODSON, I.F. (1992) (Ed) *Studying Teachers' Lives*, London, Routledge.

GOODSON, I.F. (1994) *Studying Curriculum; Cases and Methods*, New York, Teachers College Press.

GOODSON, I. (2000) 'Social histories of educational change', *Journal of Educational Change*, **2**, 1, pp. 2–15.

GOODSON, I. (2001a) 'Educational change and professional biography', Paper presented at the Annual Conference of the American Educational Research Association, Chicago.

GOODSON, I.F. (2001b) 'Social histories of educational change', *Journal of Educational Change*, **2**, 1, pp. 1–31.

GOODSON, I.F. and MARSH, C.J. (1996) *Studying School Subjects*, London, Falmer Press.

GORMAN, J.C. and BALTER, L. (1997) 'Culturally sensitive parent education: A critical review of quantitative research', *Review of Educational Research*, **67**, 3, pp. 339–369.

GRACE, G. (1995) *School Leadership*, London, Falmer Press.

GRAHAM, R.J. (1991) *Reading and Writing the Self: Autobiography in Education and the Curriculum*, New York, Teachers College Press.

GRANHEIM, M. (1990) *Evaluation as Policy Making*, London, Jessica Kingsley Press.

GREEN, A. (1994) 'Postmodernism and state education', *Journal of Education Policy*, **9**, 1, pp. 67–83.

GREEN, B. (1988) (Ed) *Metaphors and Meanings*, Perth, Australian Association for the Teaching of English.

GRESHAM, A., HESS, F., MARANTO, R. and MILLIMAN, S. (2000) 'Desert bloom: Arizona's free market in education', *Phi Delta Kappan*, **81**, 10, pp. 751–757.

GRIFFIN, D.R., COBB, J.B., FORD, M.P., GUNTER, P. and OCHS, P. (1993) *Founders of Constructive Postmodern Philosophy: Pierce, James, Bergson, Whitehead, and Hartshorne*, Albany, State University of New York Press.

GRIFFIN, P. (1998) 'Outcomes and profiles: Changes in teachers' assessment practices', *Curriculum Perspectives*, **18**, 1, pp. 9–19.

GRIFFITH, J. (1997) 'Student and parent perceptions of school social environment: Are they group based?', *Elementary School Journal*, **98**, 2, pp. 135–150.

GRIFFITH, R. (2000) *National Curriculum: National Disaster*, London, Routledge/ Falmer Press.

GRONN, P. (2000) 'Distributed properties: A new architecture for leadership', Paper presented at the Annual Conference of the American Educational Research Association, New Orleans.

GROUNDWATER-SMITH, S. (1992) 'Partnership in the professional development of teachers: Toward intercultural understanding', Paper presented at the Annual Conference of the Australian Association for Research in Education, Geelong.

GRUMET, M. (1981) 'Restitution and reconstruction of educational experience, an auto-biographical method for curriculum theory', in LAWN, M. and BARTON, L. (Eds) *Rethinking Curriculum Studies*, London, Croom Helm.

GRUMET, M. and STONE, L. (2000) 'Feminism and curriculum: Getting our act together', *Journal of Curriculum Studies*, **32**, 2, pp. 183–197.

GRUNDY, S. (1982) 'Three modes of action research', *Curriculum Perspectives*, **2**, 3, pp. 23–34.

GRUNDY, S. (1994) 'The National Curriculum debate in Australia: Discordant discourses', *South Australian Educational Leader*, **5**, 3, pp. 1–7.

GRUNDY, S. and BONSER, S. (1997) 'In whose interests? Competing discourses in the policy and practice of school restructuring', *Australian Journal of Education*, **41**, 2, pp. 150–168.

GUAN, H.K. (2000) *The implementation of an innovative computer course in Singapore: Perception and practice*, Unpublished doctoral dissertation, University of Western Australia.

GUBA, E.G. and LINCOLN, Y.W. (1989) *Fourth Generation Evaluation*, Newbury Park, CA, Sage.

GUGLIELMI, R.S. and TATROW, K. (1998) 'Occupational stress, burnout and health in teachers: A methodological and theoretical analysis', *Review of Educational Research*, **68**, 1, pp. 61–99.

GUSKEY, T. (2002) 'Does it make a difference? Evaluating professional development', *Educational Leadership*, **59**, 6, pp. 45–51.

GUSKEY, T.R. and PETERSEN, K.D. (1996) 'The road to classroom change', *Educational Leadership*, **53**, 4, pp. 10–15.

GUTHRIE, J.W. (1986) 'School-based management: The next needed education reform', *Phi Delta Kappan*, **68**, 3, pp. 208–11.

GUTTMAN, T. (1993) 'Petition to the Victorian Minister for Education regarding the mathematics national profile', May, University of Melbourne.

HABERMAS, J. (1970) *Knowledge and Human Interests*, Boston, Beacon.

HALL, G.E. and HORD, S.M. (1987) *Change in Schools: Facilitating the Process*, Albany, State University of New York Press.

HALL, G.E. and LOUCKS, S.F. (1978) 'Innovation configurations: Analysing the adaptations of innovations', In *Procedures for Adopting Educational Innovations Program*, Austin, University of Texas, Research and Development Centre for Teacher Education.

HALL, G.E., GEORGE, A.A. and RUTHERFORD, W.L. (1977) *Measuring Stages of Concern About the Innovation: A Manual for Use of the SoC questionnaire*, 2nd edn, Austin, University of Texas, Research and Development Centre for Teacher Education.

HALSTEAD, J.M. (1994) (Ed) *Parental Choice and Education*, London, Kogan Page.

HANDY, C. (1981) *Understanding Organisations*, London, Penguin.

HANEY, W. and MADAUS, G. (1989) 'Searching for alternatives to standardized tests: Whys, whats, and whithers', *Phi Delta Kappan*, **70**, 9, pp. 683–687.

HANNAN, B. (1992) 'National Curriculum: A system perspective', *Unicorn*, **18**, 3, pp. 28–31.

HANNAY, L.M. and MACFARLANE, N. (1998) 'Implementing action research: The influence of context and professional development processes', Paper presented at the Annual Conference of the American Educational Research Association, San Diego.

HANNAY, L.M. and SELLER, W. (1998) 'Action research as performance assessment', Paper presented at the Annual Conference of the American Educational Research Association, San Diego.

HANSEN, J.M. (1989) 'Outcome-based education: A smarter way to assess student learning', *Clearing House*, **63**, 4, pp. 172–174.

HARDY, T. (1990) 'Curriculum frameworks in the ACT: The case of could, should or must?' *Curriculum Perspectives*, **10**, 4, pp. 1–8.

HARGREAVES, A. (1989) *Curriculum and Assessment Reform*, Milton Keynes, Open University Press.

HARGREAVES, D. (1994) *The Mosaic of Learning*, London, Demos.

HARGREAVES, A. (1995) *Changing Teachers, Changing Times*, London, Cassell.

HARGREAVES, A. (1997) 'Culture of teaching and educational change', in FULLAN, M. (Ed) *The Challenge of School Change*, Arlington Heights, IL, Skylight Press.

HARGREAVES, A, (1998) 'The emotional politics of teaching and teacher development with implications for educational leadership', *International Journal of Leadership in Education*, **1**, 4, pp. 315–336.

HARGREAVES, A. and DAWE, R. (1990) 'Paths of professional development: Contrived collegiality, collaborative culture and the case of peer coaching', *Teaching and Teacher Education*, **6**, 3, pp. 227–241.

HARGREAVES, A. and FULLAN, M. (2000) 'Mentoring in the new millennium', *Theory into Practice*, **39**,1, pp. 1–55.

HARGREAVES, A., EARL, L., MOORE, S. and MANNING, S. (2001) *Learning to Change*, San Francisco, Jossey-Bass.

HARGREAVES, A., EARL, L. and SCHMIDT, M. (2002) 'Perspectives in alternative assessment reform', *American Educational Reform Journal*, **39**, 1, pp. 69–95.

HAROLD, B. (1997) 'Negotiating partnerships between the home and school: A New Zealand perspective', Paper presented at the Biennial Conference of the Australian Curriculum Studies Association, Perth.

HAROLD, B. (1999) 'Self-management and the curriculum framework: What have we learnt?', Paper presented at the Biennial Conference of the Australian Curriculum Studies Association, Perth.

HARRIS, D. and BELL, C. (1990) *Evaluating and Assessing for Learning*, London, Kogan Page.

HARROLD, R. (2000) 'The economic and political context of school resourcing, 1985–2000', in KARMEL, P. (Ed) *School Resourcing: Models and Practices in Changing Times*, Canberra, Australian College of Education.

HARTMEISTER, F. (1995) 'School law: What principals learn in colleges of education compared to what they need to know in the "real world"', Paper presented at the Annual Conference of the American Educational Research Association, San Francisco.

HARTY, S. (1990) 'US corporations: Still pitching after all these years', *Educational Leadership*, **47**, 4, pp. 77–78.

HATCH, T. (1998) 'How community action contributes to achievement', *Educational Leadership*, **55**, 8, pp. 16–19.

HATCH, T. (2000) 'What does it take to break the mold? Rhetoric and reality in new American schools', *Teachers College Record*, **102**, 3, pp. 561–589.

HAYES, M.T. and KELLY, M. (2000) 'Transgressed boundaries: Reflections on the problematics of culture and power in developing a collaborative relationship with teachers at an elementary school', *Curriculum Inquiry*, **30**, 4, pp. 13–37.

HAYNES, G.S., WRAGG, E.C., WRAGG, C.M. and CHAMBERLIN, R.P. (2001) 'Threshold assessment: The experiences and views of teachers', Paper presented at the Annual Conference of the British Educational Research Association, Leeds.

HEBERT, E.A. (1998) 'Lessons learned about student portfolios', *Phi Delta Kappan*, **79**, 8, pp. 583–585.

HECK, R.H. and CRISLIP, M. (2001) 'Direct and indirect writing assessments: Examining issues of equity and utility', *Educational Evaluation and Policy Analysis*, **23**, 3, pp. 275–292.

HEIBERT, J., GALLIMORE, R. and STIGLER, J.W. (2002) 'A knowledge base for the teaching profession: What would it look like and how can we get one?', *Educational Researcher*, **31**, 5, pp. 3–15.

HELLER, G.S. (1993) 'Teacher empowerment, sharing the challenge: A guide for implementation and success', *NASSP Bulletin*, **77**, 550, pp. 94–103.

HELSBY, G. (1995) *Never Mind the Quality, Feel the Width: Reforming the Curriculum the English Way*, London, Roehampton Institute Conference.

HELSBY, G. and SAUNDERS, M. (1993) 'Taylorism, Tylerism and performance indicators: Defending the indefensible', *Educational Studies*, **19**, 1, pp. 55–77.

HERMAN, J.L. and WINTERS, L. (1994) 'Synthesis of research: Portfolio research: A slim collection', *Educational Leadership*, **52**, 2, pp. 48–55.

HESS, F.M. (2003) 'The case for being mean', *Educational Leadership*, **61**, 3, pp. 22–26.

HIATT-MICHAEL, D. (2000) 'Parent involvement as a component of teacher education programs in California', Paper presented at the Annual Conference of the American Educational Research Association, New Orleans.

HILL, P.W. (1995) *Value Added Measures of Achievement*, IARTV Seminar Series, Melbourne, IARTV.

HILL, S. and HILL, T. (1990) *The Collaborative Classroom*, Melbourne, Eleanor Curtain.

HIRST, P.H. (1967) 'The logical and physiological aspects of teaching a subject', in PETERS, R. (Ed) *The Concept of Education*, London, Routledge and Kegan Paul.

HIRST, P.H. (1974) *Knowledge and the Curriculum*, London, Routledge and Kegan Paul.

HLEBOWITSH, P.S. (1992) 'Amid behavioural and behavioristic objectives: Reappraising appraisals of the Tyler rationale', *Journal of Curriculum Studies*, **24**, 6, pp. 533–547.

HLEBOWITSH, P.S. (1993) *Radical Curriculum Theory Reconsidered*. New York, Teachers College Press.

HLEBOWITSH, P.S. (1999) 'The burdens of the new curricularist', *Curriculum Inquiry*, **23**, 3, pp. 343–353.

HOLDSWORTH, R. (1993) 'Student participation: A decade of unfinished business', in SMITH, D. (Ed) *Australian Curriculum Reform: Action and Reaction*, Canberra, ACSA.

HOLT, M. (1990) 'Managing curriculum change in a comprehensive school: Conflict, compromise and deliberation', *Journal of Curriculum Studies*, **22**, 2, pp. 137–48.

HOOVER-DEMPSEY, K.V. and SANDLER, H.M. (1997) Why do parents become involved in their children's education', *Review of Educational Research*, **67**, 1, pp. 3–42.

HOPMANN, S. and KUNZLI, T. (1997) 'Close our schools! Against current trends in policy making, educational theory and curriculum studies', *Journal of Curriculum Studies*, **29**, 3, pp. 259–266.

HORD, S.M. and HULING-AUSTIN, L. (1987) 'Curriculum implementation: How to know if it's there (or not there)', *Journal of Rural and Small Schools*, **1**, 3, pp. 23–26.

HOROWITZ, P. and OTTO, D. (1973) *The Teaching Effectiveness of an Alternative Teaching Facility* (ERIC Document Reproduction Service No. ED083242), Alberta, University of Alberta.

HOUSE, E.R. (1979) 'Technology versus craft: A ten-year perspective on innovation', *Journal of Curriculum Studies*, **11**, 1, pp. 1–16.

HOUSE, E.R. (1996) 'A framework for appraising educational reforms', *Educational Researcher*, **25**, 7, pp. 6–14.

HOWARD, B.B. and MCCOLSKEY, W.H. (2001) 'Evaluating experienced teachers', *Educational Leadership*, **58**, 5, pp. 48–51.

HOY, W.K. and TARTER, C.J. (1993) 'A normative theory of participative decision making in schools', *Journal of Educational Administration*, **31**, 3, pp. 4–19.

HUBBARD, L. and DATNOW, A. (2000) 'A gendered look at educational reform', *Gender and Education*, **12**, 1, pp. 115–129.

HUBERMAN, M. (1993) *The Lives of Teachers*, New York, Teachers College Press.

HUGHES, M. and GREENHOUGH, P. (1998) 'Parents' and teachers' knowledge bases and instructional strategies', Paper presented at the Annual Conference of the American Educational Research Association, San Diego.

HUGHES, P.W. (1990) 'A national curriculum: Promise or warning?', Occasional Paper No. 14, Canberra, Australian College of Education.

HUNT, G. (1981) *The Curriculum and the Community*, Occasional Paper No. 5, Canberra, Curriculum Development Centres.

HURSH, D. (1995) 'Developing discourses and structures to support action research for educational reform', In NOFFKE, S. and STEVENSON, R. (Eds) *Educational Action Research: Becoming Practically Critical*, New York, Teachers College Press.

HURST, B., WILSON, C. and CRAMER, G. (1998) 'Professional teaching portfolios: Tools for reflection, growth and advancement', *Phi Delta Kappan*, **79**, 8, pp. 578–582.

INGVARSON, L. (2002) 'Building a learning profession, Paper No. 1, Commissioned Research Series, Canberra, Australian College of Educators.

INGVARSON, L. and CHADBOURNE, R. (1994) (Eds) *Valuing Teachers' Work: New Directions in Teacher Appraisal*, Melbourne, ACER.

INGVARSON, L. and CHADBOURNE, R. (1997) 'Will appraisal cycles and performance management lead to improvements in teaching?', *Unicorn*, **23**, 1, pp. 44–64.

IWANICKI, E.F. (2001) 'Focusing teacher evaluations on student learning', *Educational Leadership*, **58**, 5, pp. 57–59.

JACKSON, P. (1992) (Ed) *Handbook of Research on Curriculum*, New York, Macmillan.

JAMES, E.J.F. (Chairperson) (1972) *Teacher Education and Training*, London, HMSO.

JANSEN, T. and VAN DER VEGT, R. (1991) 'On lasting innovation in schools: Beyond institutionalism', *Journal of Educational Policy*, **6**, 1, pp. 33–46.

JENCKS, C. (1986) *What is Post-modernism?*, New York, St Martin's Press.

JENCKS, C. (Ed). (1992) *The Post-modern Reader*, New York, St Martin's Press.

JOBE, D.A. (2003) 'Helping girls succeed', *Educational Leadership*, **60**, 4, pp. 64–67.

JOHNSON, J. (2003) 'What does the public say about accountability?', *Educational Leadership*, **61**, 3, pp. 36–41.

JONES, B.D. (2002) 'Recommendations for implementing internet inquiry projects', *Journal of Educational Technology Systems*, **30**, 3, pp. 271–291.

JOYCE, B. and SHOWERS, B. (1988) *Student Achievement through Staff Development*, New York, Longman.

JOYCE, B. and WEIL, M. (1986) *Models of Teaching*, 3rd edn, Englewood Cliffs, Prentice-Hall.

KARSTEN, S., VISSCHER, A. and DE JONG, T. (2001) 'Another side to the coin: The unintended effects of the publication of school performance data in England and France', *Comparative Education*, **37**, 2, pp. 231–242.

KELCHTERMANS, G. and VANDENBERGHE, R. (1994) 'Teachers' professional development: A biographical perspective', *Journal of Curriculum Studies*, **26**, 1, pp. 45–62.

KEMMIS, S. (1982) 'Seven principles for program evaluation in curriculum development and innovation', *Journal of Curriculum Studies*, **14**, 3, pp. 221–240.

KEMMIS, S. and McTAGGART, R. (1984) *The Action Research Planner*, Geelong, Deakin University Press.

KEMMIS, S. and McTAGGART, R. (1988) *The Action Research Planner*, 3rd edn, Geelong, Deakin University Press.

KENNEDY, K.J. (1988) 'Creating a context for curriculum deliberation by teachers', Paper presented at the Annual Conference of the American Educational Research Association, New Orleans.

KENNEDY, K.J. (1995) 'An analysis of the policy contexts of recent curriculum reform efforts in Australia, Great Britain and the United States', in CARTER, D.S.G. and O'NEILL, M.H. (Eds) *International Perspectives on Educational Reform and Policy Implementation*, London, Falmer Press.

KENNEDY, K. (1997) (Ed) *Citizenship Education and the Modern State*, London, Falmer Press.

KENWAY, J. and LONGMEAD, D. (1998) 'Fast capitalism, fast feminism and some fast food for thought', Paper presented at the Annual Conference of the American Educational Research Association, San Diego.

KENWAY, J. and MODRA, H. (1992) 'Feminist pedagogy and emancipatory possibilities', in LUKE, C. and GORE, J. (Eds) *Feminisms and Critical Pedagogy*, New York, Routledge.

KENWAY, J. and WILLIS, S. (1997) *Answering Back: Girls, Boys and Feminism in Schools*, Sydney, Allen and Unwin.

KENWAY, J., ALDERSON, A. and GRUNDY, S. (1987) *A Process Approach to Community Participation in Schooling: The Hamilton Project*, Perth, Murdoch University.

KENWAY, J., BLACKMORE, J. and WILLIS, S. (1996) 'Beyond feminist authoritarianism and therapy in the curriculum?', *Curriculum Perspectives*, **16**, 1, pp. 1–12.

KERR, D. (1989) 'Principles underlying the dissemination implementation of curriculum', Paper presented at the Annual Cuuriculum Corporation Conference, Canberra.

KINCHELOE, J.L. (1993) *Toward a Critical Politics of Teacher Thinking: Mapping the Postmodern*, Westport, Bergin and Garvey.

KING, J.F. (1998) 'Assessment at the chalkface', Paper presented at the 24th International Congress of Applied Psychology, San Francisco.

KIRST, M.W. (1993) 'Strengths and weaknesses of American education', *Phi Delta Kappan*, **74**, 8, pp. 613–618.

KIRST, M.W. and WALKER, D.F. (1971) 'An analysis of curriculum policy making', *Review of Educational Research*, **41**, 5, pp. 486–495.

KLEIN, M.F. (1991) (Ed) *The Politics of Curriculum Decision-Making*, New York, State University of New York Press.

KLEIN, R. (1986) *The dynamics of women's studies: An exploratory study of its international ideas and practices in higher education*, Unpublished doctoral thesis, University of London, Institute of Education.

KLIEBARD, H.M. (1974) 'The development of certain key curriculum issues in the United States', in TAYLOR, P.H. and JOHNSON, M. JR (Eds), *Curriculum Development: A Comparative Study*, London, National Foundation for Educational Research.

KLIEBARD, H.M. (1977) 'Curriculum theory: Give me a "for instance"', *Curriculum Inquiry*, **6**, 4, pp. 257–268.

KLIEBARD, H.M. (1992) Forging the American Curriculum: Essays on curriculum history and theory. Routledge, New York.

KLOHR, P. (1980) 'The curriculum theory field: Gritty and ragged', *Curriculum Perspectives*, **1**, 1, pp. 1–8.

KNIGHT, T. (1995) 'Parents, the community and school governance', in EVERS, C. and CHAPMAN, J. (Eds) *Educational Administration: An Australian Perspective*, Sydney, Allen and Unwin.

KONZA, D., GRAINGER, J. and BRADSHAW, K. (2001) *Classroom Management: A Survival Guide*, Sydney, Social Science Press.

KOPRIVA, R. (1999) 'A conceptual framework for valid and comparable measurement', Paper presented at the Annual Conference of the American Educational Research Association, Montreal.

KUHN, T. (1962) *The Structure of Scientific Revolutions*, Chicago, University of Chicago Press.

LABAREE, D. (1988) *The Making of an American High School: The Credentials Market and the Central High School of Philadelphia 1838–1939*, New Haven, Yale University Press.

LAMBERT, L. (1998) *Building Leadership Capacity in Schools*, Alexandria, VA, ASCD.

LA ROCQUE, L. and COLEMAN, P. (1989) 'Quality control: School accountability and district ethos', in HOLMES, M., LEITHWOOD, K. and MUSELLA, D. (Eds) *Educational Policy for Effective Schools*, Toronto, OISE Press.

LAREAU, A.P. (1986) 'Perspectives on parents: A view from the classroom', Paper presented at the Annual Meeting of the Annual Conference of the American Educational Research Association, San Francisco.

LASKY, S. (2000) 'The cultural and emotional politics of teacher-parent interactions', *Teaching and Teacher Education*, **16**, 843–860.

LATHER, P. (1991a) *Getting Smart: Feminist Research and Pedagogy With/in the Postmodern*. London, Routledge.

LATHER, P. (1991b) 'Deconstructing/deconstructive inquiry: The politics of knowing and being known. *Educational Theory*, **41**, 2, pp. 153–173.

LATHER, P. (1998) 'Against empathy, voice and authenticity', Paper presented at the Annual Conference of the American Educational Research Association, San Diego.

LAWTON, D. (1980) *The Politics of the School Curriculum*, London, Routledge and Kegan Paul.

LAWTON, D. (1993) *Curriculum Studies and Education Planning*, London, Hodder and Stoughton.

LEA, O. and FRADD, S.H. (1998) 'Science for all, including students from non-English-language backgrounds', *Educational Researcher*, **27**, 4, pp. 12–21.

LECK, G.M. (1999) 'Afterword', in LETTS, W.J. and SEARS, J.T. (Eds) *Queering Elementary Education*, Lanham, MD, Rowman and Littlefield.

LEE, V.E., SMITH, J.B. and CIOCI, M. (1993) 'Teachers and principals: Gender-related perceptions of leadership and power in secondary schools', *Educational Evaluation and Policy Analysis*, **15**, 2, pp. 153–180.

LEITHWOOD, K.A. (1981) 'Managing the implementation of curriculum innovations', *Knowledge: Creation, Diffusion, Utilization*, **2**, 3, pp. 341–360.

LEITHWOOD, K. and MENZIES, D. (1999) 'A century's quest to understand school leadership', in MURPHY, J. and SEASHORE LOUIS, K. (Eds) *Handbook of Educational Leadership and Change*, Macmillan, Chicago.

LEITHWOOD, K.A., TOMLINSON, D. and GENGE, M. (1996) 'Transformational school leadership', in LEITHWOOD, K., CHAPMAN, J., CORSON, D., HALLINGER, P. and HART, A. (Eds) *International Handbook of Educational Leadership and Administration*, Kluwer, Dordrecht, The Netherlands.

LETTS, W.J. and SEARS, J.T. (1999) (Eds) *Queering Elementary Education*, Boulder, CO, Rowman and Littlefield.

LEVIN, H.M. (1998) 'Educational performance standards and the economy', *Educational Researcher*, **27**, 4, pp. 4–11.

LEWIN, K. (1948) *Resolving Social Conflicts*, New York, Harper and Row.

LEWIS, M.E. (1988) 'Continuation of a curriculum innovation: Salient and alterable viables', *Journal of Curriculum and Supervision*, **4**, 1, pp. 52–64.

LEZOTTE, L. (1997) *Learning for All*, Okemos, MI, Effective Schools Products.

LIEBERMAN, A. and MILLER, L. (1990) 'The social realities of teaching', in LIEBERMAN, A. (Ed) *Schools as Collaborative Cultures: Creating the Future Now*, London, Falmer Press.

LIEBERMAN, A. and MILLER, L. (2000) 'Teaching and teacher development: A new synthesis for a new century', in BRANDT, R.S. (Ed) *Education in a New Era*, Alexandria, VA, ASCD.

LIEBLE, J.A. (1980) 'Guideline recommendations for the design of training facilities', *NSPI Journal*, **19**, pp. 21–30.

LIFTER, M. and ADAMS, M.E. (1997) *Integrating Technology into the Curriculum*, Melbourne, Hawker Brownlow.

LITTLE, J.W. (1990) 'The persistence of privacy: Autonomy and initiative in teachers' professional relations', *Teachers College Record*, **91**, 4, pp. 509–536.

LIU, M. and REED, W.M. (1994) 'The relationship between the learning strategies and learning styles in a hypermedia environment', *Computers in Human Behaviour*, **10**, 4, 419–434.

LOADER, D. (1998a) *The Inner Principal*, London, Falmer Press.

LOADER, D. (1998b) 'The empty principal', *The Professional Reading Guide*, **19**, 3, pp. 1–15.

LONGSTREET, W.S. and SHANE, H.G. (1993) *Curriculum for a New Millennium*, Boston, Allyn and Bacon.

LORTIE, D. (1975) *Schoolteacher*, Chicago, University of Chicago Press.

LOUCKS, S.F. and CRANDALL, D.P. (1982) *The Practice Profile: An All-purpose Tool for Program Communication, Staff Development, Evaluation and Improvement*, Andover, MA, The Network.

LOUDEN, W. (2000) 'Standards for standards: The development of Australian professional standards for teaching', *Australian Journal of Education*, **44**, 2, pp. 118–134.

LOUDEN, W. and WILDY, H. (1997) 'Short shrift to long lists: An alternative approach to the development of performance standards for school principals', Paper presented at the Annual Conference of the American Educational Research Association, Chicago.

LOUIS, K. and MILES, M.B. (1990) *Improving the Urban High School: What Works and Why*, New York, Teachers College Press.

LOVE, D. (1986) 'Community involvement', *West Australian High School Principals Association Newsletter*, **10**, 1, 9.

LOYD, B.H. and LOYD, D.E. (1997) 'Kindergarten through grade 12 standards: A philosophy of grading', in PHYE, G.D. (Ed) *Handbook of Classroom Assessment*, San Diego, Academic Press.

LUCAS, C.A. (1999) 'Developing competent practitioners', *Educational Leadership*, **56**, 8, pp. 45–48.

LUCAS, S.E. and VALENTINE, J.W. (2002) 'Transformational leadership: Principals, leadership teams, and school culture', Paper presented at the Annual Conference of the American Educational Research Association, New Orleans.

LUI, M. and REED, W.M. (1994) 'The relationship between the learning strategies and learning styles in a hypermedia environment', *Computers in Human Behaviour*, **10**, 4, pp. 419–434.

LUNDEBERG, M. (1997) 'You guys are overreacting: Teaching prospective teachers about subtle gender bias', *Journal of Teacher Education*, **48**, 1, pp. 55–61.

LUSTED, D. (1986) 'Why pedagogy?', *Screen*, **27**, 5, pp. 2–14.

LUTZ, F.W. (1980) 'Local school board decision-making: A political-anthropological analysis', *Education and Urban Society*, **12**, 4, pp. 17–29.

LYONS, N. (1999) 'How portfolios can shape emerging practice', *Educational Leadership*, **56**, 8, pp. 63–66.

MACKAY, T. (2002) 'Challenges in perspective: Transforming secondary education, the view from the UK', Paper presented at the Invitational Curriculum Policy Seminar, Hong Kong.

MACLURE, M. and WALKER, B.M. (2000) 'Disenchanted evenings. The social organization of talk in parent–teacher consultations in UK secondary schools', *British Journal of Sociology of Education*, **21**, 1, pp. 18–22.

MACPHERSON, E.D. (1995) 'Chaos in the curriculum', *Journal of Curriculum Studies*, **27**, 3, pp. 263–280.

MACPHERSON, I. (1998) 'Creating space for the voices of significant stakeholders in curriculum leadership', Paper presented at the Annual Conference of the American Educational Research Association, San Diego.

MAGER, R.F. (1984) *Preparing Instructional Objectives*, 3rd edn, Belmont, CA, Lake Publishers.

MALE, T. (1998) 'The impact of national culture on school leadership in England', Paper presented at the Annual Conference of the American Educational Research Association, San Diego.

MANN, L. (1997) 'The learning environment', *ASCD Education Update*, September, 3–6.

MANNO, R.V., FINN, C.E. and VANOUREK, G. (2000) 'Beyond the schoolhouse door', *Phi Delta Kappan*, **81**, 10, pp. 736–744.

MARSH, C.J. (1994) 'Producing a national curriculum: Plans and paranoia, Sydney, Allen and Unwin.

MARSH, C.J. (1997) *Key Concepts for Understanding Curriculum*, London, Falmer Press.

MARSH, C.J. (2000) *Handbook for Beginning Teachers*, 2nd edn, Sydney, Longman.

MARSH, C.J. (2002) 'Engaging the hearts and minds of teachers in curriculum reform', Paper presented at the Invitational Curriculum Policy Seminar, Hong Kong.

MARSH, C.J. and STAFFORD, K. (1988) *Curriculum: Practices and Issues*, 2nd edn, Sydney, McGraw-Hill.

MARSH, C.J. and WILLIS, G. (2003) *Curriculum: Alternative Approaches, Ongoing Issues*, 3rd edn, Columbus, OH, Merrill Prentice-Hall.

MARSH, D.D. and PENN, J. (1988) 'Engaging students in innovative instruction: An application of the stages of concern framework to studying student engagement', *Journal of Classroom Interaction*, **23**, 1, pp. 8–14.

MARZANO, R.J. and KENDALL, J.S. (1996) *A Comprehensive Guide to Designing Standards-based Districts, Schools and Classrooms*, Alexandria, VA, Association for Supervision and Curriculum Development.

MATHEISON, S. (1991) 'Implementing curricular change through state-mandated testing: Ethical issues', *Journal of Curriculum and Supervision*, **6**, 3, pp. 201–212.

MATHEWS, C. and HUDSON, M. (1994) 'Teachers' own learning', *EQ Australia*, **1**, Autumn, pp. 22–24.

McCARTHY, C. (1988) 'Rethinking liberal and radical perspectives on radical inequality in schooling: Making the case for nonsynchrony', *Harvard Educational Review*, **58**, 3, pp. 265–279.

McCHESNEY, J. and HERTLING, E. (2000) 'The path to comprehensive school reform', *Educational Leadership*, **57**, 7, pp. 10–15.

McCULLOCH, G. (1998) 'The National Curriculum and the cultural politics of secondary schools in England and Wales', Paper presented at the Annual Conference of the American Educational Research Association, San Diego.

McCUTCHEON, G. (1982) 'What in the world is curriculum theory?', *Theory into Practice*, **21**, 1, pp. 18–22.

McCUTCHEON, G. (1988) 'Curriculum and the work of teachers', in BEYER, L.E. and APPLE, M.W. (Eds) *The Curriculum*, New York, State University of New York Press.

McGAW, B., PIPER, K., BANKS, D. and EVANS, B. (1992) *Making Schools More Effective*, Melbourne, ACER.

McGEHEE, J.J. and GRIFFITH, L.K. (2001) 'Large-scale assessments combined with curriculum alignment: Agents of change', *Theory into Practice*, **40**, 2, pp. 22–31.

McGILP, J. and MICHAEL, M. (1994) *The Home–School Connection*, Armadale, NSW, Eleanor Curtain Publishing.

McINERNEY, D.M. (1989) 'Urban Aboriginal parents' views on education: A comparative analysis', *Journal of Intercultural Studies*, **10**, 2, pp. 43–65.

McINNIS, J.R. and DEVLIN, M. (2002) *Assessing Learning in Australian Universities*, Canberra, Centre for the Study of Higher Education, AUTC.

McKERNAN, J. (1991) *Curriculum Action Research*, London, Kogan Page.

McKERNAN, J. (1993) 'Varieties of curriculum action research: Constraints and typologies in American, British and Irish projects', *Journal of Curriculum Studies*, **25**, 5, pp. 445–457.

McLAREN, P. and FARAHMANDPUR, R. (2000) 'Reconsidering Marx in post-Marxist times: A requiem for postmodernism', *Educational Researcher*, **29**, 3, pp. 25–33.

McLAUGHAN, M. (2001) 'Community counts', *Educational Leadership*, **58**, 7, pp. 14–18.

McLAUGHLIN, M.W. (1987) 'Learning from experience: Lessons from policy implementation', *Educational Evaluation and Policy Analysis*, **9**, 2, pp. 171–178.

McLAUGHLIN, M.W. and SHEPARD, L.A. (1995) *Improving Education Through Standards-based Reform*, Stanford, CA, National Academy of Education.

McMAHON, A. (1994) 'Teacher appraisal in England and Wales', in INGVARSON, L. and CHADBOURNE, R. (Eds) *Valuing Teachers' Work: New Directions in Teacher Appraisal*, Melbourne, ACER.

McMAHON, A. (2000) 'Managing teacher stress to enhance pupil learning', Paper presented at the Annual Conference of the American Educational Research Association, New Orleans.

McMILLAN, J., MYRAN, S. and WORKMAN, D. (2002) 'Elementary teachers' classroom assessment and grading practices, *Journal of Educational Research*, **95**, 4, pp. 203–213.

McNEIL, J.D. (1985) *Curriculum: A Comprehensive Introduction*, 3rd edn, Boston, Little Brown.

McNEIL, L. (1988) 'Contradictions of control. Part 2: Teachers, students, and curriculum', *Phi Delta Kappan*, **69**, 10, pp. 729–734.

McTAGGART, R. (1984) 'Action research and parent participation: Contradictions, concerns and consequences', *Curriculum Perspectives*, **4**, 2, pp. 7–14.

McTIGHE, J. (1997) 'What happens between assessments?', *Educational Leadership*, **54**, 4, pp. 6–13.

MEADMORE, D. (2001) 'Uniformly testing diversity? National testing examined', *Asia–Pacific Journal of Teacher Education*, **29**, 1, pp. 19–30.

MEADOWS, B.J. (1993) 'Through the eyes of parents', *Educational Leadership*, **51**, 2, pp. 31–34.

MEANS, B. (2000) 'Technology in America's Schools: Before and after Y2K', in BRANDT, R.S. (Ed) *Education in a New Era*, Alexandria, VA, ASCD.

MEANS, R. (2001) 'Technology use in tomorrow's schools', *Educational Leadership*, **58**, 4, pp. 57–61.

MEIR, D. (1998) 'Authenticity and educational change', in HARGREAVES, A., *et al.* (Eds) *International Handbook of Educational Change*, Dordrecht, The Netherlands, Kluwer.

MELARAGNO, R., LYONS, M. and SPARKS, M. (1981) *Parents and Federal Education Programs*, Vol. 6, *Parental Involvement in Title 1 Projects*, Santa Monica, Systems Development Corporation.

MELLOR, S., KENNEDY, K. and GREENWOOD, L. (2002) *Citizenship and Democracy: Students' Knowledge and Beliefs: Australian Fourteen Year Olds and the IEA Civic Education Study*, Melbourne, Australian Council for Educational Research.

MICKELSON, R.A. (1999) 'International business machinations: A case study of corporate involvement in local educational reform', *Teachers College Record*, **100**, 3, pp. 476–512.

MIDDLETON, S. (1992) 'Developing a radical pedagogy: Autobiography of a New Zealand sociologist of women's education', in GOODSON, I.F. (Ed) *Studying Teachers' Lives*, London, Routledge.

MILES, J. (1984) 'The death's head trail to teacher appraisal', *Education*, **21**, September, pp. 235–236.

MILLER, J.L. (1987) 'Women as teacher/researchers: Gaining a sense of ourselves', *Teacher Education Quarterly*, **14**, 2, pp. 52–58.

MILLER, J.L. (1990) *Creating Spaces and Finding Voices: Teachers Collaborating for Empowerment*, Albany, NY, State University of New York Press.

MILLER, J.L. (1992) 'Shifting the boundaries: Teachers challenge contemporary curriculum thought', *Theory into Practice*, **31**, 3, pp. 245–251.

MILLIGAN, S. (1994) *Women in the Teaching Profession*, Canberra, AGPS.

MISLEVY, R.J. (2002) 'The roles of technology in the assessment argument', Paper presented at the Annual Conference of the American Educational Research Association, New Orleans.

MITCHELL, J.A. (1996) *Teacher work, practices and places*, Unpublished doctoral dissertation, University of Melbourne.

MOLNAR, A. (2000) 'Zap me! Linking schoolhouse and marketplace in a seamless web', *Phi Delta Kappan*, **81**, 8, pp. 601–603.

MOORE, K.D. (2001) *Classroom Teaching Skills*, 5th edn, Boston, McGraw-Hill.

MOORE, R. (2000) 'For knowledge: Tradition, progressivism and progress in education-restructuring the curriculum debate', *Cambridge Journal of Education*, **30**, 1, pp. 17–35.

MOOS, R.H. and TRICKETT, E. (1974) *Classroom Environment Scale Manual*, Palo Alto, CA, Consulting Psychologist Press.

MORRIS, W. (1992) 'Parents and school governance', Paper presented at the Annual Conference of the Western Australian Primary Principals' Association, Perth.

MORRISON, K. and RIDLEY, K. (1988) *Curriculum Planning and the Primary School*, London, Paul Chapman.

MORTIMER, P., SAMMONS, P., STOLL, L., LEWIS, D. and ECOB, R. (1988) *School Matters: The Junior Years*, London, Open Books.

MURPHY, D. and ROSENBERG, B. (1998) 'Recent research shows major benefits of small class size', *Educational Issues Policy Brief 3*, Washington, DC, American Federation of Teachers.

MURPHY, J. and RODI, M. (2000) 'Principal evaluation: A review', Paper presented at the Annual Meeting of the American Educational Research Association, New Orleans.

MUTIMER, A. (1999) 'From home to school', *EQ Australia*, **2**, Winter, 9–10.

NAHAN, M. and RUTHERFORD, T. (1993) *Reform and Recovery*, Perth, Institute of Public Affairs.

NAISBITT, J. and ABERDENE, P. (1990) *Megatrends 1000: Ten New Directions for the 1990s*, New York, Avon Books.

NATIONAL CENTER ON EDUCATION AND THE ECONOMY (1997) *New Standards: Performance Standards: English Language, Arts, Mathematics, Science, and Applied Learning*: Vol. 1 *Elementary School*; Vol. 2 *Middle School*; Vol. 3 *High School*, Washington, DC, NCEE.

NATIONAL COMMISSION ON EXCELLENCE IN EDUCATION (1983) *A Nation at Risk: The Imperative for Educational Reform*, Washington, DC, Government Printing Office.

NATIONAL COMMISSION ON TEACHING AND AMERICA'S FUTURE (1997) *What Matters Most: Teaching for America's Future*, Woodbridge, VA, NCTAF.

NATIONAL COUNCIL OF TEACHERS OF MATHEMATICS (1991) *Professional Standards for Teaching Mathematics*, Raston, VA, NCTM.

NATIONAL WOMEN'S STUDIES ASSOCIATION (1977) *Founding Constitution*, San Francisco.

NAVE, F. (2000) 'Linking standard-based reform with student achievement', *Phi Delta Kappan*, **82**, 2, pp. 128–132.

NAVE, B., MIECH, E. and MOSTELLER, F. (2000) 'A lapse in standards', *Phi Delta Kappan*, **82**, 2, pp. 128–132.

NEVE, D. (2001) 'School evaluation: Internal or external?', *Studies in Educational Evaluation*, **27**, pp. 95–106.

NIAS, D.J. (1990) 'A deputy head observed: Findings from an ethnographic study,' in SOUTHWORTH, G. (Ed) *The study of Primary Education, A Source Book*, Vol. 3: *School Organisation and Management*, London, Falmer Press.

NIAS, J., SOUTHWORTH, G. and YEOMANS, R. (1989) *Staff Relationships in the Primary School*, London, Cassell.

NOFFKE, S. (1997) 'Professional, personal and political dimensions of action research', *Review of Research in Education*, **22**, pp. 305–343.

NORMAN, L. (1983) *The Brown and Yellow: Sydney Girls' High School 1883–1983*, Melbourne, Oxford University Press.

NORTON, P. and WIBURG, K.M. (2003) *Teaching with Technology*, 2nd edn, Belmont, CA, Thomson/Wadsworth.

O'CONNOR, C. and ROBOTHAM, M. (1991) *Towards Equity in the Queensland Core Skills Test*, Brisbane, BSSSS.

O'DONNELL, B. (2000) 'Prospects for the profession of teaching in Australia in the new millennium', *Unicorn*, **24**, 1, pp. 13–21.

OFFICE FOR STANDARDS IN EDUCATION (1997) *A Review of Inspection Report Writing*, Inspection Quality, Monitoring and Development Team, London.

OLEBE, M., JACKSON, A. and DANIELSON, C. (1999) 'Investing in beginning teachers: The California model', *Educational Leadership*, **56**, 8, pp. 41–44.

OLIVA, P.F. (1997) *Developing the Curriculum*, 4th edn, New York, Longman.

OLSON, J. (1989) 'The persistence of technical rationality', in MILBURN, G., GOODSON, I.F. and CLARK, R.J. (Eds) *Re-interpreting Curriculum Research: Images and Arguments*, London, Falmer Press.

O'NEIL, J. (1995) 'On lasting school reform: A conversation with Ted Sizer', *Educational Leadership*, **52**, 5, pp. 4–9.

ORLICH, D.C., HARDER, R.J., CALLAHAN, R.C. and GIBSON, H.W. (1998) *Teaching Strategies*, 5th edn, Boston, MA, Houghton Mifflin.

ORNSTEIN, A.C. and HUNKINS, F.P. (1988) *Curriculum: Foundations, Principles and Issues*. Upper Saddle River, NJ, Prentice-Hall.

ORNSTEIN, A.C. and HUNKINS, F. (1993) *Curriculum foundations: Principles and theory* (2nd ed.). Boston: Allyn & Bacon.

ORPWOOD, W.F. (1985) 'The reflective deliberator: A case study of curriculum policy making', *Journal of Curriculum Studies*, **17**, 1, pp. 293–304.

PAGANO, J.A. (1992) 'Women and education: In what ways does gender affect the educational process?', in KINCHELOE, J. and STEINBERG, S. (Eds) *Thirteen Questions*, New York, Lang.

PAINTER, B. (2001) 'Using teaching portfolios', *Educational Leadership*, **58**, 5, pp. 31–34.

PALINESAR, A.S. and HERRENKOOL, L.R. (2002) 'Designing collaborative learning contexts', *Theory into Practice*, **41**, 1, pp. 12–23.

PARKER, S. (1997) *Reflective Teaching in the Postmodern World*, Buckingham, Open University Press.

PARSONS, C. (1987) *The Curriculum Change Game*, London, Falmer Press.

PASSOW, A.H. (1988) 'Whither (or wither)? School reform?', *Educational Administration Quarterly*, **24**, 3, pp. 246–256.

PAYNE, D.A. (2003) *Applied Educational Assessment*, 2nd edn, Belmont, CA, Wadsworth/Thomson.

PEDDIE, R. (1995) 'Culture and economic change: The New Zealand school curriculum', in CARTER, D. and O'NEILL, M. (Eds) *Case Studies in Educational Change: An International Perspective*, London, Falmer, pp. 146–156.

PEDULLA, J.J. (2003) 'State-mandated testing: What do teachers think?', *Educational Leadership*, **61**, 3, pp. 42–49.

PERKINSON, H.J. (1993) *Teachers Without Goals, Students Without Purposes*, New York, McGraw-Hill.

PETERS, M. (1995) 'Educational reform and the politics of the curriculum in New Zealand', in CARTER, D.S.G. and O'NEILL, M.H. (Eds) *International Perspectives on Educational Reform and Policy Implementation*, London, Falmer Press.

PETERSON, K.D., WAHLQUIST, C., BONE, K., THOMPSON, J. and CHATTERTON, K. (2001) 'Using more data sources to evaluate teachers', *Educational Leadership*, **58**, 5, pp. 40–43.

PETTIT, D. (1984) 'Governing in an equal partnership: The move to school councils', *Education News*, **18**, 8, pp. 75–88.

PETTIT, D. (1987) *Schooling at a crossroad, Parent Participation in Victorian Schools*, Melbourne, Ministry of Education.

PHENIX, P.H. (1964) *Realms of Meaning: A Philosophy of the Curriculum for General Education*, New York, McGraw-Hill.

PHILLIPS, D.C. (1995) 'The good, the bad and the ugly. The many faces of constructivism, *Educational Researcher*, **24**, 7, pp. 5–12.

PINAR, W.F. (1978) 'Notes on the curriculum field', *Educational Researcher*, **7**, 8, pp. 5–11.

PINAR, W.F. (1980) 'The voyage out: Curriculum as the relationship between the knower and the known', *Journal of Curriculum Theorizing*, **2**, 1, pp. 7–11.

PINAR, W.F. (1983) 'Curriculum as gender text: Notes on reproduction, resistance, and male-made relations', *Journal of Curriculum Theorizing*, **5**, 1, pp. 26–52.

PINAR, W.F. (1994) *Autobiography, Politics and Sexuality: Essays in Curriculum Theory, 1972–1992*, New York, Peter Lang.

PINAR, W.F. (1997) 'Regimes of reason and male narrative voice', in GIERNEY, W.G. and LINCOLN, Y.S. (Eds) *Representation and the Text: Reframing the Narrative Voice*, Albany, State University of New York Press.

PINAR, W.F. (2000) 'Strange fruit: Race, sex and an autobiographics of alternativity', Paper presented at the Annual Meeting of the American Educational Research Association, New Orleans.

PINAR, W.F. and GRUMET, M. (1976) *Toward a Poor Curriculum*, Dubuque, IA, Kendall/Hunt.

PINAR, W.F., REYNOLDS, W.M., SLATTERY, P. and TAUBMAN, P.M. (1995) *Understanding Curriculum*, New York, Lang.

PIPER, K. (1976) *Evaluation and the Social Sciences*, Canberra, AGPS.

PLANK, D.N. (1988) 'Why school reform doesn't change schools: Political and organisational perspectives', in BOYD, W.L. and KERCHNER, C.T. (Eds) *The Politics of Excellence and Choice in Education,* London, Falmer Press.

POOLE, M. (1992) (Ed) *Education and Work*, Melbourne, ACER.

POPHAM, W.J. (1995) *Classroom Assessment: What Teachers Need to Know*, Boston, Allyn and Bacon.

POPPLETON, P. (2000) 'Receptiveness and resistance to education change. Experiences of English teachers in the 1990s', Paper presented at the Annual Conference of the American Educational Research Association, New Orleans.

PORTELLI, J.P. (1987) 'On defining curriculum', *Journal of Curriculum and Supervision*, **2**, 4, pp. 354–367.

PORTER, A.C. (1993) 'School delivery standards', *Educational Researcher*, **22**, 5, pp. 24–30.

PORTER, A.C., YOUNGS, P. and ODDEN, A. (2000) 'Advances in teacher assessments and their uses', in RICHARDSON, V. (Ed) *Handbook of Research on Teaching*, 4th edn, Chicago, McNally.

PORTER, P. (1994) *Women and Leadership in Education*, Occasional Paper No. 23, Canberra, Australian College of Education.

POSNER, G. (1998) 'Models of curriculum planning', in BEYER, L.E. and APPLE, M.W. (Eds), *The Curriculum: Problems, Politics and Possibilities*, 2nd edn, Albany, State University of New York Press.

POSTMAN, N. and WEINGARTNER, C. (1987) *Teaching as a Subversive Activity*, New York, Dell.

POWER, S. and CLARK, A. (2000) 'The right to know: Parents, school reports and parents' evenings', *Research Papers in Education*, **15**, 1, pp. 25–48.

PRAWAT, R.S. (2000) 'The two faces of Deweyan pragmatism: Inductionism versus social constructivism', *Teachers College Record*, **102**, 4, pp. 805–840.

PREISS, A. (1992) 'Teacher appraisal', *EQ Education Quarterly*, May, **5**, pp. 4–8.

PRESSEISEN, B.Z. (1989) *Unlearned Lessons: Current and Past Reforms for School Improvement*, London, Falmer Press.

PRICE, B. (1991) *School Industry Links*, Melbourne, ACER.

PRICE, J.N. and VALLIE, L. (2000) 'Becoming agents of change: Cases from preservice teacher education', Paper presented at the Annual Meeting of the American Educational Research Association, New Orleans.

PRYOR, J. and TORRANCE, H. (1996) 'Teacher–pupil interaction in formative assessment: Assessing the work or protecting the child?', *Curriculum Journal* **7**, 2, pp. 205–226.

RAY, H. (1992) *Summary of Mainstream Amplification Resource Room Study (MARRS) Adoption Data Validated in 1992*, Norris City, IL, Wabash and Ohio Special Education District.

REES, N.S. and JOHNSON, K. (2000) 'A lesson in smaller class sizes', Heritage Views 2000 (Online). Available: www.heritage.org/views/2000/ed053000.html

REICHMAN, J. and HEALEY, W. (1993) 'Learning disabilities and conductive hearing loss involving otitis media', *Journal of Learning Disabilities*, **16**, pp. 272–278.

REID, A. (1992) '"Accountability" and education: The great profile debate', *Curriculum Perspectives*, **12**, 1, pp. 55–56.

REID, W.A. (1999a) *Curriculum as Institution and Practice*, Mahwah, NJ, Lawrence Erlbaum.

REID, W.A. (1999b) 'The voice of the practical: Schwab as correspondent', *Journal of Curriculum Studies*, **31**, 4, pp. 385–397.

REID, W.A. (2000) 'Why globalisation may cause fundamental curriculum change: A theoretical framework', Paper presented at the Annual Meeting of the American Educational Research Association, New Orleans.

RESNICK, L.B. and KLOPFER, L.E. (Eds) (1989) *Toward the Thinking Curriculum: Current Cognitive Research*, Alexandria, VA, Association for Supervisors and Curriculum Development.

RESNICK, L. and TUCKER, M. (1992) *The New Standards Project*, Pittsburgh, University of Pittsburgh Press.

RHEDDING-JONES, J. (1995) 'What do you do after you've met poststructuralism?', *Journal of Curriculum Studies*, **27**, 5, pp. 479–500.

RIBBINS, P. (1992) *Delivering the National Curriculum: Subjects for Secondary Schooling*, London, Longman.

RICH, D. (1998) 'What parents want from teachers', *Educational Leadership*, **55**, 8, pp. 37–39.

RICHARDS, R. (1994) 'Teacher review in the Australian Capital Territory', in INGVARSON, L. and CHADBOURNE, R. (Eds) *Valuing Teachers' Work: New Directions in Teacher Appraisal*, Melbourne, ACER.

RIORDAN, G. (2001) 'Teachers working together', *The Practising Administrator*, **23**, 1, pp. 6–10.

ROBERTSON, H.J. (1992) 'Teacher development and gender equity', in HARGREAVES, A. and FULLAN, M.G. (Eds) *Understanding Teacher Development*, New York, Teachers College Press.

ROGAN, J.M. and LUCKOWSKI, J.A. (1990) 'Curriculum tests: The portrayal of the field, Part 1', *Journal of Curriculum Studies*, **22**, 1, pp. 17–39.

ROGERS, E.M. (1983) *Diffusion of Innovations*, 3rd edn, New York, Free Press.

ROGERS, G. and BADHAM, L. (1992) *Evaluation in Schools*, London, Routledge.

ROSENAU, F.S. (1973) *Tactics for the Educational Change Agent*, San Francisco, Far West Laboratory.

ROSENFELD, A. (1999) 'Natural light lets students work better', *The Weekend Australian*, 23 October, p.16.

ROSENFELD, L. (2002) 'Information architecture: Looking ahead', *Journal of the American Society for Information, Science and Technology*, June **17**, pp. 25–38.

ROSENFIELD, P., LAMBERT, N.M. and BLACK, A. (1985) 'Desk arrangement effects on pupil classroom behaviour', *Journal of Educational Psychology*, **77**, pp. 101–108.

ROSENHOLTZ, S. (1989) *Teacher's Workplace: The Social Organisation of Schools*, New York, Longman.

ROSENHOLTZ, S.J. (1991) *Teacher's Workplace: The Social Organization of Schools*, New York, Teachers College Press.

ROSENSHINE, B. (1995) 'Why do innovations come and go, and come back?', Paper presented at the Annual Meeting of the American Educational Research Association, San Francisco.

ROSS, A. (2000) *Curriculum Studies and Critique*. London, Falmer Press.

ROSS, E.W. (1993) 'Institutional constraints on curriculum deliberation', *Journal of Curriculum and Supervision*, **8**, 2, pp. 95–111.

ROSS, R.P. (1982) 'The design of educational environment: An expression of individual differences or evidence of the "press toward synomorphy?"', Paper presented at the Annual Meeting of the American Educational Research Association, New York.

ROSSI, P.H. and FREEMAN, H.E. (1993) *Evaluation: A Systematic Approach*, San Francisco, Sage.

ROWLEY, J.B. (1999) 'The good mentor', *Educational Leadership*, **56**, 8, pp. 20–22.

RUSSELL, G. and BRADLEY, G. (1996) 'Computer anxiety and student teachers: Antecedent and intervention', *Asia–Pacific Journal of Teacher Education*, **24**, 3, pp. 245–257.

RYAN, K. and COOPER, J.C. (2000) *Those Who Can, Teach*, 9th edn, Boston, Houghton Mifflin.

SADKER, M. and SADKER, D. (1986) 'Sexism in the classroom: From grade school to graduate school', *Phi Delta Kappan*, **67**, 7, pp. 512–515.

SALVIA, J. and YSSELDYKE, J.E. (1998) *Assessment*, 7th edn, Boston, Houghton Mifflin.

SAMUEL, G. (1987) 'An establish appraisal scheme', in BUNNELL, S. (Ed) *Teacher Appraisal in Practice*, London, Heinemann.

SANTROCK, J.W. (1976) 'Affect and facilitative self-control: Influence of ecological setting, cognition and social agent', *Journal of Educational Psychology*, **68**, 5, pp. 529–535.

SARASON, S.B. (1990) *The Predictable Failure of Educational Reform*, San Francisco, Jossey-Bass.

SAYLOR, J.G., ALEXANDER, W.M. and LEWIS, A.J. (1981) *Curriculum Planning for Better Teaching and Learning*, 4th edn, New York, Holt, Rinehart and Winston.

SCHERER, M. (1998) 'The shelter of each other: A conversation with Mary Papper', *Educational Leadership*, **55**, 8, pp. 6–11.

SCHILLER, K.S. and MULLER, C. (2000) 'External examinations and accountability: Educational expectations and high school graduation', *American Journal of Education*, **108**, February, pp. 73–77.

SCHMIDT, W.H., VALVERDE, G.A., HOUANG, R.T., WILEY, D.E., WOLFE, R.G. and BIANCHI, L.J. (1996) 'Studying the intended, implemented and attained curriculum: Strategies for measurement and analysis in large-scale international research', Paper presented at the annual meeting of the American Educational Research Association, New York.

SCHMOKER, M. and MARZANO, R.J. (1999) 'Realizing the promise of standards-based education', *Educational Leadership*, **56**, 6, pp. 17–21.

SCHOFIELD, J.W. and DAVIDSON, A.L. (2000) 'Internet use and teacher change', Paper presented at the Annual Meeting of the American Educational Research Association, New Orleans.

SCHON, D.A. (1987) *Educating the Reflective Practitioner*, San Francisco, Jossey-Bass.

SCHON, D. (Ed) (1991) *The Reflective Turn: Case Studies in and on Educational Practice*, New York, Teachers College Press.

SCHUBERT, W.H. (1980) *Curriculum Books: The First Eighty Years*. New York, University Press of America.

SCHUBERT, W.H. (1986) *Curriculum: Perspective, Paradigm, and Possibility*, New York, Macmillan.

SCHUBERT, W.H. (1992) 'Practitioners influence curriculum theory: Autobiographical reflections', *Theory into Practice*, **31**, 3, pp. 236–244.

SCHUBERT, W.H., SCHUBERT, A.L., THOMAS, T.P. and CARROLL, W.M. (2002) *Curriculum Books: The First Hundred Years*, 2nd edn, New York, Peter Lang.

SCHWAB, J.J. (1969) 'The practical: A language for curriculum', *School Review*, **78**, 1, pp. 1–23.

SCHWAB, J.J. (1970) *The Practical: A Language for Curriculum*, Washington, DC, National Education Association.

SCHWARTZ, G. (1996) 'The rhetoric of cyberspace and the real curriculum', *Journal of Curriculum and Supervision*, **9**, 4, pp. 326–328.

SCOTT, G. (1999) *Change Matters*. Sydney: Allen and Unwin.

SEARS, J. (Ed) (1992a) *Sexuality and the Curriculum*, New York, Teachers College Press.

SEARS, J. (1992b) 'The second wave of curriculum theorizing: Labyrinths, orthodoxies and other legacies of the glass bead game', *Theory into Practice*, **31**, 3, pp. 210–218.

SEARS, J. (1999) 'Teaching queerly: Some elementary propositions', in LETTS, W. J. and SEARS, J.T. (Eds) *Queering Elementary Education*, Lanham, MD, Rowman and Littlefield.

SEBBA, R. (1986) *Architecture as Determining the Child's Place in the School*, Washington, DC, ERIC Research in Education, ED284367.

SERGIOVANNI, D.T.J. (1998) 'Leadership as pedagogy, capital development and school effectiveness', *International Journal of Leadership in Education*, **1**, 1, pp. 37–46.

SHELDON, S.B. (2002) 'Parents' social networks and beliefs as predictors of parent involvement', *The Elementary School Journal*, **102**, 4, pp. 301–322.

SHORE, Z.L. (2001) 'Girls learning, women teaching: Dancing to different drummers', *Education Studies*, **31**, 2, pp. 132–145.

SHULMAN, L. (1994) 'Portfolios in historical perspective', Paper presented at the Portfolio Conference, Cambridge, MA, Radcliffe College.

SIMKINS, M., COLE, K., TAVALIN, F. and MWANS, B. (2002) *Increasing Student Learning through Multimedia Projects*, Alexandria, VA, ASCD.

SIMMONS, W. and RESNICK, L. (1993) 'Assessment as the catalyst of school reform', *Educational Leadership*, **50**, 5, pp. 11–15.

SIMONS, H. (1987) *Getting to Know Schools in a Democracy: The Politics and Process of Evaluation*, London, Falmer Press.

SIMPSON, G.W. (1990) 'Keeping it alive: Elements of school culture that sustain innovation', *Educational Leadership*, **47**, 8, pp. 34–37.

SIROTNIK, K.A. and KIMBALL, K. (1999) 'Standards for standards-based accountability systems', *Phi Delta Kappan*, **81**, 3, pp. 209–215.

SIZER, T. (1989) 'Diverse practice, shared ideas: The essential school', in WALBERG, H. and LANE, J.J. (Eds) *Organising for Learning: Toward the 21st Century*, Reston, VA, National Association of Secondary School Principals.

SKILBECK, M. (1982) 'The role of evaluation in curriculum development at the school level', in RUSSELL, N., HUGHES, P. and McCONACHY, D. (Eds) *Curriculum Evaluation: Selected Readings*, Canberra, Curriculum Development Centre.

SLATER, B. (1968) 'Effects of noise on pupil performance', *Journal of Educational Psychology*, **59**, 3, pp. 87–94.

SLATTERY, P. (1995) *Curriculum Development in the Postmodern Era*, New York, Garland.

SLOAN, D. (1993) *Insight-imagination: The Recovery of Thought in the Modern World*, New York, Teachers College Press.

SMITH, D. and LOVAT, T.J. (2003) *Curriculum: Action on Reflection*, 4th edn, Sydney, Social Science Press.

SMITH, J. (2004) 'Gender and schooling', in MARSH, C. (Ed) *Teaching Studies of Society and Environment*, 4th edn, Sydney, Pearson.

SMYLIE, M.A., LAZARUS, V. and BROWNLEE-CONYERS, J. (1996) 'Instructional outcomes of school-based participative decision making', *Educational Evaluation and Policy Analysis*, **18**, 3, pp. 181–198.

SMYTH, J. (1994) (Ed) *A Socially Critical View of the Self-managing School*, London, Falmer Press.

SMYTH, J. and SHACKLOCK, G. (1998) *Remaking Teaching: Ideology, Policy and Practice*, London, Routledge.

SNYDER, J., BOLIN, F. and ZUMWALT, K. (1992) 'Curriculum implementation', in JACKSON, P.W. (Ed) *Handbook of Research on Curriculum*, New York, Macmillan.

SNYDER, K.J., ACKER-HOCEVAR, M. and SNYDER, K.M. (1994) 'Organisational development in transition: The schooling perspective', Paper presented at the Annual Conference of the American Educational Research Association, New Orleans.

SODER, R. (1999) 'When words find their meaning: Renewal versus reform', *Phi Delta Kappan*, **80**, 8, pp. 568–570.

SOLTIS, J.F. (1978) *An Introduction to the Analysis of Educational Concepts*, Reading, MA, Addison-Wesley.

SOUTHWORTH, G. (2000) 'School leadership in English schools at the close of the twentieth century: Puzzles, problems and cultural insights', Paper presented at the

Annual Conference of the American Educational Research Association, New Orleans.

SPADY, W. (1993) *Outcome-based Education*, Workshop Report No. 5, Canberra, ACSA.

SPILLANE, J.P., REISER, B. and REIMER, T. (2002) 'Policy implementation and cognition: Reframing and refocusing implementation research', *Review of Educational Research*, **72**, 3, pp. 387–432.

SPIVAK, G.C. (1985) 'Strategies of vigilance', *Block*, **10**, 9, pp. 12–17.

STACEY, J. (1999) 'Gay and lesbian families are here', in COONTZ, S. (Ed) *American Families: A Multicultural Reader*, New York, Routledge.

STARRATT, R.J. (1993) *The Drama of Leadership*, London, Falmer Press.

STENHOUSE, L. (1973) 'The Humanities Curriculum Project', in BUTCHER, H. and PONT, H. (Eds) *Educational Research in Britain*, Vol. 3, London, University of London Press.

STENHOUSE, L. (1975) *An Introduction to Curriculum Research and Development*, London, Heinemann.

STENHOUSE, L. (1980) (Ed) *Curriculum Research and Development*, London, Heinemann.

STEPHENS, M. (1997) 'Negotiating the curriculum: The discursive embodiment of gender', Paper presented at the Biennial Conference of the Australian Curriculum Studies Association, Sydney.

STEVENSON, C. (1998) *Teaching Ten to Fourteen Year Olds*, 2nd edn, New York, Longman.

STUBBS, B. (1981) 'Pressures on the school curriculum', *Curriculum*, **2**, 1, pp. 15–20.

SULLA, N. (1998) 'Maximising the effectiveness of external consultants in the educational reform agenda', Paper presented at the Annual Conference of the American Educational Research Association, San Diego.

SUMARA, D. and DAVIS, B. (1999) 'Interrupting heteronormativity: Toward a queer curriculum theory', *Curriculum Inquiry*, **29**, 2, pp. 191–206.

SUTTON, R. (1992) *Assessment: A Framework for Teachers*, London, Routledge.

SWANSON, A.D. (1993) 'A framework for allocating authority in a system of schools', in BEARE, H. and BOYD, W.L. (Eds) *Restructuring Schools*, London, Falmer Press.

SWANSON, C.B. and STEVENSON, D.L. (2002) 'Standards-based reform in practice: Evidence on state policy and classroom instruction from the NAEP State Assessments', *Educational Evaluation and Policy Analysis*, **24**, 1, pp. 1–27.

TAYLOR, D. and TEDDLIE, C. (1992) 'Restructuring and the classroom: A view from a reform district', Paper presented at the Annual Meeting of the American Educational Research Association, San Francisco.

TAYLOR, W. (1979) 'Power and the curriculum', in RICHARDS, C. (Ed) *Power and the Curriculum: Issues in Curriculum Studies*, London, Nafferton.

TELL, C. (2001) 'Appreciating good teaching: A conversation with Lee Shulman', *Educational Leadership*, **58**, 5, pp. 6–11.

TESSMER, M. and RICHEY, R.C. (1997) 'The role of context in learning and instructional design', *Educational Technology, Research and Development*, **45**, 2, pp. 85–116.

THOMPSON, S. (2001) 'The authentic standards movement and its evil twin, *Phi Delta Kappan*, **85**, 5, pp. 358–362.

THORNTON, P. (2001) Is it time to review Review?', *The Practising Administrator*, **23**, 3, pp. 11–15.

TIKUNOFF, W.J., WARD, B.A. and STACEY, F. (1978) 'Toward an ecology based curriculum: Professional growth through participatory research and development', in

American Association of Teacher Educators (Eds) *Breakaway to Multidimensional Approaches: Integrating Curriculum Development and In-Service Education*, Washington, DC, American Association of Teacher Educators.

TITMAN, W. (1997) 'Special places, special people: The hidden curriculum of school grounds', Set 1, 1–4, Winchester, United Kingdom. Research paper, Educational Research Unit, University of Winchester.

TOBIAS, S. and DUCHASTEL, P. (1974) 'Behavioural objectives, sequence and anxiety in CAI', *Instructional Science*, **3**, 2, pp. 232–242.

TOFFLER, A. (1980) *The Third Wave*, New York, Bantam Books.

TOMLINSON, C.A. (2002) 'Invitations to learn', *Educational Leadership*, **60**, 1, pp. 6–11.

TOMLINSON, C.A. and KALBFLEISCH, M.L. (1998) 'Teach me, teach my brain', *Educational Leadership*, **56**, 3, pp. 53–55.

TOOMBS, W.E. and TIERNEY, W.G. (1993) 'Curriculum definitions and reference points', *Journal of Curriculum and Supervision*, **8**, 3, pp. 175–195.

TORRANCE, H. and PRYOR, J. (1995) 'Making sense of "formative assessment": Investigating the integration of assessment with teaching and learning', Paper presented at the Annual Meeting of the American Educational Research Association, San Francisco.

TREPANIER-STEET, M.L., MCNAIR, S. and DONEGAN, M.M. (2001) 'The views of teachers on assessment: A comparison of lower and upper elementary teachers, *Journal of Research in Childhood Education*, **15**, 2, pp. 234–241.

TRIPP, D.H. (1987) 'Action research and professional development', in HUGHES, P. (Ed) *Better Teachers for Better Schools*, Melbourne, Australian College of Education.

TUCKER, P. (2001) 'Helping struggling teachers', *Educational Leadership*, **58**, 5, pp. 52–56.

TUIJNMAN, A. and BOSTROM, A. (2002) 'Changing of notions of lifelong education and lifelong learning', *International Review of Education*, **48**, 1/2, pp. 93–110.

TUNSTALL, P. and GIPPS, C. (1996) "How does your teacher help you to make your work better?" Children's understanding of formative assessment', *The Curriculum Journal*, **7**, 2, pp. 185–203.

TYACK, D. and HANSOT, E. (1990) *Learning Together: A History of Coeducation in American Schools*, New Haven, Yale University Press.

TYLER, R.W. (1949) *Basic Principles of Curriculum and Instruction*, Chicago, University of Chicago Press.

TYLER, R.W. (1975) 'Specific approaches to curriculum development', in SCHAFFARZICK, J. and HAMPSON, D.H. (Eds) *Strategies for Curriculum Development*, Berkeley, CA, McCutcheon.

VALDEZ, G. (1986) 'Realizing the potential of educational technology', *Educational Leadership*, **43**, 6, pp. 4–6.

VALLANCE, E. (1982) 'The practical uses of curriculum theory', *Theory into Practice*, **21**, 1, pp. 4–10.

VALLANCE, E. (1986) 'A second look at conflicting conceptions of curriculum', *Theory into Practice*, **25**, 1, pp. 24–30.

VAN DEN BERG, R. (1993) 'The concerns-based adoption model in the Netherlands, Flanders, and the United Kingdom: State of the art and perspective', *Studies in Educational Evaluation*, **19**, pp. 51–63.

VAN DEN BERG, R. (2002) 'Teachers' meanings regarding educational practice', *Review of Educational Research*, **72**, 4, pp. 577–626.

VANDENBERGHE, R. (1983) 'Studying change in the primary and secondary schools of Belgium and the Netherlands', Paper presented at the Annual Meeting of the American Educational Research Association, Montreal.

VAN DER VEGT, S. and VANDENBERGHE, H. (1992) 'Schools implementing a central reform policy: Findings from two national educational contexts', Paper presented at the Annual Meeting of the American Educational Research Association, San Francisco.

VANTERPOOL, M. (1990) 'Innovations aren't for everyone', *Principal*, **69**, 4, pp. 38–43.

VAN WAGENEN, L. and HIBBARD, K.M. (1998) 'Building teacher portfolios', *Educational Leadership*, **55**, 5, pp. 26–29.

VAUGHAN, W. (2002) 'Professional development and the adoption and implementation of new innovations: Do teacher concerns matter?', *International Electronic Journal for Leadership in Learning*, **6**, 5, pp. 1–24.

VICK, M. (1994) 'Parents, schools and democracy', *Education Australia*, **28**, pp. 11–13.

VILLENAS, S. and DEYHLE, D. (1999) 'Critical race theory and ethnographics challenging the stereotypes: Latino families, schooling, resilience and resistance', *Curriculum Inquiry*, **29**, 4, 416–443.

VINE, K., BROWN, T. and CLARK, G. (2000) 'Which way for information technology in our schools?', *The School Principal's Handbook Series*, pp. 5–8.

VISSCHER, A.J. (2001) 'Public school performance indicators: Problems and recommendations', *Studies in Educational Evaluation*, **27**, pp. 199–214.

VON GLASERFIELD, T. (1995) *Radical Constructivism: A Way of Knowing and Learning*, London, Falmer Press.

WALKER, D.F. (1971) 'A naturalistic model of curriculum development', *School Review*, **80**, 1, pp. 51–65.

WALKER, D.F. (1980) 'A barnstorming tour of writing on curriculum', in FOSHAY, A.W. (Ed) *Considered Action for Curriculum Development*, Washington, DC, Association for Supervision and Curriculum Development.

WALKER, D.F. (1990) *Fundamentals of Curriculum*, New York, Harcourt Brace Jovanovich.

WALKER, J. (1994) *Competency-based Teacher Education: Implications for Quality in Higher Education*, II. Canberra, Higher Education Research Conference.

WALKER, R. and KUSHNER, S. (1991) 'Theorizing a curriculum', in GOODSON, I.F. and WALKER, R. (Eds) *Biography, Identity and Schooling: Episodes in Educational Research*, London, Falmer Press.

WALLACE, M. (1987) 'A historical review of action research: Some implications for the education of teachers in their managerial role', *Journal of Education for Teaching*, **13**, 2, pp. 97–116.

WALLACE, M. (1990) 'Curriculum management and organization: The collegiate approach', in SOUTHWORTH, G. and LOFTHOUSE, B. (Eds) *The Study of Primary Education, A Source Book*, Vol. 3, *School Organisation and Management*, London, Falmer Press.

WATKINS, W.H. (1993) 'Black curriculum orientations: A preliminary inquiry', *Curriculum Inquiry*, **63**, 3, pp. 321–338.

WATSON, N., FULLAN, M. and KILCHER, A. (2000) 'The role of the District: Professional learning and district reform', Paper presented at the Annual Conference of the American Educational Research Association, New Orleans.

WATT, M.G. (1998) 'National curriculum collaboration: The state of reform in the states and territories', *Curriculum Perspectives*, **18**, 1, pp. 21–34.

WATT, M. (2000) 'The National Education Agenda, 1916–1999: Its impact on curriculum reform in the states and territories', *Curriculum Perspectives*, **20**, 3, pp. 25–38.

WEAVER, R.A., KOESTER, R.J. and MCINTOSH, D. (1987) 'Collaboration in curriculum development: A case study. Paper presented at the annual meeting of the American Educational Research Association, Washington, DC.

WEE, J. (1999) *Improved student learning and leadership in Self-Managed Schools*, Unpublished Doctor of Education Thesis, University of Melbourne.

WEINSTEIN, C.S. and WEINSTEIN, N.D. (1979) 'Noise and reading performance in an open space school', *Journal of Educational Research*, **72**, 4, pp. 210–213.

WEISS, K. (1989) 'Evaluation of elementary and secondary school principals', Paper presented at the Annual Meeting of the American Association of School Administrators, Orlando, Florida.

WELLS, A.S. (1999) 'Charter school reform in California: Does it meet expectations?', *Phi Delta Kappan*, **80**, 4, pp. 305–312.

WELLS, A.S., LOPEZ, A., SCOTT, J. and HOLME, J.J. (1999) 'Charter schools as postmodern paradox: Rethinking social stratifications in an age of deregulated choice', *Harvard Educational Review*, **69**, 2, pp. 172–190.

WELLS, J.G. and ANDERSON, D.K. (1997) 'Learners in a telecommunication course: Adoption, diffusion, and stages of concern', *Journal of Research on Computing in Education*, **30**, 1, pp. 83–105.

WERNER, W. (1987) 'Training for curriculum implementation', *Pacific Education*, **1**, 1, pp. 40–53.

WEST, S. (1993) *Educational Values for School Leadership*, London, Kogan Page.

WESTBURY, I. (1999) 'The burdens and excitement of the "new" curriculum research: A response to Hlebowitsh's "The burdens of the new curricularist"', *Curriculum Inquiry*, **29**, 3, pp. 355–363.

WESTBURY, I. (2000) 'Why globalization will not cause fundamental curriculum change', Paper presented at the Annual Meeting of the American Educational Research Association, New Orleans.

WHITTY, G. (1994) *Deprofessionalising Teaching?*, Occasional Paper No. 22, Canberra, Australian College of Education.

WHITTY, G. (1995) 'School-based management and a National Curriculum: Sensible compromise or dangerous cocktail?', Paper presented at the Annual Conference of the American Educational Research Association, San Francisco.

WIDEEN, M.F. (1994) *The Struggle for Change*, London, Falmer Press.

WIEGAND, P. and RAYNER, M. (Eds) (1989) *Curriculum Progress 5–16: School Subjects and the National Curriculum Debate*, London, Falmer Press.

WIGGINS, G. (1998) *Educative Assessment*, San Francisco, Jossey-Bass.

WILCOX, B. (1992) *Time-Constrained Evaluation*, London, Routledge.

WILDY, H., LOUDEN, W. and ROBERTSON, J. (2000) 'Using cases for school principal performance standards: Australian and New Zealand experiences', Paper presented at the Annual Meeting of the American Educational Research Association, New Orleans.

WILLIAMS, M. (2000) 'Connecting teachers to the Dot. Com world', *EQ* **2**, Winter, 9–11.

WILLIAMS, R. (2001) 'Automated essay grading: An evaluation of four conceptual models', Unpublished paper, Perth, Curtin University.

WILLINGHAM, W.W. and COLE, N.S. (1997) *Gender and Fair Assessment*, Mahwah, NJ, Lawrence Erlbaum.

WILLIS, S. (1991) 'A national statement on mathematics for Australian schools: Some background', Unpublished paper, Canberra.

WILLIS, S. and KISSANE, B. (1997) *Achieving Outcome-Based Education,* Canberra, ACSA.

WILLMOTT, G. (1994) 'National collaborative curriculum development: Statements and profiles and senior secondary education', *Curriculum Perspectives*, **14**, 1, pp. 52–56.

WILSON, B. (2002) 'Curriculum — is less more?', Paper presented at the Curriculum Corporation Conference, Canberra.

WINTER, R. (1989) *Learning from Experience: Principles and Practice in Action Research,* London, Falmer Press.

WITHERS, G. and McCURRY, D. (1990) 'Student participation in assessment in a cooperative climate', in Low, B. and WITHERS, G. (Eds) *Developments in School and Public Assessment*, Melbourne, ACER.

WITKIN, H.A., MOORE, C.A., GOODENOUGH, D.R. and COX, P.W. (1977) 'Field-dependent and field-independent cognitive styles and their ed implications', *Review of Educational Research*, **47**, pp. 1–64.

WOOD, R. (1991) *Assessment and Testing*, New York, Cambridge University Press.

WOODS, P. (1988) 'A strategic view of parent participation', *Journal of Education Policy*, **3**, 4, pp. 323–334.

WOODS, P. (1990) *The Happiest Days?*, London, Falmer Press.

WOODS, P.A. (2000) 'Redefining professionality and leadership: Reflexive responses to competitive and regulatory pressures', Paper presented at the Annual Conference of the American Educational Research Association, New Orleans.

WRAGG, E.C. (1987) *Teacher Appraisal: A Practical Guide*, London, Macmillan.

WRIGHT, H.K. (2000) 'Nailing Jell-O to the wall: Pinpointing aspects of state-of-the-art curriculum theorizing', *Educational Researcher*, **29**, 5, pp. 4–13.

WROE, A. and HALSALL, R. (2001) 'School self-evaluation: Measurement and reflection in the school improvement process', *Research in Education*, **65**, 5, pp. 41–52.

YATES, L. (1998) 'Feminism's fandar go with the state revisited', Paper presented at the Annual Conference of the American Educational Research Association, San Diego.

YEH, S.S. (2001) 'Tests worth teaching to: Constructing state-mandated tests that emphasize critical thinking', *Educational Researcher*, **30**, 9, pp. 12–17.

YOUNG, M. (1971) (Ed) *Knowledge and Control*, London, Macmillan.

ZADY, M., PORTES, P., DEL CASTILLO, K. and DUNHAM, R. (1998) 'When low SES parents cannot assist their children', Paper presented at the Annual Conference of the American Educational Research Association, San Diego.

ZALTMAN, G., FLORIO, D.H. and SIKORSKI, L.A. (1977) *Dynamic Educational Change.* New York, Free Press.

ZEICHNER, K.M. (1993) 'Action research: Personal renewal and social reconstruction', *Educational Action Research*, **1**, pp. 199–219.

Index